Ran HaCohen
Reclaiming the Hebrew Bible

Studia Judaica

Forschungen zur Wissenschaft des Judentums

Begründet von
Ernst Ludwig Ehrlich

Herausgegeben von
Günter Stemberger

Band 56

De Gruyter

Ran HaCohen

Reclaiming the Hebrew Bible

German-Jewish Reception of Biblical Criticism

Translated by
M. Engel

De Gruyter

ISBN 978-3-11-024756-5
e-ISBN 978-3-11-024757-2
ISSN 0585-5306

Library of Congress Cataloging-in-Publication Data

HaCohen, Ran.
Reclaiming the Hebrew Bible : German-Jewish reception of biblical
criticism / Ran HaCohen.
p. cm. − (Studia judaica, Forschungen zur Wissenschaft des Judentums)
Includes bibliographical references and index.
ISBN 978-3-11-024756-5 (hardcover 23 × 15,5 : alk. paper)
1. Bible. O.T. − Criticism, interpretation, etc. − Germany − History −
19th century.   2. Judaism − Relations − Christianity.   3. Christianity
and other religions − Judaism.   4. Germany − Ethnic relations.   I. Title.
BS1160.H25 2010
221.6′60882960943−dc22
                                                                    2010034601

Bibliographic information published by the Deutsche Nationalbibliothek

The Deutsche Nationalbibliothek lists this publication in the Deutsche
Nationalbibliografie; detailed bibliographic data are available in the Internet
at http://dnb.d-nb.de.

Printing: Hubert & Co. GmbH & Co. KG, Göttingen
∞ Printed on acid-free paper

Printed in Germany

www.degruyter.com

Preface

This volume is based on a revised version of a Hebrew book published in 2006, which emerged from my doctoral dissertation. Its English translation was supported a generous grant by the Lucius Littauer Foundation (New York), for which I am most grateful. I would also like to thank Michelle Engel for her conscientious translation.

I wish to express my gratitude to various mentors and colleagues: First and foremost to Professor Yaacov Shavit (Tel Aviv) for his unfailing and inspiring support; to my friends Dr. Gabriele von Glasenapp (Frankfurt a.M.) and Dr. Rima Schichmanter (Tel Aviv) for their continuous encouragement and assistance; to Dr. Amnon Raz-Krakotzkin (Beer Sheva) for his helpful comments; to Professor Avraham Shapira (Tel Aviv) for his assistance in preparing the Hebrew version of this book; to Professor Günter Stemberger (Vienna), for graciously including this volume in his series Studia Judaica, and for his sagacious comments on the manuscript; and to Dr. Albrecht Döhnert and the Walter de Gruyter Verlag editorial team for their collaboration, which made the preparation of this English version an enjoyable project.

Last but not least, I am highly indebted and deeply grateful to my doctoral supervisors, Professors Paul Mendes-Flohr (Jerusalem / Chicago) and Zohar Shavit (Tel Aviv), without whom this book would not have come to fruition.

Tel Aviv, September 2010   Ran HaCohen

Contents

Introduction

Higher Criticism – Higher Anti-Semitism.

Solomon Schechter, 1903[1]

The biblical criticism of Protestant theology
is the best antidote against the hatred of Jews.

Hermann Cohen, 1907[2]

During the nineteenth century, higher biblical criticism (*Höhere Bibel-kritik*) flourished in German universities. An academic discipline centered around the biblical text, it was concerned primarily with the manner and date of its composition; consequently it also dealt with the religion and history of the ancient Israelites. Toward the end of the century the discipline achieved impressive revolutionary progress, at the heart of which was an overarching historiographical revision of the history of Israelite religion and the timeline of biblical composition. This revisionist historiography stood in sharp contrast to the historical account that was rooted in the Bible itself and which had become the traditional understanding in both Judaism and Christianity. Gradually and intermittently developed over the course of the century, the new historiography was consolidated and refined toward the century's end, becoming the dominant paradigm in the field of biblical scholarship and breaking beyond the bounds of German academia. A significant number of its methods and conclusions are accepted by biblical scholars to this day.

The field of biblical criticism did not develop in a vacuum. While in its early days it allowed room for a Jewish scholar such as Spinoza (1632–1677), as a whole it was a project of Christian Europe. Starting as early as Jerome's Vulgate in the early fifth century, there was a long tradition of Christian interest in the Hebrew Scripture; during the Mid-

---

1   Schechter 1903, 35.
2   Cohen 1907, 167.

dle Ages, the Christian study of Judaism was utilized for polemic or
missionary purposes. The Renaissance during the twelfth century saw
the birth of Hebraist discourse, which searched for the "Hebrew truth"
(*hebraica veritas*) and focused on the study of the Hebrew language and
rabbinic literature; one of its outcomes was that Christian scholars were
freed from their reliance on (Hebrew-reading) Jewish intermediaries in
order to read the Jewish holy texts. Eventually Hebraist discourse
would combine with the European Orientalist discourse, which dealt
with "Oriental" peoples in general.[3]

Modern biblical criticism was primarily a Protestant undertaking.
One of the central factors that had led to its formation was the Lutheran
Reformation's call during the sixteenth century to return to Scripture as
the sole source of religious authority (*sola scriptura*). The scholars involved in biblical criticism were for the most part theologically trained
and worked within the framework of Protestant theological faculties.
Thus in the nineteenth century, when German Jews would be required
to contend with biblical criticism, they would face a discourse concerned with Jews, their history, and their religion which nonetheless
had developed and still functioned entirely without Jewish participa-
tion – an alien, sometimes antagonistic territory. The first efforts of
German-Jewish intellectuals to enter this territory – scholars of the *Wissenschaft des Judentums* ("science of Judaism"), who were committed to
the ethos of modern scientific thought and simultaneously wished to
lead a Jewish life in the modern world – were part of the Jews' "return"
to the Bible, or of the Jewish "Bible Revolution," to use Shavit's term.[4]
These efforts form the subject of this book.

*

Academic discourse – at least within the humanities and social sciences
– takes place in the context of what Foucault called power/knowledge.
Biblical criticism is a clear example. The study by German Protestant
theologians of the texts, religion, history, and customs of the ancient
Israelites formed – whether explicitly or implicitly, directly or indirectly – part of the discussion on the nature and place of Jews in German
(and European) society, regardless of whether they were perceived as
following in the path of the ancient Israelites or as having deviated
from it. The discourse regarding the Jews' ancient roots was part of the

---

3   For a broader context on Hebraism, Orientalism, and Jewish Studies see: Raz-
     Krakotzkin 1999. On Jews' place in the Orientalist discourse see: Kalmar and Penslar
     2005.
4   Shavit and Eran 2007, 17ff.

constitution (and self-constitution) of Judaism and the Jews in modern Germany.

Recently it has been proposed that the Christian discourse about Jews, as well as the Jewish discourse it prompted, be examined through the prism of postcolonial theory that was developed toward the end of the twentieth century.[5] According to Robert Young, postcolonial studies are not a theory in the strict sense, but rather "a set of conceptual resources."[6] They derive from critical insights acquired during the colonial period and from a perspective that focuses on colonial power relations between, on the one hand, a ruling society perceiving itself as Western, modern, rational, enlightened, and so forth – and, on the other hand, the societies under its rule, perceived as „other," as non-Western (Oriental, Semitic, Indian, black, etc.) and non-modern (backward, irrational, primitive, ancient, and extra-historical, and, at times, indigenous, authentic, exotic, and the like).

A postcolonial perspective would view the Jews as a sort of colony within Germany. Indeed, Germany entered the nineteenth century as a fragmented collection of political entities with no effective central government; as a result it lacked colonies, in contrast to England and other European powers. It was for this reason that Edward Said's *Orientalism*[7] focused on English and French rather than German cultural discourse. Nonetheless, there was no lack of Orientalist discourse in Germany, and there too colonialist ambitions and fantasies were widespread.[8] The German discourse about Jews, with its Hebraist and Orientalist roots, can be described as a colonialist discourse. Incidentally, the word "colony" (*Kolonie*) served, in late eighteenth- and early nineteenth-century German, to designate the Jewish communities in Germany: David Friedländer – one of the leaders of the Berlin Jewry in the generation after Mendelssohn – wrote an article titled "On Reform of the Jewish Colonies in the Prussian States."[9] Throughout the nineteenth century Jews in Germany were perceived as "foreign elements" whose roots lay in the "Orient." Thus, for example, a Berlin lawyer wrote in 1803 that while cultured Jews could discuss Goethe, Schiller, and Schlegel to their hearts' content, they would nonetheless remain a "foreign, Oriental race" (*orientalisches Fremdlingsvolk*). Two generations later, in the late 1870s, the distinguished German historian Heinrich von Treitschke

---

5   Heschel 1998; Heschel 1999; and following her Wiese 2002.
6   Young 2001, 64. For an incisive critique of the postcolonial discourse and its political functions see: Shohat 1992.
7   Said 1978.
8   Zantop 1997; Manual 1992.
9   Friedländer 1793.

(1834–1896) would point to Jews prominent in German culture, such as the composer Felix Mendelssohn Bartholdy (1809–1847) or the politician Gabriel Riesser (1806–1863), as "uncorrupted Orientals" (*unverfälschte Orientalen*).[10] The description of Jews as "Semites" was also intended to emphasize their "Oriental" origins.[11]

Indeed, not only in the colonies were various population groups required to relinquish their identity or change it into an identity imposed upon them from the motherland: this was also the fate of numerous minority groups who were exposed to the pressures of nationalism within European countries. For example, during the nineteenth century the inhabitants of Brittany – European, Christian, and white – were required to adopt a foreign language, culture, and way of life which were perceived as "French" and imposed upon them by the central authorities in Paris. What differentiates citizens of the national periphery from colonial subjects? They are characterized differently: in the national case the criterion is geographic or economic, in contrast to ethnic or "racial" distinctions in the colonial case. And while citizens are perceived as adaptable – as able and even required to adopt the national culture in exchange for relinquishing parts of their old identity – colonial subjects are in turn classified as aliens, and their entry into the ruling group is neither possible nor even desirable from the latter's perspective. Thus, „[colonial subjects like] Slovaks were to be Magyarized, Indians Anglicized, and Koreans Japanified, but they would not be permitted to join pilgrimages which would allow them to administer Magyars, Englishmen or Japanese."[12]

Whom did German Jews most resemble – peripheral subjects who could be absorbed into the ruling culture, or colonial subjects alien by nature and unadaptable? The answer depends on whom you ask. Jews were accustomed to see themselves unambiguously as citizens – distinct, perhaps, in terms of religion, but deserving of fully equal rights in Germany; as such they differed from the typical colonial subject and better resembled minority groups in the nation-state. In contrast, many – though not all – non-Jewish Germans (and eventually Zionist Jews as well) saw Jews as a foreign element that could not be assimilated into the German environment; Jews were excluded primarily on the basis of their ethnicity, and as such more closely resembled colonial subjects.

---

10   Mendes-Flohr 1991a, 81.
11   For greater detail: Olender 1992.
12   Anderson 1991, 110. VVV.

Hence the justification for seeing Jews as a sort of "internal colony"[13] and for applying several postcolonial concepts to the discourse about and *of* German Jews. In this context, the suggestion of the Orientalist and prominent biblical scholar Michaelis at the end of the eighteenth century – namely, to concentrate Germany's Jews in the Caribbean "Sugar Islands"[14] that they might lead productive lives there and be of use to the motherland – is instructive: here Jews, members of the "internal colony," were to be transformed into "regular" colonial subjects similar to those ruled over by the other European powers during that period.

The postcolonial discourse makes frequent use of Hegel's well-known master–slave dialectic, which was derived from the unique human need to win recognition from one's fellows. In translating the master–slave relationship from the individual level to the societal, the claim is that colonialists and the colonized were also, in certain respects, each captive to the other. This dialectic is also expressed in what Homi Bhabha and others call "hybridity" or "third-space" ("in-betweenness"), which refers primarily to the obfuscation of the boundaries between rulers and ruled and to the "pollution" of each side by elements of the other. For our purposes, what is important is the insight that slaves are imprisoned within their masters' discourse about them, although it is actually the slaves who (even before the masters) tend to also develop a "dual consciousness" which enables them to see both from the rulers' dominant perspective and from that of the margins under their rule. When Jewish scholars in Germany engaged in biblical research, they had two target audiences: Jewish and non-Jewish readers alike. Even though addressing non-Jewish readers generally remained in the realm of desire, as only rarely did Christian academics take the trouble to explore the biblical research carried out by Jews,[15] this dual target was far more conspicuous in Germany – where German was the language of the *Wissenschaft des Judentums* – than it was in Eastern Europe, where Hebrew and Yiddish made it possible to write for an entirely Jewish audience.[16] It should be clarified that confessional segregation – within scholarship that aimed to be supra-confessional – was also enforced in nineteenth-century Germany in an institutionalized man-

---

13 On "internal colonialism," a concept that was developed in reference to African-Americans in the United States, Celts in Britain, Israeli Arabs (Zureik 1979), and other groups, see: Hechter 1975.

14 Hess 1998.

15 On the unidirectional nature of academic communication between Jews and Christians see: Wiese 1999.

16 See: Volkov 2006, 285.

ner: teaching and research positions in the German academia, and even admission into departments of theology, were closed to Jews, even to those few who saw themselves purely as scholars.

Colonial subjects are required to forge their identity against the backdrop of the challenge posed by power relations. This external tension is internalized and necessitates a reconstruction of the cultural and social components of the subjects' identity as well as their categorization as "self" as opposed to "other" – as elements worth preserving or which require modification. With respect to the contemporary lives of German Jews, the reorganization of identity became what Shulamit Volkov calls "inventing tradition."[17] In the case at hand, the axis of power relations in the present intersected with the axis of the past, of history. The past entered the picture in two ways: first, as the "affliction of heritage" – the past shaping the future. As much as the field of biblical study espoused scientific, modern, and unprejudiced discourse free of dogmas and confessional biases, it never disengaged from its Christian, Protestant roots (nor from its ties to the Protestant establishment). Nor was the Jewish engagement with biblical criticism able to ignore the confessional roots (and biases) of Christian criticism; and in any case it was not able, and did not desire, to disengage entirely from its own Jewish roots. Here the Jews adopted the founding principles of the dominant discourse, at times with the explicit intention of "purifying" Judaism of its "Oriental" foundations.[18]

Secondly, the depiction of the past was itself a battlefield. Now the present shaped the past. The scholars of the *Wissenschaft des Judentums*, who were pioneers of modern Jewish historiography, wished to create a picture of a Jewish past – a collective Jewish memory – that would suit their aspirations and needs in the present, both in their external struggles within German (and European) society and, internally, in the struggles taking place among Jews about the development of modern Judaism. While Christian biblical scholars proposed a revision of the traditional picture of the past, several Jewish scholars attempted to counter it with a reformed picture of the past – a revision to the revision. They did not wish to revert to the traditional image of the past (which remained the domain of conservative orthodoxy, Jewish and Christian alike), but instead to reform both the traditional image and what was perceived as anti-Jewish bias in the modern–critical picture. Here, in a manner typical of colonial power struggles, this grappling with and about the past, against the background of contemporary pow-

---

17   Volkov 1991, 276-286, following the well-known Hobsbawm and Ranger 1983.
18   Mendes-Flohr 1991a, 82.

er struggles, led to the creation of counter-histories[19] – historical narratives that rest on some of the assertions of the competing narrative, yet weave them into a fabric entirely different in nature.

The early-nineteenth-century epigraphs by Hermann Cohen and Solomon Schechter that open this chapter – each so antithetical to the other – delineate the Jewish approach to non-Jewish biblical criticism: sweeping acceptance on the one hand and thorough rejection on the other. But between these two poles exist the more interesting attempts to form hybrids – composite narratives that would enable Jews to adopt the principles and even many of the concrete conclusions of biblical criticism, thus taking part in the academic world and modern intellectual discourse; and at the same time to reform it in a manner that would allow them to "rescue" their image of the past and their own self-conception as Jews of their time.

*

Counter-histories, which nineteenth-century Jews created in contrast to – yet within the framework of – biblical criticism, are not merely a characteristic phenomenon in power relations of the colonial type but also a continuation of the traditional Jewish–Christian polemic, which has been accompanied by competing narratives and counter-narratives throughout the centuries of its existence.

The Jewish–Christian polemics revolved around several central ideas:[20] chosenness (the identity of the Chosen People, the true Israel), redemption or salvation (was it individual or national, did it belong to the past or the future; the messianic nature of Jesus), deity (its nature, the divinity of Jesus), and more. These ideas were inextricably intertwined, to the extent that any debate about one effectively touched upon all. These ties also stemmed from the analogical and metaphorical nature of medieval discourse, which tended to perceive a given pheno-

---

19   Concerning the term "counter-history" in the Jewish context see: Funkenstein 1991.

20   The literature dealing with the subjects addressed here – the history of biblical criticism, the Christian discourse on Judaism, and the Jewish-Christian polemic – is immense; to thoroughly address even a small part of it is impossible. HBOT, a joint project of Jewish and Christian scholars, attempts to provide an outline of the history of biblical exegesis, including a classified bibliography. It also includes a brief introductory chapter (and bibliography) about the place of the Hebrew Bible in this polemic (Stemberger 2000). The following, non-exhaustive survey is based primarily on comprehensive historical works such as: Rogerson 1988; Cohen 1999; Kraus 1991; Krauss 1995; TRE XIII, 40-126. More specific sources will be noted as relevant. See also an anthology of essential articles regarding the Jewish-Christian polemic: Cohen 1991.

menon as a reflection of others in a manner that organized the world
into long chains of resemblance and reflection: "The universe was
folded in upon itself: the earth echoing the sky, faces seeing themselves
reflected in the stars [...]."[21] The following eclectic summary will mention only a few general principles and motifs; each appears in one guise
or another in modern biblical criticism

The Hebrew Bible (Tanakh) – or the „Old Testament" in Christian
terminology – has stood at the center of these polemics since its incep-
tion. In a dialectical fashion, the Bible has served both as a common
foundation for Jews and Christians and as a point of controversy. On
one hand, the polemic was founded on the common ground of both
religions – chiefly their belief in the Bible as divine revelation. This
being the case, some of the qualities attributed to God were transferred,
metonymically, to the text itself, which was perceived by both religions
as holy, as absolute truth, and as an unquestioned source of legitimacy.
On the other hand, the polemic was fueled by the differences between
the Jewish concept of "written Torah" (torah she-bi-khtav) and the Christian "Old Testament." The differences were primarily hermeneutical
and exegetical, not just textual. Once it was agreed that the Bible contained divine truth, entirely disparate answers were proposed to the
question of what that truth might be and how to extract it from Scripture. This polemic in turn fostered hermeneutical differences, as each
side attempted not only to refute the exegetical conclusions of the rival
religion but also to differentiate itself from that rival and its methods.[22]

For Christianity, the central challenge posed by the "Old Testament" was the question of its relationship to the "New Testament" –
where "testament" was used both in the original sense of a covenant
forged between believers and God, and in the derived meaning of the
two canonical texts known as "Testaments." A central term in this context was "Law" – a theological term that runs like a crimson thread
throughout the Jewish–Christian polemic. "Law" – Gesetz in German,
lex in Latin – was the translation of the Greek term nomos; the latter,
since the Hellenistic period, was the prevailing if problematic translation of the Hebrew term torah, understood in Judaism as comprising
the Commandments, a way of life, and rules of behavior both valid and
binding.

In the Gospels, Jesus himself claims that his intention is not to abolish the Law but to fulfill it;[23] his criticism of the Jews' approach to the

---

21   In the words of Michel Foucault (1974, 17), who describes the importance of various
      forms of similarity in the medieval worldview.
22   See: Grossman 1986; Funkenstein 1990, 14ff.; Kamin 1991, 31-61.
23   Matthew 5:17; compare Luke 16:16ff.

Commandments stems from a desire for spiritualization but at times actually leads him to a radicalization of the Law: "You have heard that it was said to those of ancient times, 'You shall not murder' [...] But I say to you that if you are angry with a brother or sister, you will be liable to judgement"; "Again, you have heard that it was said to those of ancient times, 'You shall not swear falsely' [...] But I say to you, Do not swear at all [...]."[24] But this perception was rejected by Christianity as early as Paul. Christianity regarded the Old Testament as sacred, and the Pentateuch as the Word of God transmitted to Moses (in Jesus' words: "For Moses said, 'Honour your father and your mother'").[25] But the Old Testament laws were perceived as transitory, abolished with the advent of Jesus and superseded by belief in him – by the "Gospel." Beginning with Paul, the problem the Old Testament posed to Christianity was primarily that of the Law, and Judaism (in both biblical and later times) was identified with the Old Testament and characterized as the "Religion of the Law" (*Gesetzesreligion*) in contrast to the Christian "Religion of the Gospel." The controversy about the "Law" served as a constant and central motif in the anti-Jewish polemic;[26] in grappling with the "Law," Christianity was in fact grappling with Judaism. Eventually Spinoza too would adopt the image of Judaism as the "religion of the Law"; it would consequently make its way to Kantian philosophy and beyond and play a central role in the German perception of Judaism (and of the other great "Oriental" religion, Islam, which was similarly perceived as a "religion of Law").[27]

Paul himself is presented in the New Testament as an observant Jew.[28] He praises the Law of the Old Testament[29] and does not dispute that Jesus followed it. Yet Jesus, according to Paul, placed the Law in a new perspective that required Christians to obey it out of love and faith and not through literal observance of the commandments. In addressing the Gentiles Paul transfers the condition for redemption from the Law to faith, relying on exegesis of a verse relating to Abraham (Gene-

---

24 Matthew 5:21-22, 33-34.

25 Mark 7:10.

26 Ruether 1974, 149-165.

27 Mendes-Flohr 1991b, 342, including a bibliography on the subject.

28 Paul's approach to the Law is a complex and much-studied issue; there is no intention to address it here thoroughly. For a brief review see: Hoheisel 1978, 179ff., and for more detailed coverage see the collection of articles in: Dunn 1996; several of the authors included therein have published books on the subject (P.T. Tomson, H. Räisänen). The subject also occupied German Jews at the start of the twentieth century, following the polemic Harnack provoked regarding the "essence of Judaism." See for example: Löwy 1903 (and compare Urbach 1975, 818 N. 42).

29 Romans 7:12ff.

sis 15:6), "And he believed the Lord; and the Lord reckoned it to him as righteousness" – meaning that Abraham was justified because of his faith rather than his actions. The Law was indeed sacred, because it paved the way to redemption;[30] but the Bible (that is, the Law) was ultimately only "our disciplinarian until Christ came, so that we might be justified by faith. But now that faith has come, we are no longer subject to a disciplinarian [...]."[31]

The inherent problems created by the acceptance of the Old Testament as a sacred text, alongside the rejection of the rules of behavior it commanded, generated a central hermeneutical difference between Judaism and Christianity which was expressed in the distinction between literal and non-literal interpretation of the biblical text. Indeed, the diverse exegetical literature of both religions makes use of both forms of interpretation. The four kinds of meaning (*quattuor sensus scripturae*) in the Christian tradition since the fifth century (literal, allegorical, tropological, and anagogical) were echoed in the medieval Jewish tradition (from the fourteenth century onward) in its four methods of biblical exegesis – *peshat, remez, derash,* and *sod.*[32] Nonetheless Christianity, at least until the Reformation, was characterized by a notable preference for non-literal exegesis, in particular allegory and tropology. This is also related to the distinction between historical exegesis (considered literal) and Christological exegesis (perceived as non-literal) – that is, between the understanding of biblical passages as describing historical events and their interpretation as prophecies concerning the Messiah (in particular, Jesus). Christianity tended toward the Christological interpretation, while Judaism drew away from it.

The preference for non-literal exegesis is evident as early as in the New Testament. Following a typological approach, Jesus was identified as Melchizedek; the author of Hebrews thus presented him as a member of the priesthood.[33] Abraham's two sons – Isaac, born to Sarah in fulfillment of a divine promise, and Ishmael, born to Hagar – are seen as allegorical: of birth in a state of liberty as opposed to bondage; of spiritual as opposed to corporeal birth; of an heir as opposed to an expelled son who is not an heir; of the New Testament versus the Old; of heavenly versus earthly Jerusalem; in short, of Christianity versus Judaism.[34] Thus in Paul we find the roots of a chain of dichotomies des-

---

30 Romans 7:7ff.
31 Galatians 3:24-25.
32 Funkenstein 1990, 45ff.; Beinert 1991, 242.
33 Hebrews 5:6: "as he says also in another place, 'You are a priest for ever, according to the order of Melchizedek," following Psalms 110:4.
34 Galatians 4:21ff.

tined to serve Christianity in its approach to Judaism for many centuries. Judaism is identified with the Law, which is perceived as a curse, with the Old Testament (in both senses of the word), with bondage, and with the flesh; Christianity, in contrast, is identified with faith perceived as redemption, with the New Testament, with liberty, and with the spirit.[35] Christianity, the spiritual faith, is inscribed upon the heart ("Circumcise, then, the foreskin of your heart"[36]); Judaism, corporeal, is inscribed upon the body (physical circumcision). Jews were accused of blindness, of misreading the Bible through "a veil [laid] over their minds,"[37] and of narrow-minded observance of the Law, in contrast to Christian belief: "but Israel, who did strive for the righteousness that is based on the law, did not succeed in fulfilling that law. Why not? Because they did not strive for it on the basis of faith, but as if it were based on works."[38] The written word to which Jews were devoted signified death: Jesus "has made us competent to be ministers of a new covenant, not of letter but of spirit; for the letter kills, but the Spirit gives life."[39] All this we find already in Paul, regarding whose crucial influence on the Jews' image in the Christian perception Jeremy Cohen remarks:

> The teaching of Paul [...] defined the basic parameters for subsequent Christian reflection on the Jews [...] On one hand, Paul affirmed the veracity of Hebrew Scripture and the importance of its revelation to Israel in God's plan for the redemption of humankind. [...] On the other hand, Paul construed the continued observance of the Law of the Torah as an exercise in futility: It could not earn a person redemption; it served, rather, to accentuate the sinful depths into which postlapsarian human nature had fallen [...].[40]

The negative attitude toward the Law sharpened with the Church fathers. In an epistle (written ca. 130 CE),[41] Barnabas annulled the laws concerning sacrifice and holy days on the basis of, among other things, a verse in Jeremiah 7:22: "For on the day that I brought your ancestors out of the land of Egypt, I did not speak to them or command them concerning burnt-offerings and sacrifices"; this verse was destined for a long career in modern biblical criticism. Judaism was accused of misunderstanding and adhering to an overly literal reading of Scripture, while Barnabas interpreted them through a non-literal "spiritualiza-

---

35   Galatians 3.
36   Deuteronomy 10:16.
37   2 Corinthians 3:15.
38   Romans 9:31ff.
39   2 Corinthians 3:6.
40   Cohen 1999, 392-393.
41   Rogerson 1988, 14ff.

tion": for example, it was a mistake to think that the Bible's dietary prohibitions applied to actual foods; their true significance concerned the sort of people with whom one should not associate.

In the second century, Christian thinkers dealt not only with Roman pagans and Jews but also with Marcion of Sinope, who rejected the Law entirely along with the Old Testament and "counterfeit" sections of the New Testament. Marcion did not object to the Old Testament or its laws *per se* – they were valid for the people to whom they had been given – but he rejected any tie between the God of the Hebrew Bible and the Christian God, and denied the presence of Christological elements in the Old Testament.[42] Marcionism was declared heresy; to refute him, apologists such as Tertullian and Irenaeus emphasized Christological elements in the Old Testament. From this point on, the sanctity of the Old Testament could no longer be doubted within Christianity; only in the modern era would anyone dare to attack it again, whether to strike at Christianity or at Judaism.

Justin Martyr (100–165), in his *Dialogue with Trypho, a Jew*,[43] concluded from the biographical accounts of the generations from Abraham to Moses' mother that one need not adhere to Mosaic Law in order to be saved. The Law was imposed on the Jews because of their sins. It was not a symbol of chosenness but, on the contrary, a punishment and a mark of disgrace: the sacrifices and commandments were required because of the Jews' intransigence. Jesus, on the other hand, abolished them and replaced them with the New Testament promised by Jeremiah (31:31-32). Christianity itself was the observance of the Law; it was a state of continuous Sabbath and a return to the era before the Law. Here was a notable attempt to create a Christological continuity that passed over the "Jewish Law" and to find presages of Christianity as early as the Patriarchs.[44] The Church fathers developed a concept of religion that predated Moses and functioned as a Christian pre-history; Judaism, the Mosaic faith, thus became a strictly provisional religion, limited in time, place (the land of Israel), and applicability (to the Jews alone). According to Eusebius of Caesarea (ca. 263 – ca. 339), the Patriarchs were not Jews but rather sons of a universal stock who were virtuous without requiring the Law; this was the true spiritual and universal religion, to which Christianity was a return and a continuation. Because of his religion Abraham had been justified even before circumcision; the Jews descended from the circumcised Abraham,

---

42   About Marcion, see: Denzler and Andresen 1997, 388f. for an overview and
      bibliography.
43   See: Hirshman 1996, 31ff.
44   Ruether 1974, 150f.

while the Christians descended from Abraham before his circumcision. The more ancient religion was identified primarily with the Ten Commandments, which were perceived as eternal and universal, in contrast to the inferior, particularistic, and ephemeral Mosaic Law. This approach, which established the roots of Christianity in an earlier form of Judaism and thus passed over later Judaism, also has parallels in modern biblical criticism.

Between Jerome and Augustine – the leading figures of the Church in the early fifth century – an argument erupted regarding the interpretation of Galatians 2:11ff., in which the Jewish Peter refuses to dine with non-Jewish Christians and is then reprimanded by Paul. Jerome, following a longstanding exegetical tradition, claimed that Peter had only pretended to observe the Commandments and that Paul had only pretended to reprimand him. Augustine, on the other hand, maintained that Peter must not be ascribed such hypocrisy and declared that he did indeed observe the Jewish dietary commandments. Still, apart from this disagreement consensus reigned: both Jerome and Augustine agreed that the commandments in question no longer applied to Christians. Only to the Ten Commandments did Augustine bestow the status of a divine Law equally applicable to Christians. Augustine divided salvation history into four stages: "before the Law" (since Adam), "under the Law" (since Moses), "under grace" (since Jesus), and "in full peace" (the End of Days).

In his hermeneutics Augustine differentiated between the literal meaning of the Hebrew Bible, which he identified with the historical truth of the events of the past, and the allegorical or prophetic meaning, which alluded to events in the future. Jeremy Cohen has demonstrated[45] that during Augustine's final decades, his movement toward literal interpretation went hand-in-hand with the moderation of his hostile attitude toward the Jews and with their assignation to a "safe place" – inferior but viable – within the sacred history he developed. The Augustinian philosophy of history assigned Jews a vital role which would accompany them in the following centuries. In their subjugation to the Christians and their dispersion in the Diaspora they constituted a living testimony to the truth of Christianity and to the punishment inflicted upon them for rejecting and crucifying Jesus; typologically, the Jews represented Cain. The fact that they still observed the Law was part of their testimony to the triumph of Christianity; from here too

---

45   See: Cohen 1999, 19ff. for a thorough analysis of Augustine's attitude toward the Jews, in its historical development and hermeneutical contexts.

emerged the perception of Jews as an archaic, frozen entity whose historical development concluded with the arrival of Jesus.

Augustine's approach remained generally intact throughout the
subsequent eight centuries and began to undergo real change only in
the twelfth century. During the Renaissance in twelfth-century Europe,
the tendency toward rationalism grew stronger, contacts between
Christian and Jewish scholars increased, and Christian interest grew in
the "Hebrew truth" and in Jewish exegesis of the Hebrew Bible.[46] This
environment also saw increasing Christian recognition of the importance of literal exegesis in understanding the Bible; it would exist
alongside – not in place of – non-literal exegeses, which were developed by commentators (e.g. Hugh of Saint Victor) who simultaneously
dealt in literal exegesis. Thus, at the end of the thirteenth century, William of Auvergne defended the literal interpretation of the Law. He
vigorously rebuffed Christian allegations of contradictions and inconsistencies in biblical Law: the Law had been given by God, and even if
hidden meanings lay latent within it there was no reason to reject its
literal meaning and its thorough suitability for the Israelites of the time,
despite the fact that with the advent of Jesus it was no longer relevant.

Since Thomas Aquinas in the thirteenth century, literal exegesis has
attained a renewed status in Christianity: it is derived from the intentions of the human author of Scripture while spiritual exegesis derives
from the intentions of God. From the verse "I gave them statutes that
were not good and ordinances by which they could not live" (Ezekiel
20:25), Aquinas concluded that while the Israelites could not "live in
the Law" in the sense that it could not deliver them from their sins, the
Law was nonetheless good because it created obstacles to sin; the Law
was not perfect in an absolute sense, but it was entirely suited for its
time and place. The new Law was the grace of the Holy Spirit, granted
through belief in Jesus; the relationship between the old Law and the
new was like that between the imperfect and perfect. Aquinas – who
contended among other things with the purposes of the Commandments as presented in Maimonides' *Guide for the Perplexed* – also distinguished (like many before him) between three types of laws in the Old
Testament: moral laws, ritual laws, and judicial laws. Moral law (with
the Ten Commandments at its core) was a divine expansion of natural
law and thus applied to all men, although it was liable to historical
change and required interpretation. The two other types of law were
particular derivatives of natural law: the ritual laws were intended to

---

46   Much has been written about this period of encounteres between Jews and Chris-
     tians, including those that involved the Bible. See an overview and bibliography in:
     Talmage 1982; Kamin 1991, 141-155.

bring the Israelites to the worship of God while the judicial laws were meant to regulate their public lives. Being derivatives, their domain was not universal.

However, the Christian interest in the "Hebrew truth" and literal exegesis came at a price: when it expanded to later Jewish sources, in particular the Talmud, a new Christian accusation emerged that the Jews had distorted the biblical Law and that many of their practices had no basis in the Hebrew Bible. On the one hand, the interest in the "Hebrew truth" strengthened the relationship between Jews and the Old Testament in the eyes of Christianity; on the other hand, the recognition of the centrality Jews accorded to the oral law was translated into the claim that the Jews had breached the role that Augustine had given them as living witnesses to the old Law, had altered the Law, and had interpreted it incorrectly. Jeremy Cohen, among others, traces the decline of tolerance toward the Jews to this growing distance from the Augustinian paradigm.

*

During the Humanistic period, Hebraism – the study of the Hebrew language and Jewish texts in universities – expanded and became institutionalized; it also stood in the background of Luther's Reformation.[47] The Reformation, which to a great degree shaped modern German culture, greatly amplified the importance of Scripture.[48] The Catholic Church placed the authority of tradition side by side with the authority of Scripture; Luther, in contrast, rejected the authority of the former and declared: *sola scriptura*. The Bible must be read by everyone, not because it was open to individual interpretation but because it was, in fact, the most lucid text of all. Luther continued the preference for literal exegesis. He was greatly influenced by the work of Jacobus Faber Stapulensis (ca. 1455–1536), who had broken free entirely from the need for non-literal exegesis. In his commentary on the Psalms, Faber distinguished between two types of literal exegesis: literal-historical, which interpreted passages in their historical context, and literal–prophetic, which interpreted them as they related to Jesus. Since Christological exegesis was also considered literal, non-literal exegesis became superfluous. Following in his footsteps, Luther abandoned the four traditional forms of exegesis and focused on literal exegesis – both historical and prophetic.

---

47 In addition to the above, see: Kraeling 1969.
48 On the status of the Bible and its varied usage in Germany since the Reformation, see: Sheehan 2005.

The move toward literal exegesis was accompanied by a growing closeness to the Law itself in the more radical streams of the Reformation. Luther objected to this trend and balanced it with a counter-movement toward Marcionism. He placed faith at the center of Christianity and minimized the status of the Law in favor of the Gospel and faith.[49] Luther uncoupled faith from action: the inner self, the soul, which was inherently free, did not require action and could be saved only by faith.[50] The Law had been given to the Jews and to them alone: only they had been taken by God out of Egypt (hence God alludes to the fact in the first Commandment); the Gentiles had not. The Ten Commandments were natural law and their importance lay in the fact that they were engraved upon the heart of every man; they required no revelation. The Old Testament included commandments that should be observed – but in a purely voluntary and temporary fashion and not out of duty. Luther regarded the Law in general – even the Ten Commandments – as no more than the law of a certain people at a certain time, not unlike the Germanic constitutions in the Middle Ages.

Luther's approach to the Law was even more negative than that of the Roman Catholic Church and certainly of more radically reformed churches. The Catholic Church continued to employ the formal term "the new Law of Jesus," coined by Tertullian in the third century, in place of "Mosaic Law." At the Council of Trent (1545–1563) the Church once again declared, in opposition to Luther, that Jesus was not only a messenger but also a law-giver; it rejected the claim that the Gospel itself sufficed for salvation and that deeds were not required. The reformed churches, on the other hand, effectively adopted the biblical "moral law" as binding and even attempted in several countries to implement certain civil laws of the Old Testament in practice. Indeed, later developments in the Lutheran Church (from Melanchthon onward) somewhat softened Luther's negative attitude toward the Law, and with a certain similarity to the reformed churches Lutherans tended to adopt the "moral law" (the Ten Commandments) in part as well.

Luther subordinated Scripture to his own concept of salvation. It was not the (killing) letter of the Law that mattered, but rather the spirit of Scripture. This principle enabled him to favor certain parts of the New Testament over others; he particularly emphasized Paul's epistles and perceived the Reformation as a return to Pauline Christianity. The emphasis on the New Testament, the prominence attached to faith, and

---

49   During the twentieth century, the Swiss theologian Karl Barth (1961) would continue the process and emphasize even further the superiority of the Gospel over the Law.

50   Luther 1520, 29f.

the use of the "divine spirit" as a criterion for preferring certain parts of Scripture and rejecting others allowed Luther to approach the Old Testament with unusual liberty. He regarded it as the history of faith; the protagonists of the Old Testament, who lived their lives in faith and in hope of the coming of the Messiah, resembled the Christians of his day who lived in faith and in hope of his return. This approach – based on historical rather than allegorical interpretation – was how Christians should read the Old Testament. Within the liberal framework he granted himself, Luther downgraded several canonized books which were not included in the Jewish Bible, emphasizing their apocryphal status. He also believed that the final chapters of the Pentateuch were not written by Moses, and that in writing the Book of Genesis Moses had made use of earlier texts. Thus Luther, without being a "biblical critic," anticipated approaches that would resurface some two hundred years after his time.

*

The situation was far different within Judaism, which sanctified only the twenty-four books of the "written Torah." "If one were to seek a single term that might summon up the very essence of Judaism it would certainly be *torah*, a concept whose centrality has endured from the biblical period to the present day."[51] In the Hebrew Bible, the meaning of the term *torah* was similar to that of Law, ritual, commandment (cf. "the ritual of the burnt-offering," Leviticus 6:8; "the law for the nazirites," Numbers 6:13), collection of laws ("the law of your God," Hosea 4:6) and in particular the laws collected in the Book of Deuteronomy ("this law," Deuteronomy 1:5 and more). During the Hellenistic period the term comprehended the corpus of commandments, the teachings of the prophets, and the wisdom of the Sages; it particularly emphasized the Pentateuch in its entirety, and not necessarily the sections pertaining to commandments and laws. In post-biblical Judaism there was a duality in the concept of "Torah": on the one hand, the Torah was frequently presented in a narrow sense, i.e. the Pentateuch; the other books of the Bible were merely addenda to the Torah, and the oral law its exegesis. On the other hand, against non-conformist interpretation, the meaning of the term "Torah" gradually expanded until it applied to the entire Hebrew Bible and ultimately – as early as the talmudic period – to the oral law as well. Thus, when a Gentile asked

---

51   Kugel 1987, 995. In addition, this brief overview is based chiefly on Soloveitchik and
     Rubasheff 1925; Urbach 1975, 286 ff.; Sandler 1968; Greenberg 1982.

Hillel "How many Torahs do you have?" the latter responded: "Two, one in writing, one memorized."[52] At the same time, the Torah was also increasingly attributed to a divine source. Even though the Hebrew Bible was divided into three sections in descending order of sanctity (and in the chronological order in which they were canonized), the Torah in its broader sense, which included the oral law, was nonetheless perceived in certain contexts as the product of divine inspiration.[53] At the same time, "despite all the expansion of the meaning of the term 'Torah' underwent in Rabbinic literature, the precept remained its basic element; without commandments there could be no Torah."[54]

The trend in Judaism to see the Bible as existing outside of history and time may have been a reaction to Christianity's historicization and temporal restriction of the Law, as we have seen above. The perception already existed among the Sages that all prophecies had been given at Mount Sinai, their revelation merely postponed for later periods. Furthermore, not only "did all the Prophets receive their prophecy from Sinai, but also the Sages that have arisen in every generation received their respective teaching from Sinai."[55] The Bible was perceived as existent since the Creation and even before it;[56] Moses had simply delivered it to the Israelites.

With respect to Jewish hermeneutics, it should be noted that its basis in the Midrashic literature is very difficult to characterize. The commentators' interest in hermeneutics for its own sake was limited, and in practice the exegetical approaches they adopted were rife with contradictions; as Edward Breuer observes, "the most intriguing and historically salient feature of this interpretative mode is the lingering elusiveness of its applied hermeneutic [...] the precise interpretative discipline that fueled this literature is not at all apparent."[57] For our purposes it is important to note that Christian and Jewish exegesis had a reciprocal relationship throughout the greater part of their histories; through their reactions, Urbach identifies a Christian influence even as early as the Sages.[58] The talmudic expression "One who exposes aspects of the Torah [not in accord with the law]" – and who thus has no portion in the world to come – was, according to Urbach, directed against

---

52   Babylonian Talmud, *Shabbat* 31A.
53   For a comprehensive discussion, see: Harris 1995.
54   Urbach 1975, 315.
55   *Shemot Rabbah* 28:6 and more; quoted in Urbach 1975, 304.
56   Babylonian Talmud, *Pesahim* 54A.
57   Breuer 1996, 47.
58   Urbach 1975, 288ff., 295ff. More recently and in a wider context see: Yuval 2006.

allegorical interpretation that rejected observance of the Command-ments.

Post-talmudic Jewish exegesis – certainly from the Middle Ages onward – is characterized as a rule by a preference for literal inter-pretation and an aversion to allegory, in contrast to the Christian view that the Torah was merely a prologue to the New Testament.[59] Judaism granted a central place to literal exegesis, while typological exegesis was in contrast "peripheral and unimaginative."[60] The talmudic rule that "a verse does not abandon its simple sense"[61] also came to serve as, among other things, a "shield against the allegorical exegesis of the Christians, who wished to overrule the literal validity of the biblical commandments."[62] Judaism's self-distinction from Christianity was at times plainly apparent, e.g. when Rashi in the eleventh century explicit-ly maintained a distance from messianic interpretation: "Our Sages expounded the passage as referring to the King Messiah, but according to its apparent meaning, it is proper to interpret it as referring to David himself" (commentary on Psalms 2:1).

Judaism's emphasis on literal exegesis, as well as its derived lin-guistic and philological interests, may explain the fact that while "the concept of 'biblical research for its own sake' does not suit the Christian spiritual world, where philological criticism is rare,"[63] Jewish commen-tators over the course of generations were aware at times of the difficul-ties posed by the biblical text.[64] Philo – who represented a Hellenistic Jewish school of thought with a tendency toward allegorical exegesis – was aware of the contradiction between the two stories of Creation at the start of Genesis and interpreted them as a dual creation: of ideal man on the one hand and of corporeal man on the other. The Talmud also gives evidence of attempts to resolve contradictions that arouse during the canonization of certain books:

> That man is to be remembered for good, by name of Hanina b. Hezekiah, for if it were not for his efforts, the Book of Ezekiel would have been hid-den away, for what he says contradicts the teachings of the Torah. What

---

59   Talmage 1982, 719ff.
60   Funkenstein 1993, 98-120. For a detailed characterization of the Jewish exegetical traditions, in a context quite similar to the present one, see: Breuer 1996, 54-71. For a specific example of overt Jewish objection to allegorical exegesis see: Kamin 1991, 73-98.
61   E.g. Babylonian Talmud, *Shabbat* 63A.
62   Greenberg 1982, 645.
63   Sandler 1968, 394.
64   Even if it appears that certain attempts to construct a Jewish "prehistory" to modern biblical criticism (as in Soloveitchik and Rubasheff 1925) were themselves an apolo-getic response to modern non-Jewish biblical criticism.

did he do to save the situation? He took up three hundred barrels of oil with him to an upper room and stayed there until he had ironed out all the problems.[65]

Nevertheless, the process of shaping the canon and the struggles over it were generally forgotten and obscured. The Pentateuch was attributed to Moses and was believed to have been given to the Israelites in the desert, but the Talmud itself contains a claim that the chapters dealing with the period after the death of Moses were written by Joshua, and some talmudic scholars could not overlook even the contradictions between the two accounts of Creation. Thus in the talmudic literature we find expressions such as "considerations of chronological order do not pertain in the Torah,"[66] "The Torah speaks in the language used by ordinary men,"[67] and "The Torah uses hyperbole"[68] which were intended to settle or obscure scriptural inconsistencies – as well as more extreme views, e.g. that "the Torah was given scroll by scroll."[69]

With the growth of Karaite Judaism and the rise of Islam during the ninth century, the conflict over the text of the Bible, its inconsistencies and their resolutions, and the status of the oral law was renewed. And while very little of these conflicts has been preserved – Hiwi al-Balkhi's well-known book, which apparently enumerated two hundred questions regarding the Torah, was lost – they echo in the commentary of Saadia Gaon (882–942), who established biblical exegesis on a linguistic basis.

During the following centuries, various Jewish biblical commentators – Rashi (1040–1105), Joseph Bekhor Shor (in the twelfth century), Nahmanides (1194–1274), and others – attempted to contend with the difficulties posed by the biblical text, whether through exegesis of specific passages or by defining exegetical rules such as "[in the case of] a general statement followed by a specific act, the latter constitutes a specific [clarification] of the first [general statement]";[70] Rashi (Genesis 2:8) applied this rule to resolve the contradiction between the two stories of Creation, classifying the second story as a clarification of the first. However, the commentary of Abraham Ibn Ezra (1092–1167) is considered a clear milestone in biblical criticism *avant la lettre*, thanks in no small part to the use Spinoza would eventually make of it. Ibn

---

65   Babylonian Talmud, *Shabbat* 13B.
66   Babylonian Talmud, *Pesahim* 6B.
67   Babylonian Talmud, *Sanhedrin* 56A.
68   Babylonian Talmud, *Tamid* 29A.
69   Babylonian Talmud, *Gittin* 60A.
70   Basic exegetical rules go back to Hillel the Elder in the first century BCE, see: Tosefta, *Sanhedrin* 7:11.

Ezra's work incorporates critical material from earlier commentators; thus on the topic of Genesis 36:31 – "These are the kings who reigned in the land of Edom, before any king reigned over the Israelites" – he cites a commentator commonly identified as Isaac Ibn Castar Ben Yashush of Toledo (982–1057): "Yitzchaki said in his book that this section was written during the days of Jehoshaphat," he writes, but notes that "his book deserves to be burned." Likewise he cites Moses Gikatilla (1020–1080), who said that Isaiah should be divided and its latter half transferred to the days of the Second Temple. But Ibn Ezra's best-known remark for our purposes is found in his commentary to Deuteronomy 1:1:

> If you understand the mystery of the twelve and of „Moses wrote the Law" and „the Canaanite was then in the land" and „it will be revealed on the mountain of God" and „behold this bed, a bed of iron," then you will know the truth.

The extent to which the "truth" at which Ibn Ezra hints here is the same as the truth Spinoza attributed to it is a matter of debate; but thanks to Spinoza, who found in these words a hint to support the claim "that the Pentateuch was not written by Moses, but by one who lived many ages after him," Ibn Ezra's remark became widely known.[71]

It is important to note that despite the Bible's central place in the Jewish canon, there is evidence during the Middle Ages of an ambivalence toward it, not to mention a certain aversion to dealing with it. Rashi himself interpreted "keep your children from excessive reflection"[72] as "do not train them too much in the Bible." During the centuries prior to the Haskalah, a notable decline in Jewish study of the Bible took place in Ashkenazi communities across Europe, particularly in

---

71 Spinoza (2007 <1676> , 118 ff. [the quote is on p. 119, Chapter 8]) identified the following six clues in Ibn Ezra's works: (1) The passage "These are the words that Moses spoke to all Israel beyond the Jordan" could not have been written by Moses, who did not live to cross the Jordan. (2) "The secret of the twelve" potentially hints at an altar (Deuteronomy 27:8) which according to tradition was constructed of only twelve stones; it is impossible that the entire Pentateuch could have been written on a surface so small. (3) "Then Moses wrote down this law" (Deuteronomy 31:9) – Moses could not have written thus about himself. (4) "At that time the Canaanites were in the land" (Genesis 12:6) – from here we may infer that the text was written when the Canaanites were no longer in the land, i.e. subsequent to the death of Moses. (5) The verse "So Abraham called that place 'The Lord will provide'; as it is said to this day, 'On the mount of the Lord it shall be provided'" (Genesis 22:14) was written about a specific location, but Moses prophesied only that God would select some location. (6) "Now only King Og of Bashan was left of the remnant of the Rephaim. In fact his bed, an iron bed, can still be seen in Rabbah of the Ammonites. By the common cubit it is nine cubits long and four cubits wide" (Deuteronomy 3:11) reads as a late testimony to the existence of an ancient relic, brought to support the story.

72 Babylonian Talmud, *Berachot* 28B.

Germany.[73] Distinction in the world of biblical scholarship was measured according to proficiency and incisiveness in the study of the Talmud rather than the Bible; apart from ritual use in the synagogue, the
Bible served mainly as a basic reader for children. Thus, according to
testimony from the seventeenth century, traditional schoolteachers
would "toss the Bible behind their backs and avoid dealing with it altogether, and they [did] not educate the children and students in the
study of the Bible in their youth";[74] instead they would rapidly proceed
to the Gemara, as "He who studies the Gemara need not study the Bible nor the Mishnah nor the tannaitic Baraitot, as all intermingle in the
Gemara."[75] The return of the Bible to the forefront of Jewish scholarship
was largely a product of the Haskalah – a revolution which began, as
we have seen, with Mendelssohn's translation of the Hebrew Bible at
the end of the eighteenth century, at the very start of the establishment
and rise of biblical criticism in German academia.

*

A great deal of literature addresses the history of biblical criticism and
its development against the backdrop of the Enlightenment, the rise of
modern science, and various philosophical, theological, and cultural
developments in the West.[76] Since the seventeenth century, scholars
have emerged in Western and Central Europe in various fields – philosophers, jurists, doctors, and even priests – who dealt with the Bible
with relative freedom from Church dogmas. Despite the existing contacts between them, these pioneers of biblical criticism in various countries operated with substantially different cultural backgrounds. In
England these pioneers were Thomas Hobbes (1588–1679) and others,
who attacked the Old Testament against a rationalist–deist background
of a "natural religion" which greatly minimized the value of revelation.
In Catholic France, surprisingly, it was Richard Simon (1638–1712) who
actually attempted to attack the Protestants by casting doubt on the
credibility of the biblical text. In the Netherlands, against a background
of broad freedom of speech combined with boundless religious secta-
rianism, these were people like Hugo Grotius (1583–1645), who greatly

---

73 Fishman 1944; specifically regarding Germany, see: Shohet 1960, 89; for a revealing
     recent analysis, see: Parush 2004.
74 Horwitz 1965, 53f.
75 Weisel 1889 <1782>, 60.
76 The most detailed and comprehensive survey is: Kraus 1982. See also, among others:
     Houtman 1994; Smend 1989; Rogerson 1984; Frei 1974; Thompson 1970.

emphasized historical–literal exegesis, and first and foremost Spinoza, whom many consider to be the father of biblical criticism.

As evident by the title of his *Theological–Political Treatise*, Spinoza's biblical criticism arose in the context of liberal politics: he wished to prove that freedom of thought harmed neither state nor religion and that in fact the opposite was true – it was necessary for the state. Spinoza distilled the divine content of the Bible into the basic moral principles of love, and knowledge, of God. All the rest – the laws, rituals, and narratives – paled in importance to this primary theme. The narratives were intended only to convey the theme by means of illustration and moral lessons, while the laws and rituals were intended for the Hebrew state; with the death of that state so died their own relevance. As part of his theological–political project, Spinoza called for a historical investigation of the formation of the Bible; this investigation would need to be carried out in accordance with the principles of natural science research. In regard to miracles, he declared that all the events related in the Bible occurred naturally, as Nature does not depart from its course. Spinoza believed that it was not Moses but possibly Ezra who had composed the Pentateuch as well as the subsequent historical books, and he relied on his understanding of Ibn Ezra and additional evidence to prove his claim.

In biblical criticism Germany lagged behind the Netherlands and England. This is generally attributed to the influence of Pietism, which from the end of the seventeenth century onward emphasized the individual–experiential aspect of Christianity, as a reaction to the Lutheran orthodoxy. With respect to the composition of Scripture, Pietism adhered to the traditional approach. Despite this, the emphasis on individualism ultimately also cleared a path to individualistic criticism of the text. The philosopher Christian Wolff (1679–1754), who in 1723 was dismissed from his academic position because of his ideas, adopted Leibniz's (1646–1716) differentiation between necessary and contingent truths – the former deriving from reason and the latter, which were inferior, from history. That approach had a dangerous element with respect to the Old Testament, which expressed itself to a great extent through historical truths. Baumgarten's (1714–1762) work took place throughout the first half of the eighteenth century; he smuggled into Germany reviews of English Deism, which was hostile to the Old Testament, and declared that the biblical texts had been written by human authors (under divine inspiration) who as such were not *a priori* immune to human error with respect to historical facts. Baumgarten claimed that they were in fact free of error, but declared that this conclusion required rational proof; he did not simply derive it from faith.

Baumgarten also distinguished between two levels of scriptural interpretation: the natural, historical–philological level, where even a Lutheran scholar might err whereas a non-Lutheran scholar may hit upon a
truth; and the supernatural level, in which Scripture was read as a divine message and could be interpreted correctly only by a Lutheran
scholar. On the other hand Semler (1725–1791), a student of Baumgarten's, went one step further and rejected the supernatural level of exegesis. Semler is sometimes called the father of German biblical criticism; in his time, during the closing third of the eighteenth century, the
theological possibility of freely and critically studying the Old Testament took root in Lutheran Germany.

Starting at the end of the eighteenth century, biblical criticism in
Germany was an academic discipline that was developed almost exclusively in university theological departments. With the exception of brief
breakthroughs into the public sphere, it was not taken up by the public
at large.[77] The interest in biblical history and biblical theology was intended to rescue the Bible from the attacks of English deism: the Bible
was perceived as an authentic expression of historical and theological
attitudes that prevailed during its composition. The price of this rescue
was the abandonment of the claim of the Bible's universal applicability
– a tendency expressed most importantly in the work of Herder (1744–
1803, *The Spirit of Hebrew Poetry*)[78] – who was neither a commentator
nor an academic – and which is evident in the work of both Michaelis,
who studied the ancient Israelite law, and Eichhorn, who injected Astruc's dissection of Genesis into the academic discussion. Both will be
discussed in greater detail in the following chapter.

*

From even this short and incomplete overview, it is evident that providing a definition of biblical criticism is no simple matter: it is "a very
general term, and not easy to define."[79] From a theological standpoint,
Funkenstein's definition hits the mark:

> Biblical criticism means abandoning the premise that the biblical text was
> written through divine inspiration. No biblical scholar rejects that possibili-
> ty at the outset: he simply does not take it into account; it has no part in his
> critical considerations; it has no part in his analysis of the text. The biblical
> scholar also rejects the *a priori* premise that the text is authentic – that is,

---

77   Rogerson 1988, 97.
78   Herder 1833.
79   Barr 1993, 318.

that the text may truly be attributed to whomever it is attributed by tradi-tion.[80]

As we have seen, the Jewish and Christian traditions have long re-garded the Bible as a text written under divine inspiration, and hence the conclusion that its contents must be true; the nature of that truth and the manner of its extraction might be debated, but not the very fact of its existence. Relinquishing the assumption of divine inspiration means relinquishing the assumption of truth. One traditional biblical commentator may interpret literally the creation of man on the sixth day and consider it historical fact; another traditional commentator is apt to interpret the same passage allegorically and transfer its truth from the historical realm to another (moral, philosophical, etc.). But only a biblical critic is able to interpret a passage literally and at the same time maintain that its historical claims are false.

Such a critical approach to the Bible is bound to collide against the traditional–religious approach; that collision "is after all part of the wider problem known as 'Religion versus Science.'"[81] Two primary realms of conflict between biblical study and religious belief can be identified. One realm is the natural sciences; the conflict stems from the miracles and cosmological claims recounted in the Bible. Was the world in fact created (a question still suspended between physics and philos-ophy), and – if so – was it created at the time and in the manner de-scribed in the opening pages of Genesis? Miracles are described in the Bible, from the talking snake (Genesis 3:4) to the sun standing still at Gibeon (Joshua 10:14): can they be reconciled with science, or are they nothing but inventions; or could it be[82] that they express a subjective truth of primitive human consciousness? This conflict between Scrip-ture and the natural sciences (geology, astronomy), and later the hu-man and life sciences (biology, psychology), is not generally included in the concept of biblical criticism.[83]

The second main realm of conflict between biblical criticism and the traditional approach is the field of history. This field addresses various questions which may be divided, as customary since the nineteenth century, into the subfields of lower and higher criticism.[84]

---

80 Funkenstein 1990, 73.
81 Werblowsky 1960, 162.
82 Following Eichhorn and Gabler's suggestion at the end of the eighteenth century; see: Rogerson 1984, 17.
83 See for example Israel Ta-Shma's definition in: *Encyclopaedia Hebraica* (EH 24, 319-325).
84 For more about these concepts, see the following chapter.

Lower criticism deals with textual criticism and the history of the Bible's transmission. While the field does conflict with rigid religious perceptions that champion the literal sanctity of the text, it is not unique to modern biblical criticism. Though it will not be discussed in the present work, it is worth noting that this field – in part because the religious difficulties it poses are not immense – was particularly favored by Jewish scholars:

> There was one discipline of biblical criticism that Jews accepted more than any other, in which it seemed they even attempted to break new ground and take a leading position within the scholarly camp – namely, textual criticism.[85]

Higher criticism deals with the attribution of the biblical texts and with the chronology and manner of their composition. This subject is indivisibly intertwined with the study of the history of the Israelites and the development of their religion. It deals primarily with the historical books of the Hebrew Bible[86] – with the Pentateuch, the theories regarding its dating and composition, and the history of the period it reflects or explicitly describes, extending primarily from the Exodus to the days of Ezra and Nehemiah.

For our purposes, the following hermeneutical generalization by Rogerson is important in the characterization of higher criticism:

> Although what I am about to say is probably an over-simplification, it can be said that pre-critical scholarship accepted the primacy of the New Testament in deciding critical matters in the Old Testament. [...] For critical scholars the bond between the Old and New Testament had been loosened to the point that Old Testament critical matters were to be decided without reference to the New Testament.[87]

Higher criticism thus expressed the liberation of the Old Testament from the hermeneutical perspective of the New Testament, that is, from Christological hermeneutics. Hence the promise it held for German Jews – a promise of liberation from the overt Christological perspective; yet according to no small number of Jews it eventually evolved to a covert Christological, or anti-Jewish, bias.

From a methodological perspective, it is customary to distinguish between several streams of higher biblical criticism.[88] *Literary criticism* or *source criticism* deals with identifying the underlying sources of the text and with their historical arrangement and formation. *Form criticism* (which originated during the 1920s) attempts to identify ancient stages

---

85   Soloveitchik and Rubasheff 1925, 142; see there for greater detail.
86   Rather than with the division of Isaiah or the dating of the Psalms.
87   Rogerson 1988, 97f.
88   See for example: Barr 1993, 323f. and other introductions.

of traditions through the identification of literary genres and by deter-
mining the social context in which they functioned – their *Sitz-im-Leben*.
Tradition criticism or *redaction criticism* focuses on the later stages of
textual arrangement in which editing is evident. *Canon criticism* (originating in the 1960s) focuses on the biblical canon as a complete artifact
and investigates its influence on the community of believers. *Synchronic
criticism* (since the 1970s) reads the canon as a complete literary work.

Literary, or source, criticism was the most tempestuous and rapidly
developing field in the nineteenth century; it addressed the very holy of
holies of the Bible and the history of the Israelite people and religion. It
reached its apex in the work of Wellhausen and the school of thought
named after him, which proposed – during the final third of the century – a comprehensive historical revision of the history of the biblical
period and the Israelite and Jewish religion. The Wellhausen school
was the hegemonic approach in biblical criticism in Germany until the
start of the twentieth century.[89]

*

Nineteenth-century Germany, then, was the sphere in which the *Wissenschaft des Judentums*, which aspired to reshape and establish Judaism
on the basis of modern, "scientific" ideology, came into contact with
biblical criticism, which aspired to do the same for biblical scholarship.
This encounter held an implicit promise; but it took place in a clear
context of power relations of a colonial type, in which the Jewish minority attempted to extricate itself from its traditional inferior position
in society and German discourse and to shape its identity in a way that
would allow it to integrate in its modern surroundings without losing
its own identity. For this reason the encounter was unable to free itself
of centuries of mutually hostile Christian and Jewish readings of shared
sacred texts, nor of the Hebraist, Orientalist discourse that shaped both
Christian attitudes toward Jews and ultimately the Jews' image of
themselves, whether real or desired. The present work aims to describe
and analyze the behavior of the Jewish side of this charged German[90]
encounter.

---

89 Thompson (1970, 109) notes the year 1905 as the start of the fall of the Wellhausen
    school, with the dawning of Gunkel's form criticism and Kostermann's tradition
    criticism. Both would reach their peak only after 1925.

90 The present study focuses on biblical criticism in the German language and does not
    deal with Hebrew scholarship in Eastern Europe. See: Soloveitchik and Rubasheff
    1925, 143ff., and recently Shavit and Eran 2007.

The present study focuses on how the *Wissenschaft des Judentums* contended with higher biblical criticism and particularly with criticism of the Pentateuch, both because the issues it raised stood at the center of biblical research during the period in question and because they were the most interesting, radical, and difficult to accept – far more so than textual corrections or criticism of the Psalms. Each of the following three parts is devoted to a third of the century: Part One begins with what is commonly accepted as the birth of the *Wissenschaft des Judentums* – the establishment of the *Verein für Cultur und Wissenschaft der Juden* ("Society for Jewish Culture and Science") in 1819; Part Two deals with the second third of the century, and Part Three with its conclusion. The first chapter in each part briefly describes the status and development of biblical criticism in the Protestant academia during the period in question (chapters 1, 4, and 7). Next follows a survey of the scope and nature of Jewish engagement with biblical criticism during that period (chapters 2, 5, and 8-9). Here I attempt to examine the Jewish response in its broad, public sense – expressed not only in scholarly compositions for a limited audience, but also in articles and reviews in the more popular periodicals of the time. Each part then concludes with an expansion on the work of a single Jewish scholar of each period: the historian Isaak Markus Jost in chapter 3, the theologian Solomon Ludwig Steinheim in chapter 6, and the Reform rabbi Siegmund Maybaum in chapter 10.

Part One

Biblical Criticism in the Society for Jewish Culture and Science

> In what manner is a work diminished,
> if for intra-textual considerations
> it is determined to be younger
> by several hundreds of years?
>
> Isaak Markus Jost, 1822[1]

1   Jost 1820-1828 IIIb, 198.

Chapter 1
Christian Biblical Criticism at the Start of the Nineteenth Century

During the closing third of the eighteenth century, the field of biblical criticism became established in German universities and also won recognition outside of academia. This was thanks largely to the work of Johann Gottfried Eichhorn (1752–1827),[1] professor of Oriental languages from 1775, first at the University of Jena and then in Göttingen. Eichhorn, whose reputation had also spread beyond Germany and who even in his own time was known in England as "the founder of modern Old Testament criticism,"[2] was the first scholar to employ higher biblical criticism in an academic context. This field, as he himself defined it, dealt with the "age, reliability, completeness, and origin"[3] of the Bible, in contrast to Lower Criticism, which focused on textual criticism and purging the errors the text had accumulated over the centuries. Thanks to Eichhorn's books – in particular his *Introduction to the Old Testament*,[4] which he began to publish in 1780 – the young academic discipline entered the public consciousness in Germany and aroused interest even outside of academic–theological circles: the poet Jean Paul, the philosopher and critic Herder, and of course the polymath Goethe took interest in Eichhorn's scholarship; and he was even mentioned in a contemporary novel.[5] Eichhorn was also well-known to the Jewish intellectuals of the Haskalah: Moses Mendelssohn[6] and David Friedländer[7] were familiar with his *Introduction*, and in its wake Yehuda Leb Ben Ze'ev pub-

---

1   About Eichhorn see: Smend 1989, 25-37; Kraus 1982, 133-155.
2   Smend 1989, 25.
3   Quoted in Smend 1989, 30.
4   Eichhorn 1790. The first edition was published in Leipzig from 1780-1783, the second in 1790, the third in 1803, and the fourth from 1823-1824. For a summary and evaluation of Eichhorn's work, see: Kraus 1982, 133-151.
5   Michaelis and Semler are mentioned in *The Sorrows of Young Werther* (Goethe 1962, 89); "Professor Eichhorn" is mentioned in Jean Paul's *Flegeljahre* (Paul 1959 I/2, 656). See also Goethe's autobiography: Goethe 1987, 208, as well as Seidel 1993, 183 and Smend 1989, 29.
6   Breuer 1996, 172.
7   Friedländer 1823, 69.

lished *Mavo el mikra'e kodesh* (Introduction to the Holy Scripture),[8] in which he introduced Hebrew readers to the fundamentals of Eichhorn's work with respect to the books of Prophets and Writings – though he refrained, characteristically, from addressing the Pentateuch.

In his monumental book, Eichhorn summarized the principal conclusions of biblical criticism accepted in his time. Following Astruc's approach, he divided the Book of Genesis into two sources: the Yahwist and the Elohist, so called for the divine name each employs.[9] Eichhorn himself believed that only Moses, whom he considered a historical figure, could have authored the Bible, but other scholars of his day rejected the attribution of the Bible to Moses. The Books of Chronicles – an important internal source about the time of Samuel and Kings – were considered a product of later redaction that was nonetheless based on older sources. The Book of Isaiah was divided in two; chapters 40 and onward were attributed to a prophet who lived some two hundred years after the eighth-century Isaiah of Jerusalem. The single authorship of the Books of Zechariah and Daniel was also cast in doubt.

These were the chief issues that occupied biblical criticism at the end of the eighteenth century and the start of the nineteenth. Without diminishing their importance, it must be remembered that "The source-critical theories of the late eighteenth century did not lead to any radical theories about the history of Israelite religion,"[10] and that but for one exception, in the first decades of the nineteenth century "no history of Israel had been written which presented the course of events in a fashion radically different from what is implied in the Old Testament."[11] The exception was de Wette,[12] the most radical biblical critic of his generation, who began his work in the first decade of the nineteenth century. De Wette refuted the antiquity of Chronicles; he declared that the Pentateuch in its final form was a late composition, the only evidence to its existence dating from the days of Josiah (the seventh century BCE), and that "the Book of the Torah" was a later idea. He rejected the Pentateuch's accounts of the period before the Israelite settlement in Canaan; maintained that until the days of Josiah there were no fixed cultic site or cultic laws, nor did the priesthood exist; and

---

8   Ben Ze'ev 1810; See: Shavit and Eran 2007, 115ff.

9   Ilgen (1798) subsequently attempted to reconstruct the archives of the Jerusalem temple and in the process divided the Elohist source itself into two secondary sources. Concerning Ilgen see: Seidel 1993.

10   Rogerson 1984, 21.

11   Rogerson 1984, 24.

12   Wilhelm Martin Lebrecht de Wette, 1780–1849. On him see: Rogerson 1992, a comprehensive monograph.

conjectured that the Pentateuch had retroactively included later customs and presented them as ancient traditions – in other words, he was
the first to suggest the hypothesis that the history of Israel was entirely
different than that which emerges from an uncritical reading of the
Hebrew Bible. Nevertheless, as we shall see, de Wette was a lone radical voice.

The image of Judaism that dominated the criticism of the biblical
texts and their composition is no less important than the critical out-
looks described above. In his research on images of Judaism in German
historical writing, Christhard Hoffmann[13] distinguishes between four
approaches – "ideal types," not necessarily mutually exclusive – that
were widespread in Germany during the Enlightenment and the Romantic period. These were the traditional, enlightened, classicist, and
historicist approaches.

The traditional Christian approach – the "sacred history" (*historia
sacra*) or later "salvation history" (*Heilsgeschichte*) – whose roots can be
traced to the end of the second century CE, perceived Judaism as a
lesser, yet necessary, historical stage. The ancient Jewish people was
perceived as the harbinger of Christianity and as an important part of
world history. Its history, as related in the Old Testament, allowed the
Church to boast of a continuous lineage ranging back to the creation of
the world. The Jews' refusal to recognize Jesus as the Messiah led to the
loss of their status as the chosen people and the transfer of that status to
the Christian Church. The chosen people became intransigent and
blind; they murdered the Son of God and were punished by the destruction of the Temple and by exile. In this outlook the Hebrew Bible
is the Old Testament, read by Christological hermeneutics as a text that
presages Jesus and the New Testament.

The enlightened–rationalist approach, which developed in English
deism and the French Enlightenment as a reaction to the "sacred history," was characterized by an attack against Christianity and the role of
the Church in society and politics. Part of this attack was an anti-Jewish
and anti-biblical discourse whose true, if covert, target was the Church,
which was established on the basis of Scripture. The Jewish religion
was depicted as contradictory to the principles of reason and natural
religion (*Naturreligion*); it was the religion of a Law barbaric, cruel, into-
lerant, and unethical. The Old Testament, which was the source of the
Church's legitimacy, was attacked as an unreliable Jewish creation rife
with contradictions and accounts of miracles unacceptable to the intellect. The ancient Israelites were seen as an inferior people, unimportant

---

13   Hoffmann 1988, 8-20.

and epigonic in comparison to other ancient cultures and peoples (the Chinese, the Egyptians, the Mesopotamians).

The classicist approach dealt with Judaism by comparing it to the ideal cultures of Greece and Rome. In contrast to the classical world, which was characterized by polytheistic tolerance and perfect harmony in the fields of culture, art, politics, and religion, Judaism was accused of monotheistic fanaticism, of breaching the harmony between man and nature, of political tyranny, and of spiritual enslavement expressed in a dependent approach toward God. A characteristic representative of this approach was Hegel; we will encounter it again in later chapters.

The historicist approach, on the other hand, attempted to understand Judaism as a specific historical phenomenon rather than on the basis of *a priori* historical and value-laden assumptions. Israelite history was not judged from a dogmatic or universal–moral perspective, but was instead studied in its specific historical contexts. The Hebrew Bible was regarded as authentic testimony to the lifestyle, religion, and nature of the ancient Israelites. This context had a less polemic overtone than those discussed above, and it made possible a certain freedom from rigid Christian or rationalistic dogmas, at least with respect to *ancient* Judaism.

German biblical criticism at the start of the nineteenth century operated primarily within the framework of the historicist approach to Judaism. The work of Semler, the theologian who established the legitimacy of the critical study of the Bible in the final third of the eighteenth century, does exhibit anti-biblical rhetoric that was characteristic of the intellectual approach; he advocated a "healthy withdrawal from the Books of the Old Testament".[14] Yet in his wake there emerged an independence from the traditional Christian critical framework and an openness to historicist approaches;[15] biblical criticism was influenced by the young discipline of history and its methods, and aspired to resemble it more closely. The methods of the philological–historical investigation of the Bible, which were developed in Western Europe (Holland, England, France) beginning in the seventeenth century within the framework of deism and the Enlightenment and were the domain of "free-thinking" intellectuals such as Spinoza, Voltaire, and Astruc, were adopted in Germany within the framework of the university system by professors (primarily of theology) who had no choice but to take into account the Protestant orthodoxy. Unlike the French *philosophes*, who attacked Scripture as a roundabout way of attacking

---

14   Kraus 1982, 109f.
15   Kraus 1982, 151.

the Catholic Church, German biblical critics operated within a Protestant framework that held *sola scriptura* as one of the foundations of
Christianity. As a result of this systemic position, German biblical criticism was moderate and subdued in comparison to Western Europe's
intellectual criticism, and it attempted to reconcile the Orthodox and
critical approaches.[16] Thus most German biblical critics refrained from a
head-on confrontation with Orthodox Protestant approaches and drew
away from a sweeping invalidation of the Old Testament. Likewise the
image of ancient Judaism was not, for the most part, negative, as it was
in the intellectual tradition. In fact it was positive: the intellectual anti-
Jewish approach was rejected, Hegel's classicist approach made its way
into biblical criticism only at a later stage (with Vatke's work in the
mid-1830s), and the historicist approach, characterized by its positive
treatment of the ancient Israelites, was dominant. This was already
evident in the work of the two "forefathers" of German biblical criticism in the eighteenth century – Herder[17] and Michaelis.[18] Herder set
out to discover the original spirit of the Jewish people by way of its
ancient poetry; Michaelis attempted to reconstruct the original biblical
law, free of later Jewish interpretation, and considered it a natural law
based on intellect and reason in the spirit of the political ideals of Mon-
tesquieu. Both, in their work, idealized the ancient Israelites.

It is important to emphasize that this positive depiction of the ancient Israelites was not applied to the Jews of later periods – the post-
biblical, present-day Jews. German thinking during this period was
characterized by what is called the "German Janus":[19] a sharp dichotomy between the ancient Israelites and the later Jewish people (*Spätju-
dentum*), with the latter seen as a complete negative of the former. In
contrast to the idealization of the ancient Jewish people, later Judaism
and contemporary Jews were seen through the lens of a variety of anti-
Jewish prejudices.

In a different language and different cultural context, this approach
continued Christianity's ambivalent tradition toward the Jews; in particular it continued the Lutheran approach. Unlike the Puritan or Anglican positions, according to which the People of Israel had not lost

---

16 Hoffmann 1988, 29.

17 Herder's central work for our purposes is *The Spirit of Hebrew Poetry* of 1782 (Herder
    1833). On Herder see: Kraus 1982, 114-132. On Herder and Judaism see: Levy 1994a,
    93-213, in particular from p. 176; Manuel 1992, 263-272.

18 Johann David Michaelis, 1717–1791. His main work for our purposes is *Mosaisches
    Recht* ("Moses' Laws", Michaelis 1770-1775; English version: Michaelis 1814). About
    Michaelis see: Kraus 1982, 97-103; Smend 1989, 13-24; Hess 2000; Löwenbrück 1994;
    Löwenbrück 1995.

19 Manuel 1992, 249ff.

their status as God's chosen people – instead, their redemption was delayed only because of their sins – Lutheran theology maintained that from the moment of their rejection of Jesus the Jews had forfeited God's favor entirely. Once the Chosen People, they were now the seed of the Devil. Herder and Michaelis strove to reconstruct the biblical era in all its "purity"; they perceived any later influence as a Jewish/rabbinic corruption of the noble source. Michaelis was unconcerned with dating the creation of the Law,[20] but he claimed that rabbis and the Talmud had corrupted the laws of Moses and were therefore not a reliable source of knowledge about the ancient Law. In contrast the Arabs of Egypt and Palestine, who were described as living "outside of history" and as having remained stagnant for thousands of years, were of considerable importance to understanding the way of life of the ancient Israelites.

Hence the situation can also be viewed in the context of the Orientalist discourse, which expanded and consolidated during that period in Germany.[21] Michaelis did describe Mosaic law as natural and moral, but he described it too as primitive and Oriental (and profoundly influenced by Egyptian law); it was therefore unfit for adoption by Western, progressive Europe. This claim stood at the basis of Michaelis's lifework: he objected to the undertakings of European nations to incorporate parts of Mosaic law in their own constitutions and sought to purify European law from such primitive Oriental influences. While Christianity constantly strove to present biblical Law as particular and limited to its own time (from Moses to Jesus), its own place (the Land of Israel), and its own jurisdiction (the Israelites alone), Michaelis's Orientalism took the opposite approach: biblical Law was universal and eternal in the sense that it was the natural law of Orientals (who remained outside of history and changeless). Thus Michaelis's profound interest in the customs of Middle Eastern Arabs (and even Native American Indians) of his time becomes clear, as do his efforts to draw conclusions from these customs and apply them to the laws of the Bible.

Michaelis objected to emancipation. He saw Jews as a foreign, Oriental people whom even ten more generations could not make European. In contrast to Dohm's revolutionary initiative to grant Jews equal civil rights, Michaelis proposed establishing a separate judicial authority for the Jews and leasing them lands in unpopulated areas of Germany or sending them off to colonies ("Sugar Islands"), where they

---

20   Thompson 1970, 5.
21   On Michaelis in the context of Orientalism see: Hess 1998; Hess 2000. See also the remarks of: Raz-Krakotzkin 1999; Heschel 1998; Heschel 1999.

could live separately and be of use to the state. He accused the Jews of arrogant self-seclusion from the gentile world and warned that their acceptance as regular citizens would be harmful to the state, as they could not serve in the army (both because of the Jewish laws of the Sabbath and their dietary laws, and because of their diminutive physical stature) and would multiply endlessly and take control over the German economy.[22]

Michaelis's anti-emancipatory position did not, apparently, characterize his nineteenth-century followers in general. At the start of the century the new discipline of biblical criticism also consolidated a characteristic political identity. Early nineteenth-century German Protestantism was divided into three branches: the intellectual, the Orthodox, and the Pietist.[23] Over the course of the second decade of the century, during the period of post-Napoleonic reaction, the Orthodox and Pietist branches united into a single conservative camp and the schism that would characterize German Protestantism throughout the entire nineteenth century was forged: the liberal camp on the one hand, opposite the Orthodox, "Positivist" camp on the other.

As for the Orthodox Protestant camp, "political conservatism and religious conservatism were one and the same."[24] The Protestant orthodoxy positioned dogma above science and reason; continued the Christological line of exegesis, which read the Old Testament as a harbinger of the New; and rejected as heresy the attempt to cast doubt on the dogma of the verbal inspiration (*verbale Inspirationslehre*) of Scripture through critical historical research. This camp was also characterized by reactionary conservatism in the political arena: the Revolution was a sinful product of satanic influence, and any demands for liberty, for equality between Christians and non-Christians, for democracy, or for civil rights amounted to a revolt against the divine order.

Biblical criticism, on the other hand, was an undertaking of liberal Protestantism; the connection between biblical criticism and political liberalism is evident as early as Spinoza and would continue until the final third of the nineteenth century. During the first third of the century this camp was characterized by a habitus that integrated liberalism into theology; a modern scientific and anti-dogmatic ethos that placed theology second to reason (hence too the involvement in biblical criticism); and a liberal democratic political position.

---

22 On the polemic between Dohm and Michaelis see: Löwenbrück 1994, 326f.; Jersch-Wenzel in Meyer 1997, 11-14.

23 Nipperdey 1983, 423-440.

24 Nipperdey 1983, 436.

Eichhorn, a student of Michaelis, is an early example. His approach also considered the law of Moses good for its time; however, as the Jews and their rabbis continued to adhere to it, it increasingly became a source of harm to them. Even before they arrived in Europe, and certainly after their arrival, the Jews safeguarded their isolation and became accustomed to refraining from intermarriage with others; destruction and exile only further corrupted their national character. Jews "at-"attributed to that wisest of lawmakers [i.e., Moses] an intention not at all wise, namely that laws suited to the Orient were meant to apply in every other place."[25] The laws of Moses had been intended only to transform a nomadic people into a settled nation and gradually to accustom an idolatrous people to "the concept of a single supreme Being"; the Jews' continued adherence to these political laws corrupted their national character. It was therefore their own inability to be citizens of a state with equal rights and responsibilities before the law – and not religious hatred toward them – that accounted for the discrimination they faced. In all of these standpoints, Eichhorn followed in the footsteps of Michaelis; however, his position on Jewish emancipation was more moderate than that of his teacher. A critique written by Eichhorn in 1789 about a book by Henri Grégoire illustrates the point. Grégoire – who participated in the French polemic on Jewish emancipation on the eve of the Revolution – supported the idea of granting equal rights to Jews, as he hoped that they would convert to Christianity once the process concluded.[26] Eichhorn, in contrast, on the one hand repudiated Dohm and Grégoire's pro-emancipation position, which claimed that the Jews' debased morality stemmed from their oppression; he wondered "whether the latter is not the result of the former, and the corruption of the [Jewish] people is what forced the nations to deny Jews the full rights of citizenship, as they were unworthy of them."[27] On the other hand, he rejected absolutely the demand that Jews convert to Christianity, and proposed that "simple reform of their faith, which has been unsuited to the state of the world for millennia, will suffice; as well as (as the wiser among them also loudly recommend) the strict education of their youth, which in the space of a few generations will accomplish a miraculous refinement of their kind."[28] After such a reform, Eichhorn maintained, no nation would be able to ignore the advantages it would reap from granting equal rights to these "im-

---

25   Eichhorn 1789, 297.
26   On Grégoire and the French polemic see: Katz 1973, 71-73. On the polemic in Germany see: Katz 1973, 80-103; Katz 1980, 51-104.
27   Eichhorn 1789, 294.
28   Eichhorn 1789, 301f.

proved" Jews.[29] As opposed to Michaelis, who regarded contemporary Jews as irredeemable Orientals, Eichhorn was thus prepared to accept equal rights for Jews but set their reform as a precondition, and he opened a path for Jews' integration as Jews – reformed, but unconverted – in German society. He also alluded to Jewish figures who could assist in the satisfaction of this condition – referring, no doubt, to the *maskilim* and their descendents, the members of the *Wissenschaft des Judentums*.

---

29   Eichhorn 1789, 302.

Chapter 2
The Society for Jewish Culture and Science

In November 1819, seven young Jews in Berlin founded the *Verein zur Verbesserung des Zustandes der Juden im deutschen Bundesstaate* ("Society for the Improvement of the Jewish Condition in the German Federation"), which later became the *Verein für Cultur und Wissenschaft der Juden* ("Society for Jewish Culture and Science"). The origins of the *Wissenschaft des Judentums* are usually traced back to this Society.[1] At its peak the Society included more than eighty members in and outside of Berlin; it existed until 1824.

The Society attempted to propose a new sort of Jewish experience, theoretical and intellectual in nature, which would on the one hand enable the full integration of individual Jews in society at large and on the other hand preserve the collective Jewish identity. The need for this new form of existence stemmed on the one hand from German Jews' rapidly increasing integration into German culture – a process in which the members of the Society considered themselves the vanguard – and on the other hand from the recognition that German culture had left behind the period of rationalist Enlightenment and entered into a period of Romantic nationalism. This change in the German cultural consciousness called for a new Jewish response: the rationalist universalization of Judaism, as developed in the Haskalah since Mendelssohn, was no longer a fitting foundation for the identity of the modern Jew, who participated in early nineteenth-century German culture and demanded equal rights as a member of it.

For the Society, *Wissenschaft* ("science") – which referred first and foremost to the systematic study of history,[2] to which all other disciplines were considered auxiliary – was the key concept in the creation of this new Jewish identity. In the context of the tension between universalism and particularism – the basic problem of modern Jewish existence – the members of the Society wished to uphold Jewish particular-

---

1 On the Society, see Rachel Livnè-Freudenthal's comprehensive dissertation (1996). See also: Schorsch 1994, 205-232; Livnè-Freudenthal 1991; Ucko 1934.

2 Yerushalmi 1982, 82ff. On the central place of the study of history in nineteenth-century Germany, see: Sheehan 1989, 542ff.

ism yet base it on universal values; only such a foundation could allow the Jewish minority's existence within the majority society. *Wissenschaft* was a seen as the universal foundation upon which Jewish particularism would be based;[3] at the same time, it would make it possible to purge the Jewish identity of its Oriental character.[4] "For the first time it is not history that must prove its utility to Judaism, but Judaism that must prove its validity to history, by revealing and justifying itself historically."[5] The investigation of the past was to take the place of the traditional Jewish study of Torah and Halakhah; the historian would replace the rabbi as the highest authority.[6] Intellectual, scientific activity was intended to create a new plane of discourse in which Judaism would exist as an integral part of European culture; Judaism was seen not only as a religion but, more comprehensively, "as the gamut of relationships, special qualities, and accomplishments of the Jews in matters of philosophy, history, law, literature in general, citizenship, and all the problems of humanity."[7] As to history – the mother of all nineteenth-century disciplines – it "was the axis around which Judaism was arranged, and historiography became the instrument that granted it new substance," writes Livnè-Freudenthal;

> The members of the Society […] emphasized the importance of the historicization of Judaism. The examination of Judaism and the re-creation of its past by historical means was supposed to satisfy their primary needs: the need to integrate Judaism in European culture by re-creating and presenting its history as part of general culture and history, and the need to find – or better said to re-establish – the Judaism that had been lost so that it would be possible to grasp it once again."[8]

Historicizing Judaism was intended to establish a Judaism that could be molded and changed, that faced its past unapologetically and denied it any normative value. The paradox pointed out by Franz Schnabel – that the dawn of historical thought in nineteenth-century Germany went hand-in-hand with the thorough dismantling of traditional values and institutions[9] – thus also characterized the *Wissenschaft des Judentums* from the start.

---

3   Livnè-Freudenthal 1996, 236ff.
4   Mendes-Flohr 1991a, 82.
5   Yerushalmi 1982, 84.
6   Schorsch 1994, 218.
7   After the definition of Immanuel Wolf, a member of the Society; quoted in Mendes-Flohr 1979, 68.
8   Livnè-Freudenthal 1996, 262-263.
9   Quoted in Sheehan 1989, 543.

A customary claim is that "the birth of the *Wissenschaft des Juden-tums* lay in abandoning biblical scholarship."[10] There was indeed only minimal engagement in biblical scholarship by members of the Society. The negative image of later Judaism – rarely studied and much maligned by Christians – demanded immediate repair; the members of the Society understood that it was preferable to invest their effort in rehabilitating the negative image of rabbinic Judaism rather than in the study of biblical times.[11] The issue emerges in, among other places, a programmatic article written by Zunz in 1818 in which he noted the tremendous range of literature dealing with the Hebrew Bible and called for focus specifically on the neglected rabbinic literature, whose very future lay in peril.[12]

However a correction, or at least clarification, is required: there is no evidence among the members of the Society of any objection on principle to biblical criticism or its conclusions. On the contrary, while their contribution to the critical study of the Bible was indeed minimal, their attitude toward it was unquestionably positive. Ambivalence and even opposition to biblical criticism, which would characterize several members of the *Wissenschaft des Judentums* movement later in the century, was not yet evident among the members of the Society; their attitude toward that discipline was favorable and unambiguous. Thus Zunz, editor of the Society's journal, did not refrain from publishing an article by Lazarus Bendavid[13] in its third (and final) issue; the article claimed that Moses had not written the version of the Pentateuch known today and that even the original version of the Ten Commandments had not been preserved. This would have been a radical stance even for a Christian biblical scholar of the time; even Eichhorn believed throughout most of his life that Moses had authored the Bible.[14] This positive approach to biblical criticism is also expressed in Zunz's early work; in *Die gottesdienstlichen Vorträge der Juden* ("The Worship Sermons of the Jews," 1832) he relied on the findings of de Wette, the most radical biblical scholar of the day.[15] The same attitude is explicit in Jost's work, which will be examined at length further on.

---

10   Soloveitchik and Rubasheff 1925, 128.
11   See: Schorsch 1994, 221.
12   Zunz 1818, 3. The large part of Zunz's work was devoted, in keeping with this trend, to the post-biblical period.
13   Bendavid 1823, 491f.
14   Kraus 1982, 140.
15   The first chapter of the book deals with the books of Chronicles (Zunz 1892, 13-36). See p. 195 below.

This positive approach demands explanation, and a central factor appears to be the alliance – in the sense of similar interests and positions in the cultural and political field – that was forged between the members of the Society and the liberal Protestant camp.

As we have seen, *Wissenschaft* was the foremost universal value in the Society's project to redefine Judaism: "assimilation through science" (*Assimilation durch Wissenschaft*), in the words of Monika Richarz.[16] This was a generation of Jewish intellectuals who by and large (as in the case of Jost and Zunz) had begun their studies within the framework of traditional Jewish education and succeeded, through great effort, in filling in the gaps in their cultural and general knowledge and being accepted to regular studies at German universities in fields of study that had previously been closed to Jews.[17] During their university studies the members of this generation were introduced to modern scholarship, its achievements, and its universal image, and it is natural that, in attempting to construct a new image for Judaism, they would seek out allies within academia, which they regarded as the institutional realization of the scientific ideal.

The aspiration to integrate as modern Jews in German civil society led the members of the Society to take up a liberal political stance and to attach themselves to the liberal powers among the Protestants. Scholarship as a universalist ethos, the demand for the de-confessionalization of society, and the creation of a civil society could advance their aspirations for emancipation and absorption as citizens with equal rights in German society. "The possibility for cooperation between German liberals and Jewish activists, who yearned to achieve emancipation, led the majority of Jewish activists to join the liberal camp."[18] The alliance between Jews and liberals would continue, on the Jewish side, until the destruction of German Jewry during Nazi Germany.[19] Zunz, for example, was actively and enthusiastically engaged in political liberalism throughout his life;[20] Jost is known to have been a member of the *Burschenschaft*, a liberal nationalist student organization, in his youth.[21] In this constellation, academia also housed natural allies of the Jewish avant-garde in the liberal Protestant camp – the very camp

---

16   Richarz 1974, 100.
17   About the entry of Jews into German academia, particularly at the start of the nineteenth century, see: Richarz 1974, 83ff. Jost, for example, wrote about the experience of his introduction to the academic world in his memoirs (Jost 1854, 160ff.).
18   Toury 1960, 72.
19   See the anthology: *Das Deutsche Judentum und der Liberalismus* 1986.
20   On Zunz's political activity see: Wallach 1959, 120-140.
21   Michael 1983, 110.

that developed the field of biblical criticism. Like the liberal Protestants, who were faced with a strong conservative orthodoxy, liberal Jews were an elite minority within the general Jewish public, which for the most part adopted conservative positions on religion and loyalist positions in the political sphere.

Given the choice between these two theological camps – the conservative and the liberal – the members of the Society naturally preferred the latter to the former, which was entirely opposed to emancipation. The alliance with the liberal Protestants was thus a natural one, but this does not mean that it was free of difficulties, as the liberal Protestant camp itself did not entirely support emancipation.[22] Nor was it free of prejudice against the Jews, and its aim to "reform" the Jews was not disjoint from the Christian theological attitude toward Jews and their desired reformation. We have noted Eichhorn's reserved position above; his recommendation to postpone emancipation until after the civil reformation of the Jews (even if he held to it thirty years later) could not have been welcome to the members of the Society. Nonetheless they could certainly agree with the call to reform (rather than convert) the Jews and the Jewish religion: this was the Society's explicit goal.

The Jewish–liberal-Protestant alliance was also evident on a personal level. Remaining records testify to intimate personal relationships between two of the most prominent biblical critics, Eichhorn and de Wette, and their Jewish students, in particular Zunz and Jost, who were both of the same generation (born in 1793 and 1794 respectively). These records point to the fact that even if the two critics did not necessarily internalize the liberal idea of tolerance in full, they clearly wished to encourage those students whom they considered the desirable model – and perhaps even the standard bearers – of Jews removed from tradition and involved in German culture.[23] Incidentally, in accordance with this trend, Jost regretfully mentioned in his memoirs the "low standards to which the [non-Jewish] scholarly world held young Jews" – standards that sound almost like affirmative action: "The slightest proof of good will [on the part of Jewish students] [...] sufficed to extract from these excellent people testaments to their extraordinary intelligence [...]" Jost, who had been a student at the University of Göttin-

---

22   An unambiguously pro-emancipatory stance predominated only among the radicals, but that camp lacked representation in academia. In any case the Jewish activists were aware of their political weakness, placed their hopes for change on the government, and distanced themselves from radical positions (Livnè-Freudenthal 1991, in particular p. 119. See also: Toury 1966, 23ff.).

23   Jost 1854, 163.

gen since 1813, studied under the venerable Eichhorn, the only teacher he mentioned – with great appreciation – in his memoirs.[24] Despite their considerable difference in age – Eichhorn was forty-one years older than Jost – Jost forged a personal relationship with his teacher,[25] and it seems that the latter even encouraged him to write his *Geschichte der Israeliten* (History of the Israelites).[26] There is no evidence of tension in their relationship caused by Jost's religion, in contrast to the obvious tensions apparent between Michaelis, who taught Eichhorn, and Mendelssohn half a century earlier.[27] In the spring of 1818 Zunz visited Göttingen and also met with Eichhorn;[28] Heinrich Heine, another member of the Society, wrote fondly: "I knew old Eichhorn. He recruited me to write for the journal [...]"[29] Again, Eichhorn probably referred to Jews such as these when he wrote about "the wiser among them" who recommended "a simple reform of their faith."[30]

In 1814 Jost moved to Berlin, to be followed by Zunz one year later. Zunz studied with de Wette, who affected him profoundly; their acquaintance became more than a simple teacher–student relationship. De Wette, even more than the elderly Eichhorn, embodied the full liberal-Protestant habitus of the early nineteenth century: he was a liberal theologian and a radical biblical critic; because of his liberal democratic leanings he became so odious to the reactionary Prussian regime that he was dismissed from his post at the University of Berlin.[31] Despite his friendship with the extreme anti-Jewish philosopher Fries,[32] de Wette found a common language with his student Zunz, who was himself, as we have seen, an enthusiastic liberal political activist. The close relationship between Zunz and de Wette was no doubt strengthened by the smaller disparity in their ages: de Wette was Zunz's senior by only fourteen years. Zunz wrote of visiting de Wette in 1817,[33] and from a

---

24 Jost 1854, 161.

25 Schorsch 1994, 237; Michael 1983, 6-7.

26 ADB XIV, 578 [Brüll].

27 On the relationship between Mendelssohn and Michaelis see: Löwenbrück 1994.

28 ADB XLV, 493 [Kaufmann].

29 Letter to Moser, 1824 (Heine 1970 XX, 171). Elsewhere Heine fondly described an anonymous scholar at Göttingen; Smend (1989, 25) conjectures that the reference is to Eichhorn.

30 Eichhorn 1789, 301f.

31 For details about Zunz's academic study, in particular with de Wette, see: Bechtoldt 1995, 64ff. and: Maybaum 1894. On de Wette's political outlook and its theological associations see: Rogerson 1992, 88, 120-124.

32 Jakob Friedrich Fries, 1773–1843. On Fries' intensive anti-Jewish activities see: Michael 1993, 178-183. On the personal and philosophical ties between Fries and de Wette see: Rogerson 1984, updated in Rogerson 1992.

33 Zunz 1931, 20.

letter written in 1819 we learn that he spoke several times with de Wette about his programmatic essay "On Rabbinic Literature," written the previous year.[34] The academic and personal relationship between them continued until de Wette was dismissed from Berlin in 1819. In 1838 Zunz once again turned to de Wette in his exile in Basel and requested a letter of recommendation.[35] In his letter, Zunz mentioned the intimacy of their relationship during their days in Berlin ("I bare my heart to you as in those happy days"), thanked his teacher for opening the gates of biblical criticism to him, and emphasized his great influence on his own work: "Though the outward relationship with you was only fleeting, still the inner bonds have been remarkably long-lasting. For it is to you that I owe my understanding of biblical criticism, and, alongside Friedrich August Wolf, my scientific outlook in general." It appears that de Wette did indeed provide the requested recommendation.[36] Although in Berlin Jost and Zunz frequently studied under the same teachers,[37] I have found no evidence of a relationship between Jost and de Wette; nor did Jost mention de Wette in his writings.

It appears that the academic and political alliance formed between liberal Protestantism and the scientific–critical ethos on the one hand and the Jewish avant-garde on the other was the deciding factor in explaining the Society's positive relationship with the field of biblical criticism. The position in which the members of the Society found themselves, in both politics and academics, was characterized by a habitus that included a positive approach to biblical criticism; if they wished to adopt the scientific ethos and truly join the liberal, anti-dogmatic camp, it was necessary that they adopt the discipline of biblical criticism as well.

The alliance with liberal–critical Protestantism dictated not only a favorable approach toward biblical criticism, but also opposition to alternative approaches. This explains the antagonistic attitude of members of the Society toward the journal *Der Bibel'sche Orient* (The Biblical Orient). There is disagreement as to the identity of the writer, or writers, of this journal; only two issues were published in Munich in 1820, and its content is often unclear and rife with contradictions. There is however a consensus that it applied a Romantic approach to the Bible (the writer admired Herder) that incorporated mystical–kabbalistic

---

34   Glatzer 1964, 97.
35   Geiger, L. 1896b, 258f.
36   In a letter to the King of Prussia dated April 28, 1843 Zunz requested that the King consider, among others, de Wette's recommendation (Geiger, L. 1896b, 323).
37   Schulin 1997, 302.

foundations, looked favorably on etymological exegeses and popular name explanations, and opposed the critical approach.[38]

To the extent that a coherent program can be discerned in *Der Bibel'sche Orient*, it is the antithesis of the Society's approach. The journal also criticized David Friedländer and defended the practical Jewish commandments; Isaac Bernays, who wrote at least part of *Der Bibel'sche Orient*, would eventually become the teacher of the neo-Orthodox Samson Raphael Hirsch. *Der Bibel'sche Orient* was inundated with criticism by members and associates of the Society. A very hostile critique published in the Society's journal[39] attacked its etymological, symbolic, and mystical approach to the Bible and explicitly equated it with opposition to reform in Judaism and to Protestantism in Christianity, as well as with reactionism in general: "To Judaism it preaches Rabbinism (even as it seemingly contradicts itself), and to Christianity – Catholicism (for it hates the pure word of Protestantism); this is at least consistent. Backward! Ever only backward! That appears to be its slogan."[40] S.M. Ehrenberg, a beloved teacher of Jost and Zunz, was pleased to read this scathing critique and added that after what he had read about *Der Bibel'sche Orient* he had no wish to read it at all;[41] in 1823, Heinrich Heine dubbed Bernays a "charlatan."[42] Even Jost's objection to publishing in the Society's journal what he called "philosophical investigations of grammatical questions in the Bible"[43] may have referred to articles in the vein of *Der Bibel'sche Orient*.

As agents of the modernization, historicization, and "scientization" of Judaism, the members of the Society thus staked a comprehensive position in the political, academic, and social field – a position that

---

38 About the journal and the problems it raises see: Horwitz 1996, and the bibliography on the issue and its history therein.

39 Moser 1822. The critique is signed only "--r--"; it is attributed to Moser following Elbogen 1922, 95.

40 Moser 1822, 195.

41 Letter to Zunz dated April 29, 1822 (Glatzer 1958:31).

42 Horwitz 1996, 328.

43 *"philosophische Untersuchungen über grammatische Gegenstände der Bibel."* Elbogen (1922, 90 N. 3), who cites Jost's objection in the *Verein's* protocol, takes issue with the word "philosophical" and argues that a more reasonable choice would have been "philological"; however, he concedes that the handwriting in question is thoroughly legible. Elbogen's claim is unreasonable: why would Jost object to philological biblical research, when he supported it in his other writings? It appears to me that Jost's unusual expression does in fact refer to similar articles in their approach to the "biblical Orient," an approach that frequently included philosophical–etymological exegesis. Jost, with his rationalist approach – and perhaps even sarcasm – was certainly apt to style these "philosophical investigations of grammatical questions," objecting as he did to the inclusion of such articles in the *Verein's* organ; while Zunz replied to him that any work of a sufficiently high level would be included.

included an (incomplete) alliance with the liberal Protestant camp. Their positive approach to biblical criticism derived from this position; yet, once staked, it required them to contend with the substance and biases of biblical criticism in practice. For Jews to internalize the non-Jewish discourse about themselves was no small matter.

Chapter 3
Jost and Biblical Criticism

Notwithstanding their positive attitude toward the subject, only a few members of the Society actually engaged in biblical criticism. Lazarus Bendavid (1762–1832), a mathematician and philosopher who had studied under Kant and published the aforementioned radical article in the Society's journal,[1] was one of the last of the *maskilim* and from a generational perspective was not part of the Society; Heine, in a June 27, 1823 letter to Zunz, already complained that "Bendavid writes clearly, but what he writes is suitable for neither the period nor the periodical. These are articles that might have been appropriate for the *Theologisches Journal* in 1786."[2] Zunz himself incorporated biblical criticism into the second chapter of his *Worship Sermons of the Jews*, in which he relied on the findings of his teacher de Wette on the books of Chronicles;[3] but the bulk of his effort was directed at the "rabbinic" period, and he returned to biblical criticism only half a century after the days of the Society, at the start of the 1870s.[4] A more extensive engagement in biblical criticism can actually be found in the work of Jost, who had studied under Eichhorn. Jost, who was among the founders of the Society, had left it due to personal differences some six months after it

---

1   Bendavid 1823.
2   Heine 1970 XX, 103; the *Theologisches Journal* (formerly *Theologische Bibliothek*) was published from 1786 to 1792 and was edited by the moderate liberal theologian Johann Christoph Döderlein (1746–1792; see: ADB V:281f. [G. Frank].)
3   Zunz 1892 <1832>, 13-36. In effect, Zunz continued the work of de Wette (1806-1807), demonstrated the tendentious redaction in Chronicles, described it, and determined a late date of composition for that book. The difference between de Wette and Zunz's respective scopes of interest is instructive: while de Wette analyzed Chronicles as part of an orientation that looked "backward" to learn about the ancient Israelite religion, Zunz, who was interested in Judaism rather than Israelite religion, used de Wette's work on the book as a starting point from which to look "forward" and study the subsequent history of the Jews. For an analysis and evaluation of the chapter, see: Soloveitchik and Rubasheff 1925, 129. It is surprising that Bechtoldt, who devotes a chapter to Zunz in his book on nineteenth-century Jewish biblical criticism (Bechtoldt 1995, 64-89), altogether ignores this central evidence of the young Zunz's engagement in biblical criticism. In contrast see: Perles 1910, 317.
4   See p. 195 below.

was established;[5] but from a generational and ideological perspective he reflected the Society's membership.

Jost[6] was the first modern Jew to to write a comprehensive Jewish history; as part of this effort he addressed the subject of modern biblical criticism. This was accomplished in his two great historical monographs: *Geschichte der Israeliten* (History of the Israelites),[7] which was published in ten volumes from 1820 to 1828, and *Allgemeine Geschichte des Israelitischen Volkes* (General History of the Israelite People),[8] published in two volumes in 1832. In the following sections we shall see how – in contrast to claims that Jost's historical work was nothing but "a sort of mass of sticky crumbs"[9] – Jost created a carefully thought-out structure of Israelite versus Jewish history. This structure succeeded both in handling the complex image of Judaism and the importance of the Law within it, and in cleverly inoculating Judaism from the fundamental dangers of biblical criticism.

A "Israelites" or "Jews"?

As we have seen, biblical criticism and German historical writing in general at the turn of the eighteenth and nineteenth centuries were characterized by a relatively positive image of the ancient Israelites; one of its functions was to create a negative image of later (contemporary) Jews. This antinomy between the biblical Israelites and the Jews of the present was also expressed on a linguistic level in the distinction between "Jews" and "Israelites." The struggle over terminology is charac-

---

5   Schorsch 1994, 284.

6   Isaak Markus Jost, 1793–1860. The most comprehensive study of Jost was carried out by Reuven Michael, who dedicated to him a monograph (1983) and a chapter in his book on Jewish historical writing (Michael 1993, 217-278). See also Schorsch's article (1994, 233-254), Baron's classic 1928 article (Baron 1964), and Max Wiener on religion in Jost's writings (Wiener 1933, 209-217); likewise Dinur 1978. Jonathan Cohen analyzes and criticizes the lack of research on Jost (Cohen 1982). Cohen also rejects the accepted consensus in the field (except in Baron) that Jost was an old-fashioned enlightened historian disconnected from the developments in the field of history during his time. Cohen sees Jost as a transition figure between the Enlightenment and Historicism, not unlike his German contemporary Niebuhr.

7   Jost 1820-1828. The orphaned references from this point on (volume, page number) refer to this book. In volume III there are two separate numbering sequences: after p. 259, the page numbering begins anew from 111. I represent these sequences as IIIa and IIIb respectively.

8   Jost 1832.

9   This review by Ludwig Philippson is quoted in Michael 1983, 81, from *Allgemeine Zeitung des Judenthums* 3 (1839), 45.

teristic of social power struggles in general, and of struggles for emancipation by minority groups in a colonial context in particular; often the
power struggle between a minority and a majority group also expresses
a struggle over the identity of the minority group itself.

"Jews" (*Juden*) was a broad term denoting both the Israelites of biblical times and the Jews of the present. This was the state of things during the eighteenth century and in essence during the nineteenth century as well. According to the Grimm brothers' 1877 German
dictionary: "'Jew' refers both to an inhabitant of the Jewish land of the
Old Testament and to one who was exiled thence and retained his traits
and religion."[10] In order to escape the negative connotations that were
generally attached to this term in German culture, and in order to minimize the national aspect of Judaism and emphasize its confessional
side, German Jews began as early as the end of the eighteenth century
to call themselves "Israelites" (*Israeliten*).[11] This custom may also have
been related to the fact that they saw the current period – a time of tolerance and (prospective) equal rights – as a post-exilic age that was in
a way a return to pre-exilic times. The term "Israelites" did not entirely
displace the term "Jews," but it was frequently used by Central-
European Jews to refer to their own literature as well as religious and
cultural institutions.

During the very years in which German Jews were attempting to
adopt the term "Israelites" to designate themselves, the term also took
hold in the field of biblical criticism but with a different meaning. As
early as the eighteenth century, the term "Israelites" served to describe
those who lived during the biblical period in order to distinguish them
from the Jews – the descendents of the kingdom of Judah – who appeared after the Babylonian exile and existed to the present day. We
find this usage, for example, in Michaelis.[12] The fundamental difference
between the ancient Israelites and the later Jews required two distinct
terms in order to be firmly established. The separate usage of these
terms was not yet a regular part of the scientific discourse in the eighteenth century: thus for example the young Hegel, in a theological
work written around 1798, used "Jews" and "Israelites" interchangea-
bly when writing about the biblical period, and wrote of the "Jewish

---

10   Grimm 1877, 2352.
11   JL III, 407 ("*Jude*"), JL III, 76f.("*Israeliten*"); EJ IX, 530 ("*Jude*"); Maier 1977, 54f. From
     1811 to 1812 a debate took place in the Prussian government between those who
     argued that the term "Jew" should be replaced by "Israelite" or "Mosaist" in order
     to be rid of its negative connotations, and those who maintained that it had no such
     connotations or that they would fade away by themselves with an improvement in
     the Jews' situation (Stern 1885, 246ff.).
12   Michaelis 1770-1775 I, 44f.

monarchy" (the kingdom of Saul etc.) and "Jewish prophets" of the Bible.[13] In contrast, another non-Jewish work written in 1788 deals with "Israelite" membership in the Freemasons; here the author of course referred to contemporary German Jews.[14] It was Eichhorn, at the end of the eighteenth century, who instilled the distinction between Jews and Israelites in the scientific discourse.[15] In a brief announcement written in 1794 and published in his periodical, he objected to the trend of conflating the two terms:

> To judge by numerous new compositions, the custom of using "Israelites" as equal in meaning to "Jews," and "the Mosaic religion" as equivalent to "Judaism," is on the rise. For the sake of precision one should always refer by the term "Hebrews" or "Israelites" to the nation before its return from exile; only after the return [...] is the term "Jews" appropriate.[16]

This terminology, in which the Babylonian exile served as a chronological separator between the Israelites and the Jews, was accepted and became, over the course of the nineteenth century, a fundamental distinction within German biblical criticism.

Jost was therefore caught in a conflict between the two parts of his identity, the Jewish-German sphere and the Christian scholarly sphere – a conflict that found expression in the problematic determination of a fitting name for the members of the subordinate group. As a product of the Jewish emancipation, he preferred the term "Israelites" over "Jews" in referring to contemporary Jews. However, as a historian and a student of Eichhorn he was required to restrict the term "Israelites" to the period before the Babylonian exile alone and to use "Jews" in reference to the later periods – and in so doing to adopt not only the denotative distinction between the two terms but also the negative connotation of the term "Jews."

Jost was unable to escape this conflict without entangling himself in inconsistency. His most important book dealt with the history of the Jewish people since the days of the Maccabees – that is, the history of the people which the scholarly work of the time called "Jews." Yet the name of the book was actually *History of the Israelites* (*Geschichte der Israeliten seit der Zeit der Maccabäer bis auf unsre Tage*) – and thus in his choice of title, Jost's Jewish-German identity prevailed over his responsibility as a historian. In the preface to his book, Jost acknowledges that

---

13   Hegel 1907, 258f.
14   *Werden und können Israeliten zu Freymaurern aufgenommen werden?* was published in Hamburg in 1788 and is attributed to Hans Carl von Ecker und Eckhoffen. See: Katz 1973, 237 N. 13.
15   Smend 1958, 103-105.
16   Eichhorn 1796; see also: Schmidt 1969, 11 N. 1.

it would have been more appropriate to title it "History of the Jews" rather than "History of the Israelites"; he offers a hazy excuse for his decision.[17] Eichhorn, who reviewed the first two volumes of the book and was loyal to his approach of distinguishing between Israelite and Jewish history, praised Jost for not including as a subject "ancient Hebrew history," which in his opinion demanded an entirely different set of qualifications from those requisite to the study of Jewish history; he did, however, criticize the book's title, since during the period the book addresses there were no longer any Israelites, but only Jews.[18] Yet Eichhorn himself was also apparently a victim of slips of the pen; in that same highly laudatory review, he himself referred to Jost as an "Israelite."[19]

The distinction between "Israelites" and "Jews" was prevalent in the works of Michaelis and Eichhorn and was accepted by the members of the Society,[20] yet it is most markedly dichotomous in Jost's work and lies at the basis of his historical perspective. Despite the inconsistency in the book title, Jost adopts the sharpest distinction between "Israelites" and "Jews," but he redefines each of those terms and the relationship between them in a manner that serves the ideology of emancipation. According to his approach, these are two entirely distinct historical phenomena. His approach to the biblical period and to its relationship with post-biblical Judaism attests to a clear structure in which the Bible forms a central pillar. This structure is prominent in

---

17 "Accordingly this book should have been titled *History of the Jews*, since the Israelites no longer existed in Palestine during that period. But since it is important here to consider the *de facto* Israelites who had emigrated already with the destruction of the First Temple, the general name seems more appropriate, especially as at any rate the Jews bore this name for a short time before their general dispersion" (I, xii).

Twenty years after the publication of the ninth volume of *The History of the Israelites* in 1847, Jost began publishing *A New History of the Israelites*, which dealt with the post-Napoleonic period. On the title page, the first volume of this work is also called the tenth volume of *The History of the Israelites*. But in this work Jost refers to the subject of his research as Israelites rather than Jews; here his loyalty to the German Jews' own name for themselves overcomes his loyalty to the scholarly ethos.

18 Eichhorn 1821, 139: "And thus there is a flaw in the title the author gave to his work – *The History of the Israelites*; where he begins his history there were no more Israelites, but only Jews."

19 Eichhorn 1821, 138.

20 Zunz: "In the darkness that envelops the period between the fifth and the second century before Christ, the history of the Jews begins. Until that point we were Hebrews – […] A new people was born, though it descended from the former […] But it differed in language and custom, in its leanings and opinions, a canonized codex in its hands […]" (Zunz 1823, 114). See also: Michael 1993, 229.

Jost's second, lesser-known[21] monograph, *General History of the Israelite People*, half of which is dedicated to the biblical period; but it is also reflected, if to a more modest extent, in both *History of the Israelites* and Jost's final great work, *History of Judaism and its Sects*.[22]

B The Israelites and the Law

According to Jost, the Israelites were an ancient people similar to any other. They were in no way distinguished from other peoples except in the fact that they had, since their earliest existence, a special Law – the Law of Moses – which Jost called Moses' legislation (*Gesetzgebung*), Moses' constitution (*Verfassung*), or Mosaism (*Mosesthum*) for short. The law they had received from Moses stood at the center of Israelite existence; it expressed the people's spirit (*Volksgeist*) and uniqueness.

For Jost, then, the Law of Moses is not a natural, extra-temporal law of Eastern peoples. Michaelis, for example, tried to find a natural reason for male circumcision and argued that it must have been prevalent even in the days of Abraham; Jost rejects this argument and maintains that even if the custom was first introduced for natural reasons, Moses had commanded it solely for the symbolic value it held ever since Abraham tied circumcision to the rejection of idolatry (IIIb, 116). The Law had thus been given to the Israelites alone, and was appropriate only to their particular historical circumstances:

> The state constitution of Moses does not derive from pure Nature, just as his legal doctrines are not a product of philosophy. All of it relates to the Israelites and it is almost incapable of being applied to another people. Therefore Michaelis erred when he wanted to derive many laws from Nature [...] According to the concept that the lawmaker expresses, the law is meant to belong to the Israelites alone. It is also based only on the tradition of their ancestors; only on the manner of their exodus from Egypt, on the manner of their occupation of their place of residence, only on their manner of worshipping God. When that concept no longer prevails with respect to these matters, the law loses its value and effect. (IIIb, 116)

Jost does not rest at rejecting the universality of the law. He maintains repeatedly that the Law of Moses was never a living law:

> Mosaism was never put in practice, was never tried to its full extent; who could tell whether this was due to the law's deficiency, or to lack of will

---

21   [...] the least known of Jost's historical works today [...] it is here that Jost most fully expresses his ideas of Jewish history" (Meyer 1974, 176).

22   Jost 1857.

among the people, or whether these two should be seen as cause and effect? (IIIa, 9)

That Mosaic law did in fact exist but was never followed in practice is one of Jost's central claims. Others before him had argued that not all of Moses' laws had been implemented in full,[23] but Jost positioned this claim at the core of his historical model: "Up until the Babylonian exile we can scarcely see Israelite culture – or see it at all – as a development of Mosaism" (IIIa, 8). The centrality of this claim is also made clear by its countless repetitions[24] in the first volume of *General History of the Israelite People*, which deals with the biblical period. The monarchal period also reinforced Jost's argument (IIIa, 7): its failure to adhere to the Law displeased the Israelites and caused them to wish for a king who would observe the Law in their place and absolve them of that burden. (Note that the Law was seen as a burden!) But as soon as the Israelites had a king, the Law was abandoned entirely, and the king alone was left to (fail to) obey the Law in his people's place. Moreover, according to Jost the monarchy itself contradicted the law of Moses.

The Law was preserved only by the priests and later the prophets. Even the renewal of the covenant with God after the discovery of the Book of the Covenant during the reign of Josiah did not inspire the priests to place themselves under the Law; and imposing the Law on the entire people was impossible, as demonstrated by Jeremiah's exhortations.[25] It was only as a result of the devotion of the priests and the prophets, which was a counter-reaction to the mass unfaithfulness of the Israelites, that the Law and its history were preserved. But they too preserved nearly only the religious aspect of the Law (IIIa, 7ff.). Thus Jost distinguishes between the political aspect (constitution, *Verfassung*) and moral aspect (religion, *Gottesdienst*) of Mosaism.[26] The priests admonished the people for their failure to adhere to specifically this religious–moral aspect:

> The priests decry the neglect not of specific legal peculiarities of Mosaism, but only of the general morals of *humanity* and of the Mosaic religion (IIIa, 8).

This religious–moral aspect was destined for great importance: it would become the root of Judaism – that is, the Jewish religion.

---

23   E.g. Michaelis 1770-1775 I, 35.
24   Jost 1832 I, 123, 139, 142, 153, 174, 175, 191, 193, 195, 196, 206, 216.
25   Jost 1832 I, 381.
26   Jost 1832 I, 174.

C The Jews and the Hebrew Bible

Jews were nothing but members of a *religious community*. They were a historical phenomenon entirely different than the Israelites. The foundational element of this religious community – or these religious communities – was the Hebrew Bible.

Jews emerged on the historical stage only after the Babylonian exile. When the exiles returned (in part) from Babylon to their homeland, political circumstances prevented them from returning to Mosaism. Even had they wished to do so, they belonged to a colony that was subordinate to the Persian Empire and could not enact a full political law of their own without this being perceived as an act of rebellion. Jost cites (IIIa, 15ff.) the principles of the new pact that was established after the return to the homeland, detailed in Nehemia 10 – observance of the Mosaic teachings, in particular a prohibition on marrying Gentile women; observance of the Sabbath and the holy days; the cancellation of debts; and the payment of taxes to the Temple – and explains that it was at this moment that Judaism as a religious community was born:

> This was the entire edifice of the Jews' public obligations: how very different from the foundations of Mosaism! [...] What was created now was not, therefore, a *state*, but merely a *community* for the worship of the one God in accordance with the teachings of the law (IIIa, 16).

The Hebrew Bible formed the line of separation between the Israelites and the Jews, and was the defining feature of the Jews and Judaism. The texts that comprised the Hebrew Bible were indeed composed during the time of the Israelites, but during that period the Israelites did not observe the Law. As for the date of its composition, Jost believes that even if the Hebrew Bible included ancient fragments, those fragments were not combined into longer texts much earlier than the Babylonian exile (IIIb, 120). Only after the exile were the ancient texts compiled into the canon by a redactor, or group of redactors, who collected the copious ancient documents – possibly remnants of the Temple archive[27] – and attempted to create from them a national history that would glorify their God; later, perhaps only ca. 300 BCE, these copies of the canon began to be published (IIIb, 114).

From the time it was composed, the Hebrew Bible became not only a spiritual asset for the Jews but the feature that defined the essence of their existence:

> Beginning at this moment, when the Jewish people became the owners of this work, it became evident that they had an entirely new spiritual orien-

---

27   Jost (IIIa, 205) uses a term from Ilgen 1798: *Tempelarchiv*.

tation, and it was only at this moment that the history of Judaism and the Jews begins – fundamentally different than the history of the Israelites, which may be inferred from the work itself (IIIb, 217).

And as the biblical canon was created only in a later period, after the Babylonian exile, and yet another period was to pass before it became a shared heritage, "Only from the time of the Maccabees and onward can a more reliable history of Judaism, or of the culture of the Jews as Jews, be written" (IIIa, 18). (In this way Jost explains why he began his *History of the Israelites* during the Maccabean period.)

The Jews were not defined by the Law of Moses. Moses' laws were indeed delivered to the Jews and had a definitive effect on their character, but this effect did not take place through adherence to legal traditions transmitted without interruption from generation to generation, but rather through their written form – through the biblical text, whose laws were adapted to the new historical circumstances. For example, the Mosaic laws of war were impracticable for the Jews, while synagogues were an innovation meant to fulfill needs that Mosaic law left unaddressed (IIIa, 27-31).

The laws of Judaism were religious–moral laws and had no political dimension: "The Jews lived together to worship God, in order to leave no place for idolatry; this was something they could accomplish well, with Persian permission, even as subjects of Persian law" (IIIb, 116). Continuing in this direction, but in a different context, Jost also emphasizes with respect to the independent Jewish kingdoms that emerged in the Arab Peninsula or in India that "it is inconceivable that the Jewish faith or the Mosaic constitution were the basis for the law of these states" (V, 264).[28]

The Hebrew Bible was thus situated at the heart of the great divergence in Jewish history: it was the link that connected – but also distinguished between – the Jews and the Israelites, and its existence was what defined the Jews. The history of the Israelites in and of themselves had no importance, except that they passed on the documents that would one day influence the Jews. The Bible was a foundational text not for the Israelites but for the Jews, and it was they who brought to life the biblical heritage they had received from their Israelite forefathers. Thus, through their understanding of the Bible and by altering and adapting the Mosaic law, the rabbinate created Judaism:

> The rabbis presupposed, on the basis of the contents of the holy Scripture, that only through strict observance of the law of Moses could the Jews become worthy of such a transformation of the world [i.e., of the kingdom of the Messiah]. In the absence of the possibility of following these laws in

---

28 Quoted in Michael 1983, 51.

full, they adjusted them, insofar as their acumen allowed, and from this arose *Judaism*, newer and certainly different than *Mosaism* (IIIa, 157).

D Israelites and Jews Compared

Thus Jost adopts the sharp dichotomy between the Israelites and the Jews, and in several chapters whose names indicate their subjects – "Moses' Covenant Was Not Renewed," "The Jews Are Not a Mosaic People," "The Jews Are Not a Mosaic Priestly Kingdom" (IIIa, 18, 23, 28) – he expands on its characteristics in detail.

• The Israelites were a people with land and a state of its own; Jews were a religious community no longer tied to its historical homeland.

• The Israelites lived among pagans and thus regarded themselves as the chosen people; in fact they were in no way different than the surrounding peoples. The Jews, in contrast, differentiated themselves from the pagans only in the name of monotheism. When living in an environment that recognized the idea of a single God, they forwent the idea of chosenness and were loyal to the kingdom in which they resided.

• For the Israelites, the Covenant was only the means to maintain the state; for the Jews, the spiritual covenant – religion – was itself the ultimate goal.

• The Law of Moses required, in order to exist, a certain people – the Israelites – that would be mighty rulers of the land of Canaan, eradicating its pagans, living "the life of Arab nomads" (IIIa, 26) or working the land, and carrying out blood vengeance or punishment under the principle of "an eye for an eye." Such a people, Jost maintained, never existed. The Jews, in contrast, could not conquer the land and fight against idolatry; they engaged in a variety of professions, and consequently adjustments to Mosaic law, or reliance on foreign legal systems, were required; and blood vengeance was alien to their spirit, as it was to the spirit of their Persian rulers.

• Among the Israelites, the priests and Levites formed a sort of caste or ruling class; the cult and the Law were their domain, where the cult was centered on the Temple in Jerusalem. Among the Jews, Scripture belonged to all, the priests and Levites were simply servants at the temple, and the synagogue allowed the cult rites to be performed in any location.

"If Moses himself could have seen the remains of his people during the last century of the Second Temple, he would barely have recognized the descendents of the Israelites," Jost concludes (IIIa, 32).

E From People of the Law to Religion of the Book

The structure of Jewish history that Jost proposes reflects a highly sophisticated and modern approach to dealing with both traditional
Christian history and contemporary biblical criticism – one that expresses and serves an ideology of modern Jewish emancipation. Let us
distinguish between Jews' integration into the European historical
narrative and their political–social integration into modern European
society. As an integrative step, Jost adopts central elements of the non-
Jewish scholarly historical narrative, but he does so by means of critical
modifications that reach the point of proposing a counter-history to the
narrative, in the direction of creating a scholarly, non-confessional historical narrative that would make possible Jews' political and social
integration in Germany.

Jost adopts both the dichotomy – pervasive in Christian biblical
criticism – between Jews and Israelites, and the treatment of the Law as
a central concept in Israelite history (the description of Moses' actions
in political–legal terms reached its peak during the Enlightenment);[29]
but he reshapes them to represent Jews in a manner that suited the
needs of emancipation.

a. Jost sweeps the rug out from under the description of Judaism as
a "religion of the Law" (*Gesetzesreligion*), with the negative connotations that accompanied it, from the traditional Jewish–Christian polemic regarding biblical criticism to modern German Idealism. In his argument that the Israelites did not observe the Law at all, he rejects the
centrality of the Law as a foundational factor in Israelite history. And if
the Law did not have a substantive influence on the Israelites, it was
even less influential to the Jews: the central element of the Jewish identity was not the Law but the Hebrew Bible. Here we sense a recognition
of what Moshe Halbertal today calls the Jews' text-centeredness – their
existence as a community organized and defined by (its relationship to)
a text;[30] but no less important is Jost's idea that the Jews were not a
distorted and obsolete continuation of the Law-observing Israelites but
a new entity based on the Hebrew Bible – a text whose sanctity was
also recognized by Christians.

Eichhorn did not allow this idea of Jost's to pass unremarked. In his
review of the first two volumes of the book he rejected Jost's argument
that "the Mosaic law has never been observed, and as a result has no

---

29   Smend 1959, 54; Schorsch 1994, 239.
30   Halbertal 1997.

influence on the culture of the Jews."[31] Not by chance did Eichhorn write "Jews" and not "Israelites": he recognized that Jost's idea was not restricted to the Israelites but rather constituted a statement about the later Jews and their relationship with the Law. Eichhorn claimed that the frequent transgressions of the Law in fact proved that the Law was in force. In response, Jost wrote (in a preface to the fifth volume of *History of the Israelites*) that his argument regarding the lack of adherence to the Law – an argument he believed was original to him – was the main target for criticism, but he emphasized that he stood his ground on the matter (V: xi). Here we find the clear echo of a very old polemic tradition indeed: a Christian Eichhorn rejects a Jewish Jost's attempt to minimize the importance of the Law in Judaism.

b. Jost rejects the definition of the Jews as a nation. Judaism is solely a religion with no national dimension, and since as early a time as the Persian period Jews have been able to live in peace and loyalty to the states in which they resided. The Law of Moses was not suited for a state, nor was it observed in practice in any country; and certainly the Jewish religion had no political aspirations or ambitions to return to a state of national existence. The national–territorial period – the time of the Israelites – was shortened as much as possible and came to a close as early as the Babylonian exile.[32] The self-segregation attributed to the Jews could be explained purely by their distancing themselves from paganism and did not exist when they resided among monotheists. (Eichhorn, incidentally, addressed this matter en passant: in a glowing review of the third volume he noted, with affectionate forgiveness, that Jost saw "some things as possessing a level of importance entirely different than that observed by his Christian readers, who have no national interest in the matter; but who could ask him to renounce entirely his own national interest?"[33] And so, despite all of Jost's efforts to depict Judaism as a religion and not a nation, Eichhorn insisted on attributing to him a "national interest.")

c. Jost rejects Michaelis's Orientalist approach, which perceived Mosaic law as a natural law of the Orient. Jost specifically emphasizes the particular historical circumstances behind ancient Israelite law. The Law of Moses was not universally Oriental, but rather a particular law

---

31   "*daß das Mosaische Gesetz nie in Uebung gekommen, und daher ohne Einwirkung auf die Cultur der Juden gewesen sey*" (Eichhorn 1822, 1250).

32   In contrast to, for example, Zionist ideology, which tends to extend the Jewish national–territorial period as far as possible and end it with the destruction of the Second Temple at the earliest, and at times even much later, with the Arab conquest in the seventh century.

33   Eichhorn 1821, 138.

provided, in specific historical circumstances, to a people with well-defined characteristics, a people who in effect had never existed and certainly did not exist now; and even if they did exist they did not implement the Law, perhaps because its observation was impossible. If so, clearly Jews could not, and did not need to, return to the Law. This was a response to approaches that wished to distance Jews from Europe by "returning" them to their Oriental roots (in "Sugar Islands" of some sort, for example) and a response to anti-Jewish calls, like that of Luigi Chiarini,[34] for Jews to "return to Mosaism."

All these – the denial of the national aspect of Judaism and the emphasis on loyalty to the state, the rejection of the stereotype of a "religion of law," the rejection of Orientalist exclusion as well as the abandonment of the idea of chosenness and the recognition of monotheism beyond Judaism – served the ideology of Jews' political and social integration as citizens in modern European society. In the face of protests raised by non-Jews against emancipation – protests that were based on the definition of Jews as a nation – Jost maintains that the Jews shared only a provenance and a religion; with respect to all other human matters – political, social, economic, cultural, and especially national – they were part and parcel of the world around them.[35]

Moreover, if the Israelite period could not be considered a golden age then neither could later Judaism be seen as a decline or regression from it, a claim found in both the traditional Christian thought and biblical criticism (as well as in the traditional Jewish perception of *galut*). On the contrary, according to Jost, Judaism was the realization of the monotheistic and moral aspect of Mosaic law – the same aspect that even the prophets considered central. Judaism was perceived as the development and fulfillment of the ancient Israelite ideal, unfulfilled in its own time. Jews, not Israelites, the true "people of the book," because only during their time did the Hebrew Bible exist and become fulfilled.

Here Jost indirectly approaches the creation of a counter-history to the Christian "sacred history," elements of which also persisted in the field of biblical criticism. The Christian perception saw in the Law of Moses and in the ancient Israelite people an exalted and divine stage in the sacred history. Judaism, as far as the Christian perception was concerned, expressed a retreat from this period of grace, while Christianity, heralded by the prophets of Israel, was the true realization of the spirit

---

34 L.A. Chiarini, an Italian professor of Semitic languages who was based in Warsaw (and with whom Jost engaged in a polemic in 1830), demanded "the return of the Jews of their own will to Mosaism" (see: Michael 1983, 110-116; the quote is on p. 113).

35 On the immediate political context of this stance see: Wiener 1933, 217.

of the Hebrew Bible. In Jost's historiography, Judaism was not a retreat from Mosaic law but the implementation of its more exalted parts – the religious–moral–monotheistic aspect, the part that the prophets of Israel placed at the fore (and this is not to detract from his incisive criticism of the rabbinical establishment and its petrification). If Judaism did have Israelite roots, they must be sought in the morality of the prophets – precisely where Christianity itself had searched for its roots! – and not in state or ritual law.

In effect, Jost positions Judaism in nearly the same place as Christianity positioned itself in the sacred history – as the fulfillment of the idea of the ancient Israelite people; except that the Jewish fulfillment had begun hundreds of years *before* Christianity, after the Babylonian exile. As in Christianity, Jost too emphasizes the universality of the monotheistic idea that Judaism propagated; he even maintains that Judaism as a religion was interested in accepting converts (IIIa, 27). The Israelites were an intermediary stage in preparation for Judaism, a stage that had to die out and clear a space for its conceptual realization. Motifs from the Christian salvation history within this implicit counter-history, both parallel and contradictory to the Christian history, are found most prominently in the preface to Jost's later book, *Judaism and Its Sects*:

> From the ruins of Jerusalem there rose a spirit which, free of the trappings of the state, ushered in a new life in its believers. We call it *Judaism* or the *Jewish* religion [...]

> *Israelism* disintegrated irreversibly [...] but in its place *Judaism* appeared, [...] an emergence of the old spirit [...] This was a rebirth [...] an advance long awaited and necessary [...], a fruit of the ancient seed [...]

> [To the prophets,] the death of the state [...] seemed inevitable, but Israel's mission remains forever unshaken.[36]

The awaited and inevitable death (a metaphor for destruction), which the prophets too had foreseen; the rebirth of a fruit that had been planted in the past and was free of the trappings of state and ushered in new life – all these are remarkably reminiscent of the Christian "sacred history" and of the story of Jesus and the birth of Christianity in particular.

If we employ the metaphor of family, then Judaism to Jost is neither a direct descendent of Israel nor the begetter of Christianity. Judaism was an heir of Israel just as Christianity believed itself to be. Hence Judaism and Christianity were sister religions, born to the same mother. Jost, who died in 1866, would surely have agreed with Yehuda

---

36   Jost 1857, 1, 3-4, 5.

Liebes' writings about Judaism as the sister of Christianity; in 1983, Liebes wrote that the latter was "an alternative interpretation of a common scriptural tradition";[37] while as for I. J. Yuval, who wrote that Judaism and Christianity were "both are daughter religions of biblical Judaism, which was centered on the [Second] Temple in the days before its destruction,"[38] Jost would have amended his words to say "before the destruction of the First Temple" – thus returning to Judaism its historical primogeniture.

F Changing Attitudes toward Critical Scholarship

Following this survey of Jost's overall schema of Jewish history, the question arises as to how Judaism according to Jost would deal with the conclusions of biblical criticism about the "true" history of the Israelites and of the formation of the Hebrew Bible. To this question Jost provides two answers. The first is laid out in an "Excursus on the Study of the Period in Which the Biblical Documents Were Joined and Compiled," which appears at the end of the third volume of his *History of the Israelites*, published in 1822. The "Excursus" enthusiastically supports the approach of biblical criticism and explains why it posed no harm to the Jews. Note that in *History of the Israelites* Jost did not address the biblical era, and consequently in practice did not need to apply the conclusions of biblical criticism in his historical writing. The second answer appears in his *General History of the Israelite People*, which was published in 1832, ten years after the third volume of *History of the Israelites*. Here Jost adopts a much cooler position toward biblical criticism.

1 *History of the Israelites* (1822): A Manifesto for Biblical Criticism

The Attitude toward Biblical Criticism and its Methods

The "Excursus", which concludes the third volume of *History of the Israelites*, begins as a comprehensive manifesto (IIIb, 198-218) that issues a clear, polemic, and eager call for work in the field of in biblical criticism, and furthermore outlines a detailed and concrete textual method.

---

37   Liebes, quoted in Yuval 2006, 27.
38   Yuval 2006, 27.

This is a direct testimony to Jost's attitude toward biblical criticism. Further evidence for its importance to Jost can be found in his decision to include the "Excursus" in a work a work whose scope does not include the subject – the *History of the Israelites*, after all, begins only during the time of the Maccabees.

At the start of the "Excursus," Jost engages in a polemic in the name of the ideal of free and unbiased scholarship with the opponents of biblical criticism, whether Jewish or Christian. Their opposition appears to have been aimed primarily at the idea that the books of the Bible were composed later rather than sooner, and consequently at the rejection of the attribution of some books to their traditional authors (particularly Moses). Jost implicitly distinguishes between two types of objectors: the traditional–dogmatic and the scientific–apologetic. The dogmatic objectors rejected the very legitimacy of critical investigation of the Bible and preferred to shut their eyes to the truth: "What harm be there if, for the good of the whole, a tiny deception is carried out?" (IIIb, 199). The scientific–apologetic objectors, in contrast, did not oppose critical scholarship in itself but attempted to find, within its context, scientific justifications for their dogmatic and predetermined objections:

> The study is launched with prejudice, and from that point on they will grope, observe, compare, listen, carve, and cast aside until at last the prejudiced point is proven, and now they will waive its banner with all the greater confidence, for no longer is it the word of the dominant church – now it is borne aloft by a community of scholars on the basis of a seeming examination (IIIb, 201).

Jost furthermore maintains that these biased scholars currently hold the advantage: we may assume he was writing after the Carlsbad Decrees of 1819, de Wette's dismissal, and the introduction of censorship and strict oversight over the universities. Since those events biblical criticism had been on the defensive and in decline, as we will see in the Part Two.[39]

In defense of criticism, Jost argues that whatever damage critical challenges to the Bible might inflict on Judaism and the Jews would be minuscule: a literary work whose date of composition scholarship placed several centuries later would become no less authentic unless its authenticity was in doubt to begin with. Certainly among the knowledgeable it would become no less influential. Nor would its importance as a window to ancient times be diminished, for even if its later authors did not reflect the earlier period, they did after all reflect their own time (IIIb, 200).

---

39   Nipperdey 1983, 272-285; Rogerson 1984, 79ff.; Michael 1993, 243-244.

Following this basic defense of critical scholarship, Jost proposes a detailed critical approach to the study of the Hebrew Bible. A prerequisite is familiarity with the language of the Bible: a scholar must be aware of "the meaning of every word, every possible change and usage of the words and phrases of the Hebrew Bible"; however, "he must leave at home his knowledge of the contents of the text, of certain interpretations, of learned disputes and exegesis in general" (IIIb, 202). The rejection of all the later traditions that accompanied the biblical text was a regular practice in biblical criticism, which kept its distance both from the Christological approach to the Bible and – since Michaelis – from the Jewish exegetes (Maimonides, Rashi, Ibn Ezra) with whom the Hebraists had dealt in previous centuries.[40] Indeed, in writing the history of the biblical period – primarily the first volume of his *General History of the Israelite People* – Jost refrains entirely from employing traditional Jewish sources. Eichhorn, in his critique of this volume, praised the fact that Jost made use of Greek sources "and only here and there did he compare them to Talmudic and rabbinic sources."[41]

As a theological basis for criticism, Jost in effect reiterates the distinction that served Semler and his criticism of the Canon,[42] between what Semler called "the word of God" (the divine inspiration of Scripture) and Scripture itself (i.e., its tangible form). In Jost's formulation, "every book before our eyes is entirely the creation of one or more men and is subject to the events of its time as much as any other human creation" (IIIb, 203); this is the man-made aspect of the Hebrew Bible, which justifies treating it as any other book. In contrast, the divine aspect of the Bible is beyond human ken and consequently is the domain not of biblical criticism but of philosophy.

The method that Jost proposed was founded on analysis (fragmentation) of the text on the basis of linguistic and extra-textual criteria, followed by chronological synthesis. To begin with, the evolving versions of the biblical text as well as its integrity as a whole must be examined. Using ancient manuscripts, translations, and the like it must be determined whether the book at hand is complete, whether any text has been omitted, or whether there have been additions or deliberate corruptions in the text. Following that, an entirely "clean" manuscript of the Bible, free of any additional annotations beyond the words of the text itself, must be read from beginning to end. It immediately emerges that the Bible has not been composed all at once: otherwise it would not exhibit such grammatical variety, twice- and thrice-repeated versions of

---

40   Manuel 1992, 261.
41   Eichhorn 1821, 137f.
42   Seidel 1993, 137f.

events, and even contradictions. During the next stage the text must be divided into fragments; a new fragment begins at any point in which linguistic uniformity is interrupted. Now the authorship and date of each fragment's composition must be determined. Even if the identity of the author, or his time, is provided by the text itself, that information must not be considered reliable. Finally, the fragments must be ordered according to the date of their composition. At this stage one may expect to find disjointed fragments joined, artificially adjacent fragments separated, and many contradictions and difficulties settled. From this point on, Jost believes, it is possible to arrive at conclusions in a systematic and agreed-upon manner, by separating first the most recent fragments from the text, followed by the next most recent, and so on, using intratextual quotations in order to derive an increasingly accurate chronology. The principles of Jost's method were no different than those accepted in the biblical criticism of his time. Jost applies the method he proposes to several biblical books; he details the results of this application – the list of fragments he discovered and their characteristics – in a separate appendix (IIIb, 111-141).

Among the texts produced by the *Wissenschaft des Judentums*, none seems to have explicitly expressed such an enthusiastic, methodical, and reasoned approach toward biblical criticism, nor such an attack on its opponents, whether Jewish or Christian, as did Jost's "Excursus" at the close of the third volume of *History of the Israelites*.

The Inoculation of Judaism to Biblical Criticism

Jost inoculated Judaism to the possible results of biblical criticism by means of a sophisticated distinction between the actual history of the biblical period and the account of that history related in the Hebrew Bible. Judaism was not shaped by the history of the biblical period, but rather by the Bible itself and the view of history it presented. This was effectively Hegel's[43] distinction between the two meanings of the word "history" – between *res gestae* and *historia rerum gestarum*. The *res gestae* – the events – that formed the basis of the Hebrew Bible were the domain of historical research and biblical criticism, which operated with complete freedom and a philological–historical method. The Bible as *historia rerum gestarum* – the account of those events – and only as such was what gave form to Judaism.[44] As a result, biblical criticism was

---

43 Hegel 1961.
44 An interesting illustration of Jost's argument about the importance of the Bible as *historia rerum gestarum* was actually supplied by Siegmund Maybaum, a rabbi and follower of Wellhausen, who is discussed in chapter 10. In a book on the

unlikely to injure Judaism. Its methods did abbreviate Jewish history by a few hundred years, as it erased the entire biblical period; but, Jost argues, better for Jews to be of a young line, brimming with vitality and youth, than of a more ancient but withered and bloodless foundation (IIIb, 200). This solution of Jost's, which proposes to "save" Judaism and the Bible by separating the historicist examination of the Bible from the Bible's influence as a complete literary work, was, on the one hand, absolutely modern and furthermore similar to the insights that formed the basis of the literary study of the Bible as it would develop years later during the twentieth century;[45] on the other hand, basing Jewish history on the interpretation of texts and not on historical truth was in fact a reflection of age-old Jewish tradition, which was unconcerned with the texts as a historical source and instead transformed the substance of Judaism into something a-historical and extra-temporal.

Jost does not expand on the Hebrew Bible's influence on the Jews as *historia rerum gestarum*: its essence was the monotheistic idea and the glorification of God through the national history of the ancient Israelite people. These were what determined the shape of Judaism. Jost shows little restraint in criticizing the flaws in the Hebrew Bible:

> The Jews have been supplied a work [...] that includes strange and most prominent contradictions, that refutes on one page what is written on another, that jumbles together the divine and the mortal, that offers calculations incompatible with the four basic arithmetic operations, that casts doubt even on the concept of the divine being in whose honor and for whose glory it was composed, that presents the history of its people in the least sequential order – in short, a work that remains in aggregate and in detail incomprehensible and impenetrable (IIIb, 216).

---

methodology of religious instruction, Maybaum suggested that Jewish teachers (and even sermonizers) pay no mind to the conclusions of biblical criticism: "The teacher need suffer no harm from the fact that one or another biblical figure was granted legendary status only at an advanced date, or that an ancient biblical institution was established in a far later period than that indicated by the Bible [...] The composition of Scripture, regardless of when it occurred, was clearly accomplished for religious purposes, and these purposes have thus far been fulfilled through the Bible in its traditional form in a manner so satisfactory, that we have all the reasons in the world to leave the story unaltered in our religious instruction" (Maybaum 1896, 26f.).

45 For example, *God: A Biography*, by Jack Miles (1995, 416-418 N. 9; the quote is on p. 418): "The conclusions of 'New Historicist' Bible scholarship, because they derive from hard-won erudition, are on their own terms beyond refutation [...] But historicist terms are by no means the only terms available [...] historical scholarship believes that Joshua never fought the Battle of Jericho [...] but literary criticism is free to accept [the claim] and move on, reclaiming the story of the Battle of Jericho as literature from its relative wreckage as history."

How had this come to pass? Had the redactor (or redactors) of the He-brew Bible led astray the people? Jost, at least in this manifesto, rejects this possibility. The redactor had approached his task faithfully[46] but with the hope that future generations would not refrain from criticizing him or his work, which was neither perfect nor free of error. Yet this was not to be. The fruits of his work quickly became a property that must not be amended, and the spirit of the people (*Volksgeist*) devel-oped from that point on through the reading of the work in its entirety. The audience's ignorance forced them to depend on the redactor with blind, unbending faith and to shield their eyes when confronted with the truth. The cardinal aim was now to protect this property from all attack; since its bareness was so clearly vulnerable, numerous scarves – exegetical maneuvers – would be required to conceal it. The Jewish intellectuals devoted all their efforts toward this goal.

The *res gestae*, on the other hand – that is, the actual history of the people of Israel – was different than that related in the Bible; the Bible thus contained a distorted history of the Israelites. This distortion (*Entstellung*) – perhaps, the theologization of history – was created by the redactor or redactors of the Bible and was preserved with the help of "Jewish rabbis, and later Christian ones as well" (IIIb, 217). There was a need for critical scholarship to reconstruct the real history of the Jews, and this was the task of biblical criticism. The results of this his-torical research – and Jost was aware that such research was still far from complete – would be very different than the history told in the Bible. Again, however, this would pose no harm to Judaism.

With this fundamental attitude, which essentially "conceded" the ancient history of Israel, Jost set the gates wide open to the discipline of biblical criticism. From his writing about "the rabbis" it appears that he hoped to rely on the conclusions of the field in his attacks against the rabbinical establishment. His lack of nostalgia for the biblical period and readiness to let Jewish history begin at such a late date allowed him to accept almost any radical conclusion from biblical criticism, whether about the authenticity of the books of the Hebrew Bible, the manner and date of their composition, or the real history of the Jews, even if all these differed greatly from the traditional account. This was not enough to solve the problem of the divine foundation of the Bible – but, as we have seen, Jost announced in advance that this problem was the domain not of the critical historian but rather of the philosopher.

---

46   Though elsewhere Jost conjectured that "A fair amount of time was required to endow the new books with the appearance of antiquity, and especially to treat later poetry as ancient prophecy" (Jost 1820-1828 IIIb, 114).

2 *General History of the Israelite People* (1832):[47] A Conservative Retreat

Jost's enthusiasm for biblical criticism was somewhat dampened in his book *General History of the Israelite People*, which was published a decade after his "Excursus" in 1832. During this period, biblical criticism in Germany was in decline: already in 1819 de Wette had been dismissed from Berlin, and in 1830 Hengstenberg, an anti-critical conservative, was appointed editor of the periodical *Evangelische Kirchenzeitung*, which waged war against rationalism of any flavor.[48] The atmosphere in reactionary Prussia thus changed for the worse with respect to critical–radical scholarship, and Jost's book also reflects this trend.

The work comprises two volumes, the first of which is dedicated entirely to the biblical period. This time, Jost addresses the actual history of the period. It is important to remember that at the time, no revisionist history of the biblical period had yet been written based on documentary hypotheses.[49] It was possible to derive such a revision from the work of de Wette; it is not clear to what extent Jost was familiar with it.[50] At any rate, Jost himself did not undertake that enormous task, and his readiness to accept the historical revision of the biblical period in *History of the Israelites* bore no fruit in the *General History of the Israelite People*; there Jost remains loyal to the biblical historiography.[51] His academic ethos is expressed in his disregard of traditional Jewish sources and his attempts to provide a rationalist explanation for miracles[52] and to criticize biblical exaggerations.[53]

At the conclusion of the chapter on the history of Pentateuchal times, Jost devotes a special chapter to the subject of the criticism of

---

47 Jost 1832. The orphaned references in this section refer to the two volumes of this work.

48 Rogerson 1984, 79-90. See also the following part for a broader treatment.

49 Hoheisel 1978, 12. The first to write such a history was Vatke (1835).

50 Surprisingly, I could find no evidence that Jost – who explicitly mentioned Michaelis, Eichhorn, Ilgen, Ewald, and many other biblical scholars before them – was acquainted with the work of de Wette (who was, as noted above, Zunz's teacher). It is hard to doubt that he had heard of de Wette. It is possible that he consciously decided to ignore the work of the radical exiled professor, whose star had dimmed during the reactionary era, as many Christian scholars of that generation and even later also neglected his work.

51 "And when Jost came forth to bring order to the Jewish history throughout the ages, he neglected to say anything new about the biblical period" (Soloveitchik and Rubasheff 1925, 128).

52 For examples and harsh criticism of Jost's descriptions of miracles, see: Wiener 1933, 210f.

53 For example, the immense quantities of plunder acquired from the Midianites (Numbers 31:32ff.) seemed highly exaggerated to Jost (I, 146).

that text (I, 147-156); his temperance is evident here both in substance and in style. This time, Jost distinguishes between four approaches to the Pentateuch. Two of these he rejects at the outset: the approach of the believers, who follow only the path of their faith, and the approach of those who ridicule the text and scorn all tradition. The two approaches worthy of serious consideration are those of the "true and honest scholars." One such type found in the Pentateuch a consistent and homogeneous text that had in fact been written by Moses and delivered to the priests; the other saw it as a collection of ancient stories and laws that had been anthologized, and approached them with skepticism. Without specifically naming names, Jost is obviously referring to confessional (orthodox) scholars on the one hand and to rationalist (critical) scholars on the other.

Yet if in *History of the Israelites* there was no doubt regarding which camp Jost placed himself in, now – as the fortunes of the liberal camp declined, and alliance with it no longer seemed so promising and could even hold danger – Jost adopted an entirely different stance: both approaches, he said, left much still unilluminated, and "the means to reconcile them is the philosopher's stone" (I, 149). Jost attempts to discover this philosopher's stone and refrain from passing judgment on the division between the confessionals and the rationalists in the field of biblical criticism,[54] at least with respect to the Pentateuch.[55] He accepts the basic historical events of the Pentateuch at face value, but argues that the Pentateuch had not been composed in order to relate a history but rather to describe, in general lines and by means of historical stories, God's intentions towards the people of Israel; hence the incompleteness and lack of coherence in the text. As for whether Scripture described the time of Moses or a later period, Jost proposes to bypass the issue by assuming that the author of the Pentateuch had imagined an audience that lived hundreds of years after Moses. He also proposes to bypass the question of prophecies; whether the prophecies were issued in advance (as the confessionals believe) or composed in

---

54   Wiener (1933, 210) attacked Jost on the grounds that "[t]he fundamental critical question, namely who was the author of the five books of the Pentateuch, is evaded here in the typical fashion of most Jewish scholars of the previous century, whose thinking was muddled by a combination of a measure of apprehensiveness and critical tendencies," but he did not mention that there was a withdrawal here from the highly critical position that Jost had adopted in his first book, and he ignored the suppression of criticism in the German academia.

55   But he maintains his critical position with respect to the other books: "Joshua, Judges, Samuel, Kings – all these are very late books in general, written to all appearances after the fall of the kingdom, as is evident by their contents." (I, 157 N. 1).

retrospect (according to the rationalists), one may approach their contents as historical truths, since the fact of their preservation testifies to their fulfillment.

After these proposals Jost declares that he will issue no judgment as to the date of the Pentateuch's composition (I, 153). However, he emphasizes, both camps concur that the books Moses had written (according to conservatives), or that were attributed to Moses but had in fact been written later (according to the critics), were not known to the people until centuries after Moses. Thus Jost succeeds in simultaneously eluding the controversy around when the Pentateuch was composed and protecting the essential foundation of his historical approach, which we have seen above – the claim that the Israelites neither knew nor observed the law of Moses.

There is one subject regarding which Jost departs from his neutrality and flatly rules out critical claims; this is the revelation on Mount Sinai and Moses' delivery of the Ten Commandments. Here Jost rejects any attempt at a naturalist, mythological, or other explanation that might dispute the authenticity of the Ten Commandments and their exact phrasing. It is impossible, according to Jost, to consider them a later fabrication: they are cited again and again by later voices in the Bible. Had there been any suspicion of forgery, the many idolaters among the people of Israel would quickly have taken advantage of it; the fact that the prophets made no mention of such a claim proves that none had ever disputed their authenticity. The Commandments' pithiness and polish was "also proof of the antiquity and originality attributed to them. They were not polished by any school of thought; no Gentile law was their example, as some have suggested" (I, 113). They were the foundation on which all other laws and regulations could be developed. The Ten Commandments were "the most important memory of ancient times and worthy of the honor given them. Through them Moses tied the people completely to God and set them apart from all neighboring nations" (I, 111). Here Jost attempts to define the biblical spirit that was fulfilled in Judaism, or the essence of the Torah, Bible, and Judaism in general. Regarding that essence – namely the Ten Commandments, and, in another section, the union between the people and the one God ("everything else, regardless of its attribution, is merely an expansion of this idea" [I, 121]) – Jost refuses to compromise. He is willing to accept the claim that the Pentateuch had been composed at a very late date, but he insists on the authenticity of its monotheistic core. This was the limit Jost placed on biblical criticism, and the limit of the line he tried to draw between historical scholarship and theology or philosophy.

Part Two

Biblical Criticism in the Second Third of the Nineteenth Century

> [...] Biblical criticism,
> which must be avoided
> like boiling porridge.
>
> Abraham Geiger, 1846[1]

---

1   Geiger, L. 1878, 188.

Chapter 4
The Conservative Turn in German Academia

Biblical criticism's entry into German academia and its flowering during the early part of the nineteenth century came to a halt during the reactionary period that began with the fall of Napoleon and the Congress of Vienna (June 1815). In all spheres of life, the ruling powers attempted to turn back the wheel to the days before the French Revolution and its ramifications. This was also a time of suppression and retreat with respect to critical approaches in German academia. During the early years of the reactionary period, German universities were still a center of liberal and nationalist activity. In October 1817 a celebration was carried out by students at Wartburg. This was both a patriotic celebration commemorating the historic victory over Napoleon in the "Battle of Nations" near Leipzig in 1813, and a religious–Protestant one commemorating three hundred years since the Lutheran Reformation. It honored the nation's liberation from the yoke of foreign conquest and its religious and spiritual liberation from the tyranny of the Catholic Church; simultaneously it was a political demonstration – a call for national unity, for a constitution and constitutional freedoms, and for dismantling feudal institutions as well as police and surveillance bodies. When the radical-liberal student Karl Ludwig Sand assassinated the conservative writer August von Kotzebue about a year and a half later – on March 23, 1819 – the conservative authorities singled out universities as subversive sites meriting close supervision. Later that year the Carlsbad Decrees were enacted; these, alongside censorship of newspapers and books, were directed first and foremost against the universities. Lecturers who disseminated revolutionary or "subversive" ideas were discharged, the nationalist student organizations – the *Burschenschaften* – were banned, and the civil service was closed to any members of these organizations. Each university was appointed a commissioner to oversee it.[1]

Political reactionism seeped into the academic world; the theological faculties and the field of biblical criticism were no exception. As we have seen, biblical criticism was predominantly identified with political

---

1   Nipperdey 1983, 273-285; Volkov 1997, 47-56.

liberalism. After Kotzebue's assassination, de Wette, the prominent biblical critic of his time and a political liberal, was accused of sending a letter of consolation to the mother of the assassin, Sand – a letter which conveyed support for the assassination. The accusation led to his dismissal from the University of Berlin in 1819 and to his exile in Switzerland, where he remained (at the University of Basel) to the end of his days. His position at Berlin remained vacant for nearly a decade, until 1828. That year, the conservative Ernst Wilhelm Hengstenberg was appointed to the position; he would become the dominant figure in German biblical scholarship for the next thirty years.[2] That de Wette's position was passed on to a conservative theologian whose views were diametrically opposed to de Wette's is a good illustration of the *Zeitgeist*.

Hengstenberg (1802–1869) was a characteristic theologian of the Restoration period. His contribution to biblical criticism was extensive – but adversely so; more than any other theologian of his time, he worked successfully to obstruct and delay progress in his field. Hengstenberg rejected the rationalist theology developed by Semler and his followers, from de Wette to David Friedrich Strauss (the latter "a heartless man," according to Hengstenberg), and he regarded rationalism as the enemy of theology. According to his approach, reason must recognize its limitations and its own blindness, because of which Man must demonstrate "religious obedience" to Scripture and its binding authority. Hengstenberg also rejected the historical approach to the study of the Bible which regarded it as evidence of the existence of the ancient Israelite religion, and he retreated – as the name of his central book, *Christologie des Alten Testaments* (Christology of the Old Testament, 1829-1835), makes clear – to a Christological approach that read the Old Testament from the perspective of the New. Naturally, Hengstenberg also adhered to traditional views regarding the authorship and authenticity of the books of the Bible. The Pentateuch, in his opinion, was written by Moses; one could prove that it already existed during the monarchic period using Judges, Kings, Amos, and Hosea. Isaiah was written by a single author. The books of Chronicles were an authentic description of the Levitical religion, and "Jehovah" and "Elohim" were both ancient names of God, their difference theological rather than one of historical origin.[3]

Hengstenberg's power did not derive from his academic position alone. In 1827 he began to publish the *Evangelische Kirchenzeitung*,

---

2   Rogerson 1984, 79-90. About Hengstenberg see also: Kraus 1982, 222-226. Schorsch (1994, 25) wrote about him briefly in a Jewish context.

3   Rogerson 1984, 87f.; Rohls 1997, 514f.

which became the foremost theological journal in Germany and was dedicated to fighting against rationalism of any form. Hengstenberg's duties in connection with the journal included not only editing but also copious composition of articles and book reviews. He was the confidant of Ministers of Culture both in Prussia and beyond when they were called on to appoint professors of theology; throughout Germany the fate of biblical scholars in particular and theologians in general rested largely in his hands. The careers of his opponents – critical biblical scholars – were obstructed. Thus the critical biblical scholar Vatke, who will be discussed below, was denied the professorship he had hoped for after the publication of his book on Old Testament theology; he had to rely on his wife's income and soon ceased to publish. The academic advancement of George, another prominent critical scholar, was also impeded, until he was at last obliged to transfer to the philosophy faculty. At the same time, Hengstenberg's disciples or those who held similar views occupied an increasing number of positions in universities throughout Germany.[4]

Throughout this period, from 1830 to 1860, an environment antagonistic to biblical criticism prevailed in most German universities, and the dogmatic, orthodox Protestant approach gained in power. This is not to say that critical activity came to a halt; alongside the critical books of Vatke and George, which appeared in 1835, other critical scholars continued to work during this period, including Ewald, Bleek, Hupfeld, Hitzig, and others. But hegemony lay in the hands of the anti-critical conservatives. This also had a moderating influence on the few active critical scholars, and as a result some of the findings of de Wette and his students were marginalized or forgotten altogether. They would be "rediscovered" only a generation later, during the closing third of the century.

---

4   Nipperdey 1983, 426; Rogerson 1984, 69, 88f. Of the long line of Old Testament scholars close to Hengstenberg, Rogerson lists C.F. Keil, H.C.A. Hävernick, M. Baumgarten, F. Delitsch, J.C.K. von Hoffmann, G.F. Oehler, F.W. Schulz, A.F. Kleinert, and J. Bachmann; many of their students may be included.

Chapter 5
Wissenschaft des Judentum's Departure from Biblical Criticism

German academia's retreat from biblical criticism was accompanied by a similar retreat among German Jews. The three decades beginning in 1830 are characterized by an almost complete silence by the *Wissenschaft des Judentums* on the subject of biblical criticism. The turning point appears to have been heralded as early as 1832 by the retreat to the conservative extreme in Jost's second major book, discussed in chapter 3; from that point on, Jost's work no longer dealt with the biblical era. Zunz, de Wette's student, also fell silent. While he dealt with biblical criticism in the first chapter of his *Die gottesdienstlichen Vorträge*, he then abandoned the field entirely and returned to it (or at least published work in it) only forty years later, during the 1870s.[1] Zunz's limited involvement in biblical scholarship is admittedly consistent with his declaration in his first programmatic article, *"Etwas über die rabbinische Literatur"* (Something about Rabbinic Literature),[2] that scholars should concentrate on postbiblical Judaism, whose texts were neglected, rather than the Bible, which attracted numerous Christian scholars. Still, this alone cannot account for the fact that Zunz's two works dealing with biblical criticism are separated by such a wide interval – the first, which dealt with Chronicles, was published in 1832, while the second, which included extremely radical conclusions about the composition of the Pentateuch, appeared only in 1873. Unsurprisingly, the Bible translation that Zunz published in 1837-1838 seems to be entirely faithful to tradition.[3]

Geiger's central work, *Urschrift und Übersetzungen der Bibel* (Text and Translations of the Bible),[4] which was published toward the end of the period examined in this part (1857), adhered to the same mold. According to Michael Meyer,

> What Geiger did not discuss in his volume was pre-exilic biblical history. This was clearly the most ticklish subject of all – "too hot to handle," he be-

---

1   Zunz 1892 <1832>, 13-36 (see note 75 in the previous chapter); Zunz 1873; Zunz 1875 (see also the next chapter).
2   Zunz 1818, 3.
3   Sarna 1975, 19.
4   Geiger, A. 1928 <1857>. See chapter 8 for a broader discussion of Geiger.

lieved at first. It was one thing to suggest variant versions of the received text, quite another to take an unorthodox position on its origins.[5]

And indeed, in a later review published in 1862 Geiger himself divided biblical criticism into three parts – the first the study of the text's creation, the second of its arrangement, and the third of its transmission – and emphasized that his *Urschrift* dealt only with the last enterprise and not the first two.[6]

Steinheim's polemic book against Vatke (1840), which will be discussed below, is the exception that proves the rule, as Steinheim himself was a marginal and exceptional figure in the Jewish intellectual arena.

We can thus conclude that the retreat from biblical criticism in German academia and culture coincided with a similar retreat among the scholars of the *Wissenschaft des Judentums*. How might we explain this parallel? Why did Jews abstain from biblical criticism during the period in question? In the case of the more conservative Jewish streams, the answer is simple: while Christian scholarship and the progressive *Wissenschaft des Judentums* were not questioning the Pentateuch's authenticity, there was no reason for an Orthodox scholar or rabbi to deal with such a sensitive issue. But how can we explain this abstention on the part of the Reform movement, particularly given the *Verein*'s formerly positive attitude toward biblical criticism?

It appears that the *Wissenschaft des Judentums*' ambition for integration dictated its accommodation of the central non-Jewish narrative. To accommodate or support a marginal, oppressed, or persecuted narrative would have been of little use to progressive Jewish scholars. Here the boundary also became evident between, on the one hand, participating in biblical scholarship on the basis of shared scholarly premises that were considered non-confessional, and on the other hand fully adopting the Christian approach. The aspiration to take part in the academic narrative was based on a belief in modern scholarship's rationalism and transcendence over confessionalism, and consequently attracted Jewish scholars. As the central stream of Christian scholarship retreated toward dogmatic Christological premises and its legitimization became clearly confessional, the attraction for Jews of the academic debate lessened considerably. To put it another way, scholars of the *Wissenschaft des Judentums* could contend with an *a posteriori* anti-Jewish bias in a discourse whose legitimization was at its core academic (as did Jost, for example, and many after him starting in the latter third of

---

5   Meyer 1988, 93.
6   Geiger, A. 1862a, 124f.

the century). But as the anti-Jewish bias became *a priori*, and the legitimization of the discourse became based primarily on dogmatic Christology, the main Archimedean point supporting the Jewish position – rationalism that superseded confessionalism – was lost, and we may assume that Jews saw no use in entering a dialogue whose outcome could only sharpen the differences between Christians and themselves and emphasize their own foreignness.

A polemic tract by Steinheim against the conservative theologian Franz Delitzsch written in the 1860s illustrates this point.[7] In this polemic (which took place after that with Vatke discussed below) Steinheim had no need to defend the authenticity of Scripture, since Delitzsch believed in that authenticity perhaps even more than Steinheim himself. Delitzsch actually declared that "the Jewish people [. . .] are the trustworthy, living papyrus on which the Bible has been inscribed by God's will,"[8] but defended this authenticity with explicit and declared Christological motives that Steinheim could not accept: he clarified that denying the authenticity of the Old Testament would undermine that of the New Testament and the stories of Jesus, and as a result "Mosaical history (*Moseïde*) would serve only to subvert [Jesus'] Messianic history (*Messiade*)."[9] Delitzsch's Christology served as an axiom that delineated his work in advance. Steinheim felt that he and Delitzsch lacked a shared academic foundation, and insisted that the study of the Old Testament be conducted as though there were no New Testament; that is, he called for autonomization and the renewal of the academic approach to biblical scholarship.[10] The Christology of the Protestant orthodoxy abandoned the common rational background and once again transformed the Jewish–Christian debate into a dogmatic polemic bereft of academic orientation; no wonder that Jewish scholars chose to avoid it.

However, even without a basis for scholarly dialogue with the Protestant orthodoxy, Jewish scholars could in theory have continued to take part in biblical criticism without connection to the orthodox hegemony, whether independently or as a continuation of the work of critical Christian scholars. Why did they refrain from doing so? Did the almost complete absence of Jewish publications in the field of biblical

---

7   The polemic was published in two versions, one short – "Das alte Testament und seine neuen Ausleger" (Steinheim 1863, 398-411) – and one long – "Monomachie gegen den Commentar zur Genesis von Prof. Dr. Fr. Delitzsch" (Steinheim 1865, 139-185).

8   Quoted in: Steinheim 1865, 173.

9   Quoted in: Steinheim 1865, 144 = Steinheim 1863, 399.

10 Steinheim 1863, 400.

criticism during the second third of the century stem from a lack of interest on the part Jewish scholars, or from their concerns about extraneous factors? It is generally difficult to provide a solid answer to such a question, which attempts to distinguish between the personal and the societal. Nonetheless some evidence has been preserved which may shed light on this issue.

The Jewish historian Levi Herzfeld (who in 1834, as a student, was denied an academic award by Hengstenberg because he described a biblical story as an anecdote!)[11] admits in 1863 that "Seventeen years ago a religious Jew still could not study the Bible critically without assuming significant risk."[12] "Significant risk" here means difficulty in obtaining a position as a rabbi, whether because of opposition from congregations or from the government. Note that Herzfeld, at least in retrospect, does not claim that he had no wish to engage in biblical criticism, but rather that he wished to do so but was afraid. The context of this testimony is his earlier book about Ecclesiastes, whose authorship he attributed to King Solomon; if Ecclesiastes could rouse such a reaction, surely biblical criticism of the Pentateuch would invite even greater risk.[13]

Similarly, in 1861 the Jewish schoolteacher Julius Popper, in a preface to a book of his which dealt with biblical criticism (and will be discussed in chapter 8), writes that "This work has by and large, since 1843, lain written and set in the form you see today" – its publication has been delayed for 18 years – and notes that until then (that is, until 1861!) Jewish theologians refrained from recognizing the findings of scholarly criticism in the fields of biblical history and literature. Popper accounts for their silence as the result of "irremediable fear or shameful cowardice."[14] Again the problem was fear rather than lack of desire or interest.

During this period Abraham Geiger also issued – specifically in personal letters that were not published until after his death – similar and even more detailed comments. In a personal letter to Joseph Dérenbourg written April 10, 1837, he mentions of a letter he received S.Y. Rapoport, who complained about the "Reformist slant" of Geiger's

---

11 Schorsch 1994, 320.

12 Herzfeld 1863 II, 66.

13 Seventeen years before 1863 is 1846; Herzfeld appears to have been mistaken in his calculations and intended to write "27 years ago," i.e. 1836, during which year he worked on his translation and exegesis of Ecclesiastes (which would be published in 1838).

14 Popper 1862, XII-XIII.

journal (referring to the *Wissenschaftliche Zeitschrift für jüdische Theologie*, which Geiger edited during those years). Geiger writes:

> You will at least observe from this that even in the field of literature it is impossible to rush forward with giant steps and it is still forbidden to let biblical criticism be placed at the fore and to expose it in full, without denial. At any rate it will do no good to condemn the application of criticism to the Talmud, as still no one speaks of it with regard to the Bible. You know that I am certainly not known for my restraint, but still we must to some degree act tactically; the polemic against the Talmud began only in the sixth number [. . .] Consequently, reviews of works of biblical research will be very good; if you already have something of the sort about Vatke, it will be excellent, and if not I will gather what Zunz wrote about Chronicles and Ezekiel, about George and Vatke, and in the preface I will talk about the different types of biblical criticism and show to what extent they have already been employed by Jews in the past. This last point will require some reading that certainly bids to be not at all dreary.[15]

Geiger himself – who had met Vatke and George in Berlin in 1838-1839,[16] who regarded the Bible as a work of Man and some of its stories as mere anecdotes ("For how long can we persist in this lie, presenting the stories of the Bible time and again as real events of history [. . .]?"),[17] and whose interest in biblical criticism is beyond doubt – thus wished to publish critical material but was unable to do so because of the pressure upon him. As a tactical approach, Geiger intended to circumvent the difficulty by publishing reviews in place of real articles; yet in contrast to the intentions he declared in his letter, the subsequent issues of his journal did not include any articles or reviews on the subject of biblical criticism! (This did not, incidentally, satisfy Rapoport, who nonetheless left the journal's editorial board because of its "slant."[18])

Such was the situation in 1837; it would remain unchanged nearly a decade later. In January 1846 Geiger writes a personal letter to Jacob Auerbach:

> Indeed I have long thought about an encyclopedia of Jewish theology; beyond the difficulty of the undertaking, an obstruction to this – and other – works is biblical criticism, which must be avoided like boiling porridge.[19]

Here we again find a clear expression of the fear of addressing that sensitive topic rather than a lack of interest in doing so. In a public text, in contrast – a review in his journal published a year later – Geiger emphasizes the importance of biblical criticism but clarifies that Jews have

---

15   Geiger, L. 1896a, 188.
16   Geiger, L. et al. 1910, 67.
17   Letter from November 1836, in: Wiener 1962, 86.
18   *Wissenschaftliche Zeitschrift für jüdische Theologie* 4 (1839), 427f.
19   Geiger, L. 1878, 188.

not yet taken up this approach: "The time will come, certainly sooner than some believe; but it is not here yet."[20] It seems that the time had still not come in 1857, when Geiger published his *Urschrift*; despite his caution, as we have seen above,

> The book was not well received even in his own country and circles. Even the monthly *Monatsschrift für Geschichte und Wissenschaft des Judentums*, which was published in Geiger's hometown, passed over it in silence. Leopold Löw, who fought for the Reform in Hungary, was the only Jew to praise the book.[21]

The three figures whose voices have been brought here in testimony – Geiger, Popper, and Herzfeld – all belonged to the Reform stream. Among the reformists there was an evident desire to take up biblical criticism, but this desire was never put into practice. The primary reason for this was what we might call political pressures – that is, forces that were heteronomous to pure scholarship. It is difficult, and apparently unnecessary, to distinguish here between pressures internal and external to the Jewish community, since they all operated in the same direction: in their opposition to appointing a rabbi suspected of critical work, Jewish opponents could rely on the aid of the non-Jewish authorities, and the opposite was likely true as well. Germany's conservative political field controlled the academic world, the overarching culture, and the Jewish sub-culture in a manner that created a climate antagonistic to biblical criticism. Reform Jewish scholars internalized the message and preferred to remain silent or to undertake critical work strictly behind closed doors.

A similar conclusion also emerges from the well-known polemic[22] that took place among German Jews in 1842 in the wake of Geiger's article[23] which challenged the foundations of *midrash halakhah* and argued that generations of rabbis had derived commandments from Scripture by means of forced and arbitrary logic. Both sides of the debate – and especially the Reform rabbis[24] who came out to defend Geiger and emphasized his right (both as a rabbi and as a private individual) to engage freely in scholarship – focused on critical examinations of the applicability of the oral law and approached the Bible as an agreed-upon foundation which was indisputable and was not itself susceptible to critical study.

---

20   Geiger, A. 1847, 114.
21   Soloveitchik and Rubasheff 1925, 131-132.
22   Schorsch 1994, 23-26; Meyer 1988, 112f.; Harris 1995, 164f.
23   Geiger, A. 1844. Schorsch (1994, 46 N. 60) shows that the article had already been published in 1842.
24   Their articles were published in two volumes: *Rabbinische Gutachten* 1842-1843.

In January 1857, at the end of the reactionary period and on the eve of the new flowering of biblical criticism during the final third of the century (and just a moment before the publication of Geiger's *Urschrift*), Ludwig Philippson published a front-page article in the *Allgemeine Zeitung des Judenthums* titled *"Die Bibel und ihre Auslegung"* (The Bible and Its Interpretation).[25] This short article is a good demonstration of biblical criticism's image at the time after decades of suppression; and as Liebeschütz writes,[26] "Ludwig Philippson fills an important role as spokesman for the view that prevails among the educated Jewish middle-class."

Philippson traces the roots of critical exegesis back to Ibn Ezra; these roots "found in Spinoza their true articulation." Since the middle of the eighteenth century this approach took over the exegetical field, but

> If we examine its results today, when the field of criticism has more or less been exhausted, it is impossible not to recognize that in exchange for two or three certain and unquestionable successes, it has left us with a terrible mess [. . .] torn the books themselves to shreds, rent them into pieces and scattered them across the centuries. Thus we have lost all our certainty; and because every critic occasionally relied on entirely arbitrary and unimportant details and arrived at altogether different conclusions, the work of the critical school may be seen as worthless on the one hand and harmful on the other. The chief reason for which criticism has not achieved real successes was [. . . that] instead of first demanding proof against tradition and examining it in an unbiased way, it demanded that tradition provide evidence in its favor; and in doing so, with the aid of every weapon of Sophist ingenuity, it strove to make it impossible to provide that evidence [. . .]

> We do not claim that the critical work has been in vain, because it was necessary, or: it is still necessary, in order to return us to rational discussion of questions [. . .] In any case this benefit is beyond comparison with the damage it has inflicted in severely injuring the prestige of the Bible and making a complete chaos of the history of the biblical texts.

Beyond the conventional arguments about criticism's questionable and conflicting findings, a fact that stands out is that throughout the passage Philippson speaks of biblical criticism in the past tense, as though it were something that once existed but had since passed away from the world; the dying field of criticism does not pose any threat to Judaism or require Judaism to deal with it. Philippson essentially regards Jews' previous attraction to criticism as a matter of foolishness, and this too he expresses in the past tense:

---

25   Philippson 1857.
26   Liebeschütz 1978, 5.

It was very foolish on the part of modern Jews, and does not testify to the depth of spirit with which they approached the task; from the moment they ceased to fear punishment by one authority or another, they rushed to leap into this critical storm.

To summarize, in parallel to the suppression of criticism in German academia, biblical criticism was almost a taboo among German Jews during the period in question, to the extent that as that period concluded the discipline was considered the domain of the past alone. It is possible to see this as a testament to the reactive character of the *Wissenschaft des Judentums*; but by the same measure we might say that the relationship demonstrates to what extent it was ultimately part and parcel of the German intellectual world in which it operated. Either way, we have a special interest in perhaps the only work from this period to deal with biblical criticism directly – specifically with one of its most important and radical books.

Chapter 6
Steinheim versus Vatke

1835 was an *annus mirabilis* in German theology. During that single year three highly important books in the field of Old and New Testament scholarship were published. Foremost among these was David Friedrich Strauss's revolutionary *Life of Jesus*, which stirred a considerable scandal when it shattered the historical reliability of the New Testament's accounts of Jesus' life. Less scandalous but still unquestionably radical were two major books in the field of Old Testament scholarship which relied in great measure on the work of de Wette: George's book on the Jewish festivals, and Wilhelm Vatke's *Biblical Theology*.[1]

As we have seen above, 1835 cannot by any means be regarded as the apogee of any critical momentum in the field of Old Testament scholarship, a momentum whose great path-breaker was de Wette. The restorative trends that began to take shape immediately after the end of the Napoleonic period were entirely evident by 1835: the critical era had come to a close and now made way for an extended period of anti-critical conservatism. It is more correct to regard the publications of that year, and the work of Vatke in particular, as a last glimmer of the critical period – a reality that was expressed in, among other ways, the hostile reception these works experienced. Vatke published his research entirely ahead of his time, and the book had no influence at the time of its publication. It owed its later renown primarily to Wellhausen, who rediscovered its conclusions more than forty years later, adopted several of them, and developed them while giving credit to his forerunner.

We have seen that the retreat of criticism among Christian theologians led to its decline among Jewish scholars as well. The German-Jewish theologian Salomon Ludwig Steinheim, whose reaction in 1840 to Vatke's book will be examined in this chapter, is almost the sole exception to this silence. Somewhat like Vatke, Steinheim's work also had little impact during his lifetime. He was rediscovered only during the latter half of the twentieth century. Thus we are faced with a polemic between two scholars who were forgotten and subsequently redisco-

---

1   Strauss 1835; George 1835; Vatke 1835.

vered after some time. Vatke, scholars agree, preceded his time; we will see that the same is also true of Steinheim.

A. Wilhelm Vatke

The biblical scholar Johann Karl Wilhelm Vatke (1806–1882)[2] studied with Gesenius at Halle, with Ewald at Göttingen, and with Neander, Schleiermacher, and Hegel at Berlin. David F. Strauss was a friend. Beginning in 1830 he worked as a *Privatdozent* at the University of Berlin. The first part of his *Biblische Theologie wissenschaftlich dargestellt* (Biblical Theology Scientifically Described), titled *Die Religion des Alten Testaments nach den kanonischen Büchern entwickelt* (The Religion of the Old Testament Developed According to the Canonical Books), was published in 1835; additional sections remained unpublished.

Vatke was active during the peak of the anti-critical Restoration period, but he extended de Wette's critical tradition and generalized his insights using a Hegelian philosophical–historical framework. His intention was to abolish (*aufheben* in the Hegelian sense) the dichotomy between medieval dogmatism ("objectivity") and negative criticism ("subjectivity") by means of a systematic and scholarly method. He took it upon himself to describe the *forms* – "ideas" – that religion could take in their true relation to the *concept* of religion (*Begriff der Religion*). This pair of concepts is defined as follows: "The concept of religion is its divine objective; the idea of religion is the fulfillment of that objective in history."[3]

While the concept of religion is unique, its manifestations are numerous and varied. Every religion before Christianity, Judaism included, was a preliminary phase (*Vorstufe*) of the one true religion, and they are revealed in their true light only when examined from the perspective of Christianity. It is the nature of the concept of religion – which is Man's conception of God, where that in turn is simultaneously God himself – to expand and develop and never to recede.

The principle of development was the central part of Vatke's description of religion. The development of the Old Testament faith, like the development of religions in general, proceeds according to a dialectical structure from natural religion (*Naturreligion*) to Christianity. The stages of the development of religion are the stages of the development

---

2   About Vatke see: Benecke 1883; Perlitt 1965; Brömse 1973; Kraus 1982, 194-198; Rogerson 1984, 69-78.

3   Vatke 1835, 18.

of consciousness: "Natural consciousness is characterized, to begin with, by a direct union of the spiritual and the natural, [. . .] secondly it distinguishes itself from the natural and places itself as a subject [. . .] and thirdly it develops into self-awareness, into a spirit [. . .] and in this movement it is thoroughly free."[4] As with the Hegelians, development here serves as a clear normative concept of progress: each stage of development is perceived not only as chronologically advanced but as superior to the stage preceding it. The conclusion of the process is clear, but its origins are nebulous: Vatke rejects the existence of a "primeval revelation" (*Ur-Offenbarung*) and recognizes only a long line of contiguous stages of development. "As with Hegel, here too there lurks the danger of pantheism; in order to avoid the necessity of conceiving of God as an absolute entity in and of itself or as a material being, Vatke rejects a 'disconnected' deity existing outside of the world, [and instead] places Him *inside* history [. . .] The active God is revealed in the progress (i.e., development) of history as a *deus revelatus*."[5]

Vatke identified reliable sources about the history of the Israelites starting only from the time of the Judges. The biblical tales of creation and of the patriarchs are myths with no historical foundation, but he accepts the account of the Egyptian exodus as historical. In accordance with the developmental model, he believes that during their years in the desert the Israelites were a nomadic people who worshiped nature. Their primary God was Saturn, whose bull-shaped idol they transported in a tent.

Vatke's Moses is divested of many of his unique attributes. The laws he enacted could not apply to the conditions of an agricultural society settled in its own land, and hence Moses could legislate at most only a partial version of the Decalogue, but not the commandment "You shall not make for yourself an idol" (Exodus 20:4), since the descriptions of the bronze serpent[6] and cherubs in the Tabernacle[7] contradict it. Moses introduced the worship of God as a national deity and purged it of the elements of nature worship, but the worship of the two national deities, Jehovah and Saturn, continued to coexist among the people.

During the period of Judges, according to Vatke, the Israelites abandoned their nomadic lifestyle for a settled one and simultaneously

---

4   Vatke 1835, 100.

5   Perlitt 1965, 97.

6   "He broke in pieces the bronze serpent that Moses had made, for until those days the people of Israel had made offerings to it; it was called Nehushtan" (2 Kings 18:4).

7   "The cherubim shall spread out their wings above, overshadowing the mercy-seat with their wings" (Exodus 25:20).

experienced legal and moral, but not political, development. From a religious perspective, this period was characterized by a struggle between the worship of Jehovah – a minority religion – and the prevailing cult of Baal and Astarte. Here too there emerged initial signs of prophecy, albeit only in the form of fortune tellers and Nazarites.

The crowning event during the period of the united monarchy was the construction of the Temple, and Vatke attributes great importance to the fact that the architect of the Temple was not an Israelite but a Phoenician. The Temple did express a rejection of Baal-worship, but it incorporated symbols of the sun god. It did not testify to any real development on a religious level but merely increased the grandeur of the worship. The status of the Levites, who were never a tribe unto themselves but rather religious officials lower in status to the priests, was established only during this period.

During the Assyrian period, worship of the sun god increased but at the same time the Israelite laws continued to develop, and prophetic activity expanded. The prophets introduced an abstract element that helped distance the people from nature worship. Jehovah's transcendence was expressed in the concepts of "the day of the Lord" and "the end of days." Jehovah was perceived as the lawgiver, Lord, and patron of the people; theocracy too developed during this time.

Josiah's reform during the Babylonian period was a prophetic reform aided by laws that regulated day-to-day life. Vatke doubts the discovery of the Book of the Torah in the Temple and believes that the scroll, whether discovered or simply composed, contained only a few chapters of the Book of Exodus (13, 19-24, and 32-34). The Passover festival that Josiah enacted was a variation on astrolatrous motifs; a connection to the Exodus was drawn only later.

During the Babylonian exile paganism, whether Canaanite or Babylonian, persisted, but particularly during the days of Jeremiah and Isaiah there was a development of religious awareness alongside the development of the idea of Israel's mission to disseminate the true faith among all nations.

Following the Babylonian exile a further religious development took shape: laws and rites were now attributed to Moses, and belief in Satan, demons, and resurrection was adopted from Babylon and Persia, as well as myths including those of the Great Flood and the Tower of Babel. The Day of Atonement also originated during this period, as evidenced by the connection to the demon Azazel – the Israelites had not believed in demons before this period.

During the Persian period idolatry vanished. Religious and political life was regulated according to the Law and the rituals of religious observance; prayer began to develop. Vatke points specifically to this period as the pinnacle of the Old Testament faith. It is important to note that in contrast to the Lutheran tradition and to many biblical critics before and after him, Vatke does not view the Law and the rituals as a retreat or decline, but rather as a positive development. The Law freed religious life from idolatry and nature worship and expressed a high degree of awareness, on the part of believers, of the distance between them and the transcendental divinity.

The Hellenistic period was a time of transition from the Israelite religion to Judaism. This was a fateful transition that occurred gradually.[8] Judaism itself was born only during the middle of the second century BCE, when the canon was sealed and the Pharisees and Sadducees split apart, rather than after the Babylonian exile as other scholars believed. In Vatke's opinion, Judaism is a degeneration of the religion of the Old Testament dialectically leading to the religion of the New Testament. Judaism stands in dialectical contrast to the religion of the Old Testament:

> If we examine the two periods of development of the Old Testament, and the status of the New Testament, as moments in a higher unity, then the positive assessment applies only to the first and third moments, abstractly to the first and concretely to the third – while the second contains the negation, the contradiction of the universality that was set in the first moment and the dialectical progression to the true concrete universality.[9]

In summary, we should note that Vatke puts forth a comprehensive description of the Israelites' religious as well as moral and political development during the biblical period, and does so according to higher theoretical standards than was customary before that time.[10] In accordance with the developmental approach, he rejects the possibility that Moses composed the Pentateuch; as proof, he points to the fact that the historical books of the Bible, and the prophets, are not aware of the Law. He does not see the Law as a negative phenomenon, but he is the first to claim that the Law emerged only after a period subsequent to that of the prophets. He declares that the final consolidation of the Pentateuch occurred only after the Babylonian exile: *lex post prophetas* – a slogan that would become the trademark of Wellhausen's hypothesis during the 1890s.[11]

It is generally agreed that Vatke's influence, upon the publication of his book, was minimal. The date of its publication contributed to this –

---

8   Kusche 1991, 63ff.
9   Vatke 1835, 170.
10   Rogerson 1984, 78.
11   Morgan 1988, 79.

it coincided with the publication of Strauss's *Life of Jesus*, with the result that Vatke was overshadowed (Hengstenberg attacked him as the "Strauss of the Old Testament") – as did Vatke's adherence to Hegel's philosophy. But the main reason the book was marginalized – both in hostile reviews and in terms of general recognition within the field – was the conservative hegemony that ruled over German theology during the second third of the century. The professorship that Vatke had hoped to obtain on the merits of his book was denied him, the five remaining volumes he had planned to add to his book remained unwritten, and his scholarly activity declined until in 1850 it ceased entirely. As already said, Wellhausen would return to several of his insights and conclusions half a century later, and the result is that Vatke has retroactively attained a central position in the history of biblical criticism.[12]

B. Salomon Ludwig Steinheim

Salomon Ludwig Steinheim (1789–1866),[13] sometimes called "the Philo of the nineteenth century,"[14] is often regarded as the first Jewish theologian of the modern era.[15] He was born in Westphalia and moved in 1804 to Altona. In 1807 he began his medical studies at the University of Kiel and from 1810 he studied at the fledgling University of Berlin. During his studies he joined a group of (Christian) students interested in philosophy and theology, among them August Detlef Twesten, a theologian who in 1835 would take Schleiermacher's place in Berlin; Steinheim would maintain a friendship with him for the rest of his life. It seems Steinheim also studied under Wilhelm Vatke.[16] In 1813 he left Berlin and returned to Altona, and thus was unaffiliated with the *Society for Jewish Culture and Science* that was established in Berlin in 1819, though he knew several of its members. Until 1833 he occupied himself primarily with his profession as a doctor; after that year he expanded his activities as a philosopher, theologian, and activist for emancipation. Most of his theological work was written before 1845 and pub-

---

12 For a broader discussion see: Rogerson 1984, 68ff.

13 About Steinheim see the following monographs: Shear-Yashuv 1986; Haberman 1990; and anthologies: Shear-Yashuv 1994; Schoeps 1966; Schoeps et al. 1993; Wiederbach and Winkelmann 2002.

14 The epithet is attributed to either Zunz (Werblowsky 1990, 46) or Graetz (Lease 1993, 282). Geiger objected to it on the grounds that Steinheim, unlike Philo, had been forgotten. Either way, the epithet is ironic considering Steinheim's hostile treatment of Philo – see, for example: Steinheim 1840 and Shear-Yashuv 1986, 75.

15 Shear-Yashuv 1994a, 48; Shear-Yashuv 1993, 77.

16 Wiederbach and Winkelmann 2002, xiv.

lished in books and in Christian and Jewish periodicals. In 1845 he settled in Rome, where he wrote the final two volumes of his great four-
volume work, *Die Offenbarung nach dem Lehrbegriff der Synagoge* (Revelation According to the Doctrine of the Synagogue).

> The core of Steinheim's theology may be described as follows: constitutive
> reason is unable to see the truth, because it is forever entangled in antino-
> mies. In contrast, critical reason is capable of knowing the divine matters
> that we are given, through Revelation, as fundamental concepts – God,
> freedom, and the Creation for example – because they are characterized by
> a special identifying sign, a 'shibboleth' of their own.[17]

This "shibboleth," the identifying sign of Revelation, is clearly incom-
patible with and opposed to reason: "Revelation is not 'transcendence'
above human knowledge, nor a 'supplement' to it, but its absolute opposite," writes Steinheim.[18] Reason masters the necessary and general
(Euclidean geometry, for instance) through its own efforts. But natural,
factual reality is paradoxical: it is the slave of the coincidental, the arbitrary, the surprising; it does not derive from the necessary. As a result,
a form of knowledge is necessary beyond rational knowledge – one that
grasps the factual "to the degree of certainty that its own existence af-
fords."[19] The agent of this knowledge is faith.

Revelation on its own is not the main part of faith but rather an instrument by which its fundamental principles are communicated from
God to Man. The content of Revelation is summarized in three principles: God's uniqueness; the Creation; and freedom.[20] "The One God
created the world from nothing, of His free will, and so granted absolute freedom to Man; and He is the only possible basis for any theoretical truth and every moral action."[21] There is but one God, personal rather than philosophical, and His existence is not given to proof; it is
expressed in the phrase *Shema Israel* ("Hear, O Israel"). Creation is
stated in the first sentence of the Bible and stands in opposition to rational logic, which declares *"ex nihilo nihil"* – "from nothing, nothing."
Freedom, whether of God or Man, derives from the Creation.

How does Revelation make its way into the consciousness of a be-
liever? Steinheim considers himself exempt from the need to answer
the question, and even refuses to do so. Just as a scientist finds the facts

---

17   Shear-Yashuv 1994a, 54.
18   Quoted in Schwartz 1967, 69.
19   Schwartz 1967, 73.
20   Schwartz 1967, 74ff. A fourth principle is the eternal nature of the soul: Shear-
     Yashuv 1986, 41-52; regarding this see Levy's remark, "This is unclear (as well as
     unconvincing)" (1994b, 117 N. 8).
21   Steinheim 1835, 348, quoted in Schwartz 1967, 75.

available to him beyond his own mind and senses and is not required to explain how they became available, so Steinheim maintains that all he needs as a scholar is the fact that he found within his consciousness, or within religious tradition, truths that testify that they could have come only from an external source and not from reason itself; he does not need to explain in what manner they appeared. Religious life, according to Steinheim, is based not on direct experience of Revelation or direct encounters with the divine, but on knowledge of the conceptual substance of Revelation, familiarity with the imperatives that arose from it, and the fulfillment of these. Eliezer Schweid,[22] who sheds light on this issue, attributes to it the meager extent of Steinheim's influence: "There is no religious life without the occurrence of Revelation and without the presence created thereby between Man and his God. Jews who searched for full religious lives were thus unable to find guidance in [Steinheim's] words."

Through this Revelation free of an occurrence-of-revelation, Steinheim absolves himself of the need to rely on "Torah from heaven." He rejects the sweeping divineness both of the written and oral law and in particular of the Pentateuch itself,[23] parts of which Steinheim considers pagan in spirit. Remarks of this sort are strewn throughout his work: in the second volume of his most important book, printed in 1856, Steinheim wonders how long the doctrine of Revelation existed among the Israelites; his answer is that it is impossible to determine its exact origin, but he attempts to identify the earliest possible date by which there was no doubt that it was already known. By counting backward from the destruction of the First Temple to the time of Isaiah (the first), he arrives at the conclusion that already circa 1000 BCE, "The doctrine of Revelation, that is, either the first four books of the Pentateuch [. . .] or Deuteronomy [. . .] or all of them together were included in that manuscript, in the Torah, in the same form and with the same contents as those we have before us today."[24] In the fourth volume of his book Steinheim explicitly uses the phrase "the author or authors of the ancient document."[25] Steinheim understands Scripture as a collection of texts subject to historical development and to errata, that even included elements alien to Revelation. Nevertheless, parts of the Pentateuch and

---

22   Schweid 1994. The quote is on p. 112.
23   Meyer 1993, 148.
24   Steinheim 1856, 283.
25   Steinheim 1865, 41.

Prophets did contain the core truths of Revelation, which is not subject to historical development.[26]

The laws – the practical commandments – are in Steinheim's opinion not part of Revelation . Unlike the approaches of non-Jewish and Jewish thinkers alike (in particular Mendelssohn), Steinheim does not see the Law as the essence of Judaism; nor does he regard the Bible as a "law book." He objects to "the Law" as an alternate name for the Hebrew Bible, because the term "Law" implies an element of coercion (external or internal) or of necessity, whether with regard to human laws or to laws of nature. In contrast, a true moral law does not coerce but only compels; hence it deserves the name "commandment" (*Gebot*) rather than "law." The Bible is not a book of laws nor a book of commandments; it includes commandments, but they are not its chief subject. The appropriate name for the Hebrew Bible is "the teachings of Moses," because its concern is instruction rather than legislation. On the contrary, several of the instructions in Scripture, such as the sacrificial laws in the Book of Leviticus, even contradict the principles of Revelation.[27] When Steinheim discusses practical issues central to Judaism, he is not interested in the commandments those issues are intertwined with but in their theoretical derivation from Revelation and in the principle of Revelation they express. The Sabbath, for example, was not given to the Israelites alone; it is derived from the principle of Creation. The principal occupation on that day is *diagoge* – a term Steinheim borrows from Aristotle – which means the exchange of physical for spiritual labor; Steinheim is not concerned with the specific rituals of the Sabbath. Dietary laws were given to the Israelites in order to ready their spirit to accept and fulfill the teachings of God; they are not eternal, but subject to change. The most important commandment of Revelation is "love your neighbor as yourself," and here too Steinheim does not delve into its practical substance.[28] Graupe points out that

> Steinheim's attempt to include religious law in his theory of revelation is certainly the weakest part of his work, because from the first he overlooked or perhaps did not wish to take advantage of the methodological possibilities of that inclusion.[29]

And indeed, it seems that Steinheim need not have had particular difficulty in incorporating the practical commandments into his method: he could easily have presented, for example, what Saadya Gaon had called

---

26   On the ahistoricity of revelation see the beginning of the first volume: Steinheim 1835, 17ff.
27   Steinheim 1865, 110f.
28   Shear-Yashuv 1986, 54-58.
29   Graupe 1966, 68, quoted (in German) in: Shear-Yashuv 1986, 63.

"commandments of revelation" as a shibboleth that proved Revelation. Yet Steinheim did not do this, as Shear-Yashuv observes:

> It is not quite clear why Steinheim did not include the biblical legislation within his system. [...] Indeed, the question of legislation is a very weak point in Steinheim's system. But it might be that in his *magnum opus*, because of its epistemological character, he did not try to develop a theology of *Halakhah* on purpose, but he only describes the theological ground of Judaism.[30]

The starting point for many of Steinheim's works – and specifically of that analyzed herein – was polemical, and polemics was an essential motive of his work.[31] The main part of Steinheim's polemic was aimed at the great enemy of Revelation: the *Philosophem*, a philosophical–pagan approach which Steinheim traces throughout the entire history of human thought and religion. In effect, Steinheim creates a sophisticated system of binary oppositions, at one pole of which he places Revelation and on the other *Philosophem*, which appears not only throughout the entire history of philosophy (particularly among those whom Steinheim considers philosophy's most important representatives: Plato, Leibniz, German idealism, and Schleiermacher), but also in the ancient Eastern religions (Brahmanism and Buddhism) as well as Christianity, in which paganism overshadows Revelation (from the Gospel of John to Luther and ultimately Schleiermacher). The antinomies between *Philosophem* and Revelation are summarized in a well-known table.[32] So, among other things, *Philosophem* is identified with the eternal nature of the material; with a God who merely arranged the material from which the world was made and did not create it; with the subjugation of Man and God to necessity; and with belief in fate. Revelation, on the other hand, stands for the very opposite: a God who created the world and all things material; Man who was created free and a God who created freely; and faith in divine providence.

Steinheim's position among the German-Jewish camps was problematic. He debated both the Reform and Orthodox camps and belonged to neither of them. In his opinion, the Orthodox stream placed issues of marginal importance at the center of Judaism; he accused it of both rote thought and utter obfuscation. He believed that pagan principles had infiltrated the Orthodox prayer book, and consequently supported the reform of the cult and the universalization of Judaism, which he believed was intended for all of humanity. On the other hand, he also despised the theology of the reformists, who he claimed were

---

30   Shear-Yashuv 1986, 62f.
31   Shear-Yashuv 1994a; Schöps 1966.
32   Shear-Yashuv 1994a, 52-53.

ashamed to present the idea of Revelation to their supporters and at times, because of their fervor for emancipation, even committed the sin of identifying the principles of Judaism with modern anti-revelatory streams of thought such as pantheism or idealism. Another fundamental difference between Steinheim's approach and that of the Reform movement was his nearly absolute disregard of post-biblical Judaism and his rejection of its religious development – two issues that the reformists placed at the fore.

Michael Meyer credits Steinheim's minimal influence on his peers not necessarily to the fact that he abandoned the religious praxis but primarily to the small amount of Jewish content in his work.[33] Steinheim was not deeply versed in the traditional Jewish canon, and his work rarely cited Jewish sources – something that particularly stands out in contrast to his copious references to non-Jewish philosophy, from ancient Greece to German idealism. Occasionally he quoted from the Bible, but even in his day critics remarked on his limited command of Hebrew.[34]

Scholars agree that Steinheim's influence on his contemporaries was minimal, and he was rediscovered only in the twentieth century with the work of J.H. Schoeps.[35] It was Steinheim's marginality which may have enabled him to grapple explicitly with biblical criticism during a time when most German-Jewish scholars preferred to avoid that subject.

C. Steinheim on Vatke

In 1840 Steinheim published a response to Vatke's book, titled *Die Offenbarung vom Standpuncte der höheren Kritik. Eine Prüfung der Darstellung des Herrn Professors W. Vatke in dessen Schrift: "Die Religion des Alten Testaments nach den kanonischen Büchern entwickelt"* (Revelation from the Standpoint of Higher Criticism. An Examination of Prof. W. Vatke's Description in his "The Religion of the Old Testament Developed According to the Canonical Books"). Initially published in two parts in a theological journal[36] edited by Pelt, a student of Twesten (who was, again, a friend of Steinheim's), it was republished later that year as a 190-page book.[37] The response begins with a short preface (pp. I-VIII,

---

33   Meyer 1988, 69; Werblowsky 1990, 42; Meyer 1993.
34   E.g.: Joël 1857.
35   Lease 1984 wrote about Steinheim's similarity to his "discoverer," Schoeps.
36   See: Schoeps 1966, 270 N. 8.
37   Steinheim 1840. The orphaned references in the rest of the chapter refer to this work.

signed Altona, July 1840) and, after a brief introduction (pp. 1-3), continues with "General Commentary" (pp. 3-68), which discusses Vatke's preface on general theory; "Specific Commentary" (pp. 68-159), which examines the history of biblical religion according to Vatke; and finally a conclusion (pp. 159-180). In truth, Steinheim's arguments were not laid out in a particularly orderly fashion, and the same ideas recur repeatedly in different variations and in occasionally hazy contexts. His cumbersome and convoluted style – manifested in lengthy sentences and a profusion of rhetorical questions – and the copious Greek and Latin phrases with which he peppered his work make for difficult reading indeed; of Steinheim's stylistic shortcomings, which also affected his other books, contemporary critics wrote: "[. . .] endless redundant repetitions, rhetorical flourishes, and digressions which needlessly delay the arrival at the destination itself hinder the curious reader who wishes to get to the root of the matter, and not infrequently leave him baffled."[38]

In his preface, Steinheim argues that many Jewish alleged intellectuals were drawn to Philosophy's hostile approach to the Old Testament[39] (more on this later), and it is his desire to curb that attraction that motivated him to write and republish the work in question so that it may reach the Jewish public at large. Though the entire book deals with the work of a Christian theologian and biblical scholar, Steinheim primarily addresses Jewish readers. This may explain certain flaws in his book, which may have stemmed from his preference to influence Jewish readers even at the cost of inaccuracy.

Thus, for example, Steinheim points in his preface to the importance of Vatke's book and to the recognition it received. He mentions de Wette's "appreciative and endorsing" review of the book (p. 1). This reference to de Wette's praise may derive from a desire to inflate Vatke's importance in the eyes of his readers, so that Steinheim himself would not appear insignificant but rather as one dealing with the successor of a prominent, critical, and even persecuted biblical scholar (de Wette was living in exile in Switzerland at that time). However, it should be noted that in fact de Wette's review was not positive in the least; on the contrary, he argued that Vatke had crossed almost every line in his critical work and fiercely criticized his abstruse philosophy.[40]

---

38   Joël 1857, 79.
39   Throughout his work, Steinheim freely employs the Christian term "Old Testament".
40   Quoted in: Perlitt 1965, 140. More on de Wette's negative review can be found in: Brömse 1973, 41.

Steinheim begins with a survey of the history of higher biblical criticism (p. 8ff.). After a number of attempts, which he himself rejects, to
define the subject, he provides a definition using the metaphor "teles-
copic," in contrast to the "microscopic" lower criticism. Steinheim places the beginnings of higher criticism outside of theology, in the work of
Astruc: the physician, he argues, dared to write openly what conscience
and self-preservation forbade clerics to express (one cannot help reading this as a self-allusion by Steinheim the doctor). As a reaction to
negative criticism, the Protestant orthodoxy entrenched itself in an
extreme literal theopneustic[41] position (*Buchstaben-Theopneustie*) and
sentenced itself to willful blindness and a complete subjugation of the
intellect to faith, out of the conviction that admitting any flaw in Scripture would deny its sanctity entirely and render it a mere collection of
anecdotes. Ewald emerged as a synthesis between the two camps to
reconcile the critical and anti-critical approaches,[42] and in his wake P.
von Bohlen published an essay on the Book of Genesis which Steinheim
praises for its attention to the doctrine of Revelation.[43]

Here Steinheim discusses what he calls "Old Testament criticism in
the Domain of the Old Testament" (p. 16ff.), by which he means biblical
criticism in Judaism. This is an attempt to describe – or construct – a
Jewish parallel to Christian biblical criticism.[44] Steinheim differentiates
between the nature of the "struggle" in Christianity and that in Judaism. Judaism lacked the mania for destruction that reached its peak
in English and French Christianity during the eighteenth century, a
mania accompanied by *Schadenfreude* and the arrogance of victory: biblical criticism "dragged the vanquished hero in the mud and contami-
nated him with mud after it felled him, in its opinion" (p. 17ff.). In this
unrestrained frenzy, Steinheim claims, biblical critics behave as though
the fault lay in Scripture itself rather than in their ill usage, and forget
that what is best and most holy is always the most easily employed for
evil. All this Steinheim contrasts to the serene, temperate, and respectable spirit of Manasseh ben Israel (1604–1657).[45] Higher criticism was
seldom practiced in Judaism. Steinheim offers several reasons for the

41   Theopneusty, the doctrine of the literal dictation of Scripture by God.
42   This was written before the publication of Ewald's (1843-1859) central book. Stein-
      heim mentioned an earlier work by Ewald on Genesis. On the intermediate critical
      position of Ewald, who objected to Vatke's position on the lateness of the Law, see:
      Rogerson 1984, 91-103.
43   The reference is to Bohlen 1835.
44   Cf. Geiger's similar suggestion in the previous chapter.
45   Manasseh ben Israel (1972) – Spinoza's teacher in the seventeenth century –
      enumerated 470 contradictions in Scripture and resolved them using Kabbalistic
      techniques.

dearth and moderation of Jewish biblical criticism: first of all, the Jewish critics' cautiousness and consideration stemmed from the spell that Revelation casts upon those who know its secret. Secondly, Jews' attitude toward the Bible was an internal one – the attitude of "citizens" rather than mere "visitors" as in Christianity, and as a result they showed restraint in attacking it. Thirdly, Jewish critics feared that their criticism would harm the final refuge of the Jewish people, who had preserved it throughout millennia of suffering. Fourth, since the days of the "more comprehensive spiritual education" that was widespread in the Sephardic communities of Spain and Portugal, the in-depth study of language and history in the "Synagogue" increasingly declined,[46] and this was due to the historical circumstances that forced Jews to attend first and foremost to their physical survival and did not allow them to devote themselves to scholarly study.

Even at the beginning of this book (p. 22), following the description of the disagreement between the critics and their opponents, Steinheim poses his "means of reconciliation," which is the starting point for his criticism and its main organizing principle. Is it possible, Steinheim asks, to identify a "tenable idea" – an Archimedean point of sorts, higher than and external to the opposing sides – that could indeed allow for criticism while defining its permissible boundaries? Steinheim believes it is possible, and here he lays forth the basis and aim of his book:

> But precisely in doing so we could mark the point from which we must judge Vatke's work. Let us further add, that Vatke believes that he has found this life principle not so much in the realm of Revelation itself but rather [. . .] in a philosophy attained externally to it and without its influence. But this is exactly what appears to the author of this work [i.e., to Steinheim] to be the flaw of higher criticism. The certainty that some other, special thing, not only alien to philosophy but also entirely beyond its reach, exists as a pure religious moment in the doctrine of Revelation itself, and simultaneously his conviction that it is possible to find, isolate, and grasp this moment by means of unmistakable signs, are the motivation and substance of these pages. This also marks the point at which the author [i.e., Vatke] and the reviewer differ. Both seek a third, higher thing, but they do so in different realms. Both believe they have found it: the author in a primeval idea of the purely human (*Urgedanken des Reinmenschlichen*); the reviewer in information delivered from outside. So the two are separated in their origins and conclusions, and parallel to each other in their method and their unshakable love of truth (p. 23ff.).

---

46 By "Synagogue" Steinheim denoted Judaism as a whole. See Werblowsky's (1990, 45) penetrating criticism of Steinheim's terminology: "First of all there is no ‚Synagogue'; that is, the concept is the invention of Christian theologians who required an analogy to the concept of the Church [...]."

In so writing, Steinheim clarifies the fundamental difference between himself and Vatke. Both sought an "Archimedean point" for their work, but each found it in a different place: Vatke in philosophy, Steinheim in Revelation. Steinheim correctly notes that their approaches are "parallel," and hence any dialogue between them is inherently problematic. Steinheim rejects one of the basic premises of biblical criticism, which strives to study Scripture without resorting to Revelation, and he accuses biblical criticism as a whole of the fact that one of its most prominent "conclusions" is "an absolute rejection of the substance of our canon as Revelation" (p. 159).

In principle Steinheim could have concluded his book at this point. Having pointed out the axiomatic epistemological difference between him and Vatke, there seemed to be no room left for dialogue between them. However, Steinheim did go on to raise a long litany of complaints against Vatke and the Hegelian approach. The greater part of his arguments, which are scattered with frequent repetition throughout his book, may be divided into (1) criticism of the principles of Hegelian philosophy and of Vatke's methodology which derived from it, and (2) specific criticism of the conclusions of Vatke's study of Moses and the Law.

(1) The Philosophy and Methodology of Biblical Criticism

Steinheim's criticism of Vatke's methodology is particularly interesting because of the latter's influence on Wellhausen's approach. In Steinheim's criticism three main issues can be identified: criticism of Vatke's philosophical primacy; criticism of the particularism of Hegel and Vatke's philosophical–historical model; and criticism of the developmental approach to Scripture.

Criticism of Vatke's philosophical primacy

As we have seen, Steinheim rejects on principle the preeminence that Vatke granted his (Hegelian)[47] philosophical framework. The subordination of biblical history to this framework is mistaken because it rejects Revelation *a priori*: the idea that Revelation from beyond is impossible (p. 123) is an old and harmful view that betrays shades of paganism because it places Man and his reason in the rightful place of Revelation. Here Steinheim reiterates his well-known claim[48] that *Philo-*

---

47   For Steinheim's criticism of Hegel see: Steinheim 1863, 293-298.
48   See: Shear-Yashuv 1986, 64ff.

sophem is a form of paganism, while "The doctrine of Revelation is a protest against philosophy and paganism" (p. 57).

Vatke's concept of religion attempted primarily to blur the distinction between God and Man and regarded religion as "self-awareness of God in the spirit of the community" (p. 51). But this attempt to conciliate between God and Man necessarily leads to the rejection of a God external to Man (how, Steinheim asks, can one speak in the spirit of Lessing about "the education of the human race" in the absence of an educator? [p. 70]). From here derives Man's deification and his pretension that he is knowledge, God, and world all at once: "I am wisdom! I am God and the world, I and you, you and I! All is one, all is one!" (p. 56). Thus Steinheim reiterates his general, familiar argument against the pagan element in *Philosophem*, and in effect largely rejects humanist rationalism as a whole.

Criticism of Particularism

Moreover, Vatke's concept of religion, which developed over the course of history, did so in a specific location – in the spirit of certain communities and not others. Regarding this Steinheim begins with a comprehensive discussion of "the objectivity of the new school" (that is, the school of Hegel and Vatke; p. 41ff.) – objectivity attributed to the concept of religion. Steinheim maintains that that school's use of the term "objective" is both incorrect and misleading. His argument runs as follows: the objective concept of religion according to Vatke was, in fact, God. Not God in the abstract philosophical–rational sense, but a specific God as He was manifested in practice – in the world and in the human spirit – throughout history, taking on and shedding various forms over its course. This abstract primeval entity – the concept – rejected its abstract essence and seemingly crystallized – congealed, as it were – into a tangible substance (*Substanz*) in the world. "The concept thinks itself into the world," Steinheim writes; in other words, the concept brings itself into the world by means of thought. This substantiation – the transformation of concept into substance – contradicts the usual philosophical use of the term "concept." In effect the concept is the fulfillment of the thing-in-itself (*Ding an sich*) in the (Kantian) critical school. This school despaired of finding the thing-in-itself, and out of this desperation emerged the "dogmatic restoration" of Hegel (and Fichte). Hegel attempted to create an "absolute" unification of subject and object, of the expanding and the contracting, of the thing-in-itself. But in the process, Steinheim argues, he became trapped in two contradictions: first, it was impossible to determine what had prompted the

absolute's division in the first place – and, if such motivation were discovered, it would contradict the entire method; and secondly, the principle of identity (A = A) prevented the abstract and the thinking – that
is, the object and the subject, which were distinct (to use Steinheim's
term – heterogeneous) – from existing together in the same primeval
absolute. In order to extricate himself from these contradictions, Hegel
chose a solution that avoided them, namely turning concept into substance. Because of this he declared that it was the nature of the concept
to change, to roll over itself ("turn somersaults") and thereby to enter
the world and stand on its feet within thought, and to continue rolling
onward and onward until it arrived at the spirit of the community and
there became manifested in its full form. And thus, Steinheim explains
sarcastically,

> In the religion that the eminent teacher teaches us from his armchair, the
> eternally moving "concept" [Begriff] would come to a rest; after its restless
> bifurcations and unifications it became God as the spirit of the community,
> its living description this community's cult; the cult is the revealed spirit,
> the God who arrived at Himself in the evangelical Christian community of
> the philosophical school – this is the thought, the objective concept in its
> full, self-aware development, in its perfect manifestation (p. 44).

The problem, Steinheim continues, is that the entire extended journey
of the concept takes place in the material and spiritual world; because
of that it culminated among humans, and particularly among the part
of humanity that thinks in one particular way, and this culmination
could not have taken place in any other community.

Steinheim points out a double problem in this context. The first is
conceptual confusion, not to mention misdirection: that which takes
place only inside a person's thoughts is generally called "subjective" in
order to distinguish it from what exists outside of thought, rather than
"objective" as Hegel and Vatke called their "concept." Hegel inter-
changed object and subject, which would not have been a problem in
itself (since one may define one's terms as one pleases) had it not also
been misleading: it was in contrast to the accepted usage of the terms
and created an impression of objectivity with regard to a subjective
concept.

Secondly, this subjectivity, which conceals itself behind the claim of
objectivity, is clearly particularistic – it is a subjectivity that specifically
names the Protestant–philosophical Christianity of Hegel or Vatke
themselves as the ultimate stage of religion:

> The history of the world and of the spirit is the history of God, His epige-
> nesis, His formation beginning in the embryonic era and culminating in
> His philosophical completion in Hegel's work! A bag full of worms on a
> drop in a bucket imagines to itself that in it God becomes spirit and, having

overcome all contradictions, joins with the concept and becomes Truth. This is a madhouse of the first order, *insanire cum ratione*, the dead end of the wisest stupidity! (p. 170).

Steinheim refrained from expanding on the Christian bias of this philosophical approach, and simply indicated it in general and rejected its claim to universal objectivity – perhaps because its bias was indeed trivially obvious.

Criticism of the Developmental Approach to Scripture

As noted, Vatke's model was developmental and normative. Steinheim comments that the gradual development of Vatke's idea of religion is a biological analogy, similar to the Aristotelian concept of *omne animal ex verme* – that all animals developed from the worm (recall that Darwin would publish his theory of evolution only later, in 1858). Steinheim does not object in any way to this physical–organic analogy in itself (p. 34), but at several points in his book he points out flaws, limitations, and contradictions inherent in the model or in the manner in which Vatke used it.

First, again, Steinheim clarifies that the developmental approach rejects Revelation at the outset. Revelation means, to Steinheim, a sudden communication from a divine source to Man, a communication that radically alters its recipient. In describing the impact of Revelation Steinheim even uses the term "rebirth," with all its connotations (particularly in Christianity): "It is requisite that natural Man change entirely, and he will emerge from this process as though born anew in all his intellectual and emotional faculties."

Clearly the model of organic development rejects such radical change at the outset, as Steinheim emphasizes again and again (pp. 38-40, 76, 86, 159). Steinheim regards monotheism as an entirely innovative and revolutionary idea; there was no way it could have developed from the pagan religions that preceded it in history. The principles of the religion of Revelation contradict even common sense, and consequently their origin must have been be external to human reason. "There is no transition between the dogma of reason to the doctrine of Revelation" (p. 40); the denial of the absence of such a transition was the "grave mistake" of contemporary philosophy as a whole. This was not gradual development – advancement to the next level – but a break, an extreme change in relation to all before it:

> How could the doctrine of unity, freedom, and creation suit the entirely naturally-developing contemplative results of pluralism (at least dualism), necessity, and becoming, to such an extent that it is supposed to be only a continuation, a higher stage of the pagan–philosophical concept? How can

one even say that a self-sufficient life (*vita propria*) such as that of the concept and of its course of life could suddenly absorb into its subtance something totally foreign, something new and even opposed to it, and merge with it into a single entity – which contradicts every analogy in the development of any other organism and simultaneously breaches the intellectual principle of logical contradiction? (pp. 38-39).

Secondly, Steinheim hints briefly and rather ironically at the arbitrariness in the choice of the "concept"'s subject community. About the fact that the "concept" made its way from the generation of Moses to his heir Joshua, Steinheim notes: "Why, this concept must truly be mad, if it wants to continue through ours of all nations!" (p. 94). Not only is the final harbor of the concept (i.e., Protestantism) thus subjective, as noted above, but the path of its historical journey between human communities was determined arbitrarily and derived from the needs of the developmental model. Steinheim considers particularly problematic the idea of the Persian cult of light as the stage preceeding that of the religion of the Old Testament within the development of the concept of religion: this Persian religion, he argues, was actually later to the Old Testament or was at the least of the same age, and thus there is no justification for placing it earlier, whether chronologically or conceptually (pp. 37-38).

A third problem that Steinheim indicates lay in the fact that Vatke's developmental approach negated the possibility of retreat or decline in the concept of religion.[49] So, for example, Steinheim sees stagnation in the development of the Israelite concept of religion during the prophetic period, because the community largely devolved into paganism; after it, however, there began a new awakening of the concept during the Babylonian exile – "and this is a historical fact, supplying clear evidence against [Vatke's] model" (p. 89), which rejected a decline followed by additional development. Elsewhere (p. 142), in a certain contradiction of his own argument (but still as a counter-argument to Vatke), Steinheim declares that before, during, and after the exile there was no progress in the Israelites' concept of religion, but rather a decline. It appears that Steinheim agrees with the normativeness in Vatke's concept of development, but disagrees about the details of its applicability to history.

---

49   In truth, this is not a separate problem but another facet of the earlier problem. Whenever Vatke found decline, he exchanged the subject community of the concept of religion for another community in which he identified the continuation of the concept's development.

(2) The Lateness of the Law and the Image of Moses

Beyond these methodological arguments, Steinheim objects to a good deal more of Vatke's specific conclusions. The most important of these, in his eyes, are summarized in four emphatic "protests" that Steinheim makes toward the midpoint of his book (pp. 80-81). In the first place, he "protests" against the conclusion that derived from the Hegelian approach in which Moses (and the patriarchs) supposedly were pagans "like – – the philosophy and theology of our time" (p. 80). Secondly, he protests against the claim that the doctrine of the one God had not yet come of age during the time of Moses, a claim that in his opinion derived from confusion between the human and the divine, or from two-bit anthropomorphism, as though God needed to keep track of a global clock in order to know whether the bells had chimed and it was time to reveal His teachings to Man. Thirdly, he protests against Vatke's remark that to assume that the traditional accounts of Moses were correct, even if only for the most part, meant assuming a miracle even greater than that of Jesus: Steinheim responds that Moses was not miraculous in the least, but was rather a regular mortal in every way; his only distinction is that he experienced divine revelation. Finally, in the fourth place, he protests against Vatke's remarks that the creation of the Law took place no earlier than the time of the prophets.

Steinheim's second and fourth "protests" touch on a central issue in Vatke's work: the lateness of the Law, a question destined to become Vatke's main contribution to the history of biblical criticism. As we have seen, Vatke argued that Moses had enacted at most the Decalogue (with the exception of the commandment against making a graven image of God),[50] and that the Law was created only later, not before Josiah's reforms and in part even after the Babylonian exile; he upended the accepted historical chronology and proposed that the prophets predated the composition of the Pentateuch. Vatke worded this in various ways, but Steinheim latches on to one specific formulation of his (p. 75 and again 81), which he quotes: "The profound idea of the Old Testament, that the Law exists between the promises and their fulfillment, may be justified historically, because the Pentateuch really was completed later than the promises of most of the prophets" (p. 75).[51]

---

50 Vatke rejected specifically this commandment, of which Kant, in his *Critique of Judgement*, wrote that "Perhaps there is no more sublime passage in the Jewish Law" and which served as the basis of Steinheim's entire approach to paganism. On this subject see: Kochan 1993 (the quote by Kant is on p. 137).

51 Vatke 1835.

Steinheim declares that this is a highly particularistic position (p. 81). Here Steinheim – admittedly following in Vatke's footsteps – does take the bull by its horns. In this formulation Vatke revealed the proximity of the modern, scholarly *lex post prophetas* approach to the traditional Christological perspective. His formulation evokes Paul's epistle to the Romans (5:20): "But Law entered in-between,[52] with the result that the trespass multiplied; but where sin increased, grace abounded all the more, so that, just as sin exercised dominion in death, so grace might also exercise dominion through justification leading to eternal life through Jesus Christ our Lord." This, of course, summarizes the negative Christian (Pauline, Lutheran) attitude toward Judaism and the Law.

Steinheim explicitly insists on the Christian nature of this perspective and anchors his claim in his overall conception of the biblical Law. Again, Steinheim refuses to view the Law as the essence of the Bible, or even to see it as a set of "laws". In such approaches he finds "a unilaterality bias two thousand years old" (p. 109), which apparently began at the end of the period of the Second Temple and perhaps originated in the purely legislative nature of "what is called" the oral law. This approach cannot be found in the Old Testament – neither in the Pentateuch nor in the Prophets or Writings – nor in later Judaism:

> Neither Samuel nor Isaiah, neither the major nor the minor prophets, neither the psalmists nor the Maccabees, neither the Talmudists nor the rabbis up to this very day were so foolish and mistaken as to see the entire apparatus of forms, prayers, and laws as the essential part of the Old Testament (p. 81).

Because of such expressions – "the Law from Sinai" (p. 109) – these prejudices about necessity, force, degeneration, and so forth took form and were attributed to the Old Testament in contrast to the New Testament. "Whoever subsumes the collection of laws in the expression 'Law' – as designator and characteristic of the Old Testament – diverts our perspective at the expense of the Old Testament and in favor of the New" (p. 110). Moreover, reducing the Old Testament to the concept of "the Law" is not helpful to Christianity either. Steinheim notes Jesus' claim that his purpose was to confirm and not to abolish even a single letter of the Torah; hence what Jesus did abolish did not in his view belong to the Torah, which he wanted to perpetuate. The true essence of Judaism was not "the Law," but – "as is still written in Mark 12:29-30" – "Hear, O Israel: the Lord our God, the Lord is one," and "You shall love the Lord your God with all your heart, and with all your

---

52   This phrase is a literal translation of Luther's German translation ("*Das Gesetz ist aber dazwischen hineingekommen*"), to which both Vatke and Steinheim probably referred.

soul, and with all your mind, and with all your strength" (p. 110). In short, "The term 'Law' for the Old Testament must be abandoned entirely" (p. 111).

As for the laws and political arrangements that Moses enacted, Steinheim rejects their divine–revelatory origins out of hand. In this he was in complete agreement with Vatke: "To introduce good and coherent politics – that did not in truth require passage through the desert and Revelation at Sinai" (p. 98). Steinheim attributes many of the laws to the influence of Jethro (Moses' father-in-law), "the first politician in the full sense of the word," and recalls that the prophets already declared that these laws were the work of Man, or else rejected them entirely. As evidence he cites (p. 99) the well-known verses of Isaiah and Jeremiah[53] – the same verses which served in the long Christian tradition to attack the Jewish adherence to the Law, and were used in biblical criticism to prove the lateness of the Law.

As for the remaining biblical laws, Steinheim does not consider them laws at all: they had no aspect of compulsion or force, and so were more fittingly called commandments or directives (*Gebote*), similar to moral directives. Either way, they were of marginal importance from a religious aspect: "The Pythagorean religion also included dietary laws, but no one ever thought to consider them its essence" (p. 110). Here Steinheim seizes the opportunity to criticize Mendelssohn as well: only because he denied true Revelation could Mendelssohn boil Judaism down to "a beard and a prayerbook" (p. 124).

Steinheim thus rejects the Pauline equivalence between "Torah" and "Law," as well as between them and the essence of Judaism. For him this was one way to grapple with the lateness of the Law in Vatke's view: to deny the legitimacy of the very usage of this comprehensive term, which he considered deceptive, Christological, and highly biased. Hence his task would not be to prove the antiquity of the Law, but rather that of the Pentateuch; this would go some way toward proving the antiquity of what he considered its essence – namely Revelation, expressed in the principles of Creation and monotheism; the Sabbath which represented them; and certain moral principles.

Following this Steinheim attempts, through narrow, particular arguments, to refute the arguments on which Vatke based the lateness of

---

53   Isaiah 29:13 ("The Lord said: Because these people draw near with their mouths and honour me with their lips, while their hearts are far from me, and their worship of me is a human commandment learned by rote"); Jeremiah 7:21 (properly 7:22: "For on the day that I brought your ancestors out of the land of Egypt, I did not speak to them or command them concerning burnt-offerings and sacrifices"), 8:8 ("in fact, the false pen of the scribes has made it into a lie").

the Pentateuch. To the claim that the prophets neither knew of nor mentioned the Pentateuch, Steinheim responds (p. 133) that their entire activity was aimed against paganism. They did not mention the rituals described in the Pentateuch because the rituals themselves were unimportant in their eyes. All their work was intended only to protest against "public and private paganism" (p. 133) and the cult that had degenerated into meaningless ritual – what Steinheim calls *opera operata* (pp. 134, 139). The choice of this theological term is not accidental; *opera operata* was a Catholic term[54] attacked during the Reformation. Steinheim thus creates an analogy between the prophets' attack on the Israelites and Luther's attack on Catholicism, and places Judaism in the same position in which Protestantism positioned itself: basing religion on faith (in the deeds) and discounting the religious value of the deeds themselves.

In contrast, the prophets did mention the Sabbath because it was not solely a ritual but was also deeply symbolic of the belief in Creation and the relationship to God (p. 134). And what right would Nathan the prophet have had before David, Steinheim asks, had the prohibitions against murder and adultery not existed? "Any other Oriental ruler would simply have laughed at him!" (p. 140); hence the Pentateuch must have existed during his time. In contrast to Vatke's argument, Steinheim maintains that the famous verse in Jeremiah 7:22[55] was no proof that sacrifice was not mentioned in the Torah available to the prophet, but rather that he intended to protest the fact that sacrifices had become the most essential point of their faith to the Israelites (p. 139);[56] as we have seen, Steinheim considers sacrifice an element alien to the doctrine of Revelation. Steinheim also minimizes the importance of Hezekiah's reforms: "Hezekiah's reform was not real reform" (p. 136). There is also no reason to suppose, as Vatke did, that parts of the

---

54 "ex opere operato: *by the work performed*; with reference to the sacraments, the assumption of medieval scholasticism and Roman Catholicism that the correct and churchly performance of the rite conveys grace to the recipient [. . .] Sacraments themselves, therefore, have a *virtus operativa*, or operative power. This view of sacraments is denied by both Lutherans and Reformed, who maintain that faith must be present in the recipient if the sacraments are to function as a means to grace; the mere performance of the rite will not convey grace" (Muller 1985, 108).

55 "For on the day that I brought your ancestors out of the land of Egypt, I did not speak to them or command them concerning burnt-offerings and sacrifices."

56 In this Steinheim does not depart greatly from the traditional Jewish interpretation of the verse, which read it as a critique by Jeremiah of the over-emphasis on sacrificial practice in his time. According to Rashi: "The beginning of the condition was only: 'If you hearken to My voice' [...]"; David Kimhi (1160–1235): "the crux of the commandment was not concerning burnt-offerings and sacrifices, but rather 'Obey my voice, and you shall be my people'".

Pentateuch were composed when they were "discovered" during Josiah's reforms, since in reality books were apt to be forgotten during a time of paganism and rediscovered later (p. 140). There was no justification to assume on the basis of 2 Kings 23:22[57] that the festival of Passover had first been created during the days of Josiah, since first of all such a conclusion does not follow from the verse at all,[58] and secondly even during the present day holidays tend to be forgotten quickly and discovered anew after many years (p. 137).

The first and third "protests" touch on another issue that occupied Steinheim intensely throughout his book, namely the depiction of Moses. Vatke maintained that no individual – particularly not Moses – could stand out too far above the rest of his generation. A too-large gap between an individual and his community was unacceptable, and if Scripture described such a gap the description must not be historical. In such a case, critical scholarship must pare down the degree of development of the individual and bring it closer to that of his community, as well as fill in the missing links for the sake of continuity in the historical description.[59] If Moses' community had become devoted to paganism, as described in the Pentateuch, Moses could not have deviated too far from them, and the majority of his work, according to Vatke, consisted of introducing the cult of Jehovah as the national God. Steinheim rejects Vatke's fundamental argument – which derived from his developmental approach – and storms: if Moses could be demoted so, how low would the patriarchs be demoted? Steinheim reiterates his argument against demotion and writes that Vatke's developmental framework precluded Revelation; but furthermore, Steinheim argues, his claim has no hold: an individual certainly can stand out above the members of his generation. If 2000 years later Hegel's approach would be as prevalent as Moses' teachings, Steinheim wonders, at what conclusion may a historian of philosophy arrive if he acts like Vatke and tries to learn about Hegel's method from the current religious state of Christianity as a whole, or of the Germans, or Prussia, or Berlin alone (p. 77)? Certainly the Israelites in general could be immersed in the cult of Molekh while Moses arrived at a consciousness of monotheism. Vatke's deduction from the concept to the community's cult and from the community to the individual is therefore unjustified.

---

57   "No such passover had been kept since the days of the judges."

58   Steinheim clarifies that in contrast to Vatke's claim, the verse actually reads "*since the days of the judges*" and not "*in the days of the judges*," meaning that the festival *was* celebrated in the days of the judges; this was also Michaelis's interpretation (p. 137).

59   Vatke 1835, 183.

Steinheim argues further: if it was not Moses who had arrived at a consciousness of monotheism, it must have been someone else, someone who lived later – and Scripture made no mention of such a figure (p. 93). This argument again relies on his stance that Revelation is a conscious–religious leap; Vatke, who considered Revelation a gradual process taking place over a series of small steps and transitions, would have objected to this.

But more than any other argument of Vatke's, what riled Steinheim was the claim that Moses worshiped Molekh. By the cult of Molekh both Vatke and Steinheim referred to human sacrifice, in particular the sacrifice of children or boys. Steinheim mentions this claim even in his introduction (p. IV) as a first example of Vatke's unacceptable arguments, and returns to it in spirited protest many times throughout his book (pp. 74, 80, 97, 100, 112). His outrage at the idea that Moses (and all the more so the patriarchs, who preceded Moses and were therefore necessarily less religiously advanced) practiced human sacrifice is fairly understandable in the context of his position that Moses brought Revelation to the people – the cornerstone of Steinheim's method; but here it appears to exceed even those considerations.

The symbolism of blood appears in another context in the book, where Steinheim rebels against Vatke's accusation that the Israelites practiced cannibalism (Vatke based this on I Samuel 14:33: "Look, the troops are sinning against the Lord by eating with the blood"). Steinheim responds that the sin in question was that warriors, ravenous after a hard day of battle, ate meat that was still bloody without salting it and making it kosher, exactly like "Professor Vatke consuming his steak or roast beef" (p. 118) in the manner currently accepted throughout the Christian world; thus Vatke's attempts to read this as proof of Israelite crudity or cannibalism is unjustified.

There is good reason to assume that Steinheim believed that ascribing the cult of Molekh to Moses carried as subtext a similar accusation against Jews in general. Indeed, the motif of human sacrifice and Molekh worship was widespread during his time in anti-Jewish propaganda. Some works in this vein were written by Ghillany and Daumer,[60] both in 1842; to the polemic against the latter Steinheim later devoted a separate article.[61] Let us also recall that the preface to Stein-

---

60 i.e. Georg Friedrich Daumer, *Der Feuer- und Molekhdienst der alten Hebräer*, 1842; Friedrich Wilhelm Ghillany, *Der Menschenopfer der alten Hebräer*, 1842 (see: Tal 1963, 262 N. 136; Meyer 1997, 172).

61 *Ikonoklasis. Der Phalluskult im antiken und modernen Heidenthum. Antagonisma gegen F. Daumers Molekhideen, niederlegt in seiner Schrift "Der Feuer- und Molekhdienst der alten*

heim's book is dated July 1840, while the blood libel of the Damascus Affair – which the book does not mention – began to unfold six months earlier, in February. But with respect to Moses, it seems that Steinheim's eager efforts to reject any argument that might taint Judaism with the shadow of blood libel injured his own argument, because Steinheim took liberties with his words: nowhere in Vatke's book could I locate an instance in which he accused Moses of Molekh worship. Vatke did ascribe the cult of Molekh to the Israelites during Moses' time (and Steinheim did not altogether disagree [p. 84]), but he did not relate it to Moses, who he in fact claimed introduced the cult of Jehovah.

Evaluation

Steinheim contended with Vatke as one theologian against another. But while Steinheim was a Jewish theologian–philosopher who lacked real interest or training in history and biblical scholarship, Vatke was a theologian who specialized in the study of the Old Testament and biblical history. It is possible to distinguish between Vatke the theologian and Vatke the biblical scholar; Rogerson[62] notes that despite his Hegelianism, it is largely possible to read the main, historical part of Vatke's book independent of its theoretical–philosophical preface and conclusion. Thus, if Steinheim's contention with Vatke's philosophical–theological framework is fairly successful, his response to Vatke's alternative historiography reveals his limitations: he mostly reiterates his conclusions with respect to the general philosophical framework, and is content with specific refutations of certain of Vatke's views. He is unable to propose an alternative historical narrative to Vatke's, even though he himself rejects the traditional account of "Torah from heaven."

Thus Steinheim, who was neither a historian nor a biblical scholar, could offer only a destructive response. His is not a study in biblical scholarship – Steinheim lacks the requisite scholarly tools to provide that – but rather a critical essay about the Hegel–Vatke school of biblical criticism. As a critique of Vatke's theoretical framework it is overlong; Steinheim's conclusions may be summarized in a few sentences, and they represent an approach whose basic premise (i.e. Revelation) so contradicts those of Vatke that dialogue between them is impossible.

Hebraeer als unwiderleglicher orthodoxer Cultus historisch-kritisch nachgewiesen." Neapel/Rom 1864/65, 46 pages (following Shear-Yashuv 1986, 93).

62   Rogerson 1984, 70.

As a critique of Vatke's historical conclusions, furthermore, Steinheim's work proves inadequate. He repeatedly reiterates his main theological thesis of the fundamental antinomy between Revelation and *Philosophem*, and focuses on Vatke's philosophical framework rather than his alternative historiography. He apparently lacks the tools necessary to truly engage with Vatke's alternative historiography.

Furthermore: while he clarifies the axiomatic chasm between himself and Vatke – the chasm between the axiomatic assumption of Revelation (Steinheim) and the absence of such an assumption (Vatke) – the question arises as to why Steinheim needed to go on to contend with Vatke's conclusions as well, which derived from his axiomatic framework? After all, in rejecting the foundations of Vatke's work he invalidates any specific conclusion Vatke constructed upon that framework. The answer appears to lie in the nature of Steinheim's book and intended audience: this was a polemic–apologetic work written for a Jewish audience rather than a work of academic theology. Perhaps because of this he addressed as much as he could, with the goal of providing ready responses to any reader confronted with Vatke's work. It thus seems that Steinheim's interest lay more in shaping and contending with the *image* of Vatke in his readers' eyes than in a polemic with the real Vatke. Consequently he permitted himself certain inaccuracies when citing Vatke, like accusing him of the prevailing anti-Semitic motif of ascribing the cult of Molekh to Moses when this was not the case. Steinheim engages the real Vatke less than he does his image as the "Strauss of the Old Testament" – a name that stuck to Vatke and which Steinheim mentions at the very start of his book (p. I). Strauss shattered the historical image of Jesus; Steinheim devotes the great part of his effort to rehabilitating the image of Moses, as though shattering that image were Vatke's main intention, in analogy to Strauss.

Still, it appears that Steinheim was the first Jewish thinker to explicitly point out the Christian bias in modern biblical criticism. He identified this bias not only in the general Hegelian framework, which placed Protestant Christianity at the apex of religious development (a fairly transparent bias, which would die out with the decline of Hegel's philosophy) but also in modern biblical criticism as a whole, which Steinheim perceived as new incarnation of Marcion's anti-biblical Gnosticism (p. VII) – particularly in the approach of *lex post prophetas*, which defined Judaism as Law, distinguished between the Law and Moses, and positioned the Law at the historical "midpoint" after Moses but before Christianity. From a historical perspective, the criticism of this approach is highly significant; not only because of the reappearance of

Marcionist Gnosticism during the 1920s, but because it would eventually be taken up by Wellhausen.

Interestingly, Steinheim identified the Christian bias of this approach specifically in the work of Vatke, who was not hostile toward
the Law as so many other Christian scholars. Steinheim's sensitivity to
the Christian character of biblical scholarship undoubtedly derived
from his general theological–philosophical framework, which constructed a dichotomy between Revelation and *Philosophem* and considered the latter an overarching name for paganism, philosophy, and
Christianity all at once. And so, while Vatke placed Judaism on the
same level as paganism, Steinheim responded in the same vein (p. 34)
and bound together paganism and Christianity – as well as the biblical
criticism of Vatke himself.

Part Three

The Graf-Wellhausen Era

The great struggle between prophets and priests,
which would be resumed later again and again
in different forms and between different parties
and continues to this very day,
revolved around the content of the "Torah."

Siegmund Maybaum, 1880[1]

---

1   Maybaum 1880, 62.

Chapter 7
Biblical Criticism in the Final Third of the Century

In the final third of the 19th century the reactionary period in the unit-ing German states came to a close. Biblical criticism too reawoke. Dur-ing the 1880s, with the work of Wellhausen and the paradigm shift he fueled, the discipline underwent a sensational development that swept far beyond the borders of its place and time. Its main achievement was the creation of an alternative historiographical framework for the bibli-cal period, which determined that the legal parts of the Pentateuch – the "Law" – were composed after the Babylonian exile.

The reactionary period ended gradually, about a decade after the failed revolution of 1848. Thomas Nipperdey and other historians call this period, on the eve of the establishment of the Second Reich, the "New Era" (*Die Neue Ära*).[1] The weakening and disintegration of the reactionary regimes was a complex, gradual process which took place not only in Prussia but also – in one form or another – in the other German states. Nipperdey offers several reasons for this process: the relatively liberal Wilhelm I's rise to power in Prussia[2] and the genera-tional transitions involved therein; the formation of a conservative–liberal group of monarchs; rifts among the conservatives; tensions be-tween the Catholic Church and the State (in the Southern states) – all these contributed to the rise of liberalism.

Whatever the reasons for this turning point, in Prussia – the leading German state and home to the highest concentration of Jews – liberal-ism and nationalism became newly influential; a Conservative–Liberal cabinet came into power against conservatism and the absolutist–bureaucratic reaction; the new king, in contrast to his predecessor, swore loyalty to a Constitution; the Conservatives' power in Parliament declined considerably after free elections were held; and in the other German states the reactionary laws were also weakened, liberal eco-nomic and educational reforms were advanced, civil liberties were granted, and citizens increasingly participated in the government.

With the unification of the Reich under Prussian hegemony the Jews attained full legal emancipation – in 1869 in Prussia and in 1871 in

---

1 Nipperdey 1983, 697ff.
2 Initially, in 1858, as Regent (in place of Friedrich Wilhelm IV); from 1861 as King.

Germany as a whole. But beginning in the 1880s the political sphere began to change. Bismarck broke off from the National Liberal Party, and liberalism splintered and was cast out from the center of the political and cultural map, to be replaced by nationalist values and institutions. To illustrate: the National Liberal Party in the Reichstag shrank from about 30% of the vote in 1871 to less than 15% in 1881.[3] Starting from the end of the 1880s, nationalist forces with an anti-pluralistic bent gained in power; they hoped to strengthen the Prussian–Protestant state and objected to increasing the power and freedoms of minorities. As part of this trend, anti-Semitic sentiments gathered force; the *Berliner Antisemitismusstreit* (Dispute on Anti-Semitism) stirred by Heinrich von Treitschke in 1880 is considered a milepost in the "return of old hatreds."[4] The traditional alliance between the Jews and Protestant liberalism had broken.[5]

The changing *Zeitgeist* was also reflected in biblical criticism. During the 1860s, the conservative "Hengstenberg era" came to a close. A radical development occurred in biblical criticism, primarily through the work of the German scholars Karl Heinrich Graf (1815–1869) and Julius Wellhausen (1844–1917) and the Dutch Abraham Kuenen (1828–1891). At the heart of this revolution was the emergence of an alternative history of the biblical period that differed radically from the historical narrative recounted in Scripture itself. That narrative had been adopted by both the Jewish and Christian religious traditions and was also in principle accepted, despite some local objections, by biblical scholars until the mid-19th century (with a few exceptions, such as Vatke, who were relegated to the margins of the discourse). The new narrative will be discussed in detail in the survey of Wellhausen's work.

If at the start of the century historicism was the prevailing academic approach toward the history of ancient Israel, at the end of the century biblical criticism showed signs of making inroads through an approach that Christhard Hoffmann[6] has described as "classicistic" – a Hegelian approach that, despite the historical importance it attributed to ancient Israel as a positive stage in spiritual development, tended to regard later Judaism as a fossilized, anachronistic, and fanatical phenomenon[7] – an approach that was evident beginning with Vatke, an unmistakable

---

3   Nipperdey 1992 II, 314ff.
4   The phrasing is Peter Pulzer's; he surveys the process in Meyer 1997, 196-251.
5   On the break and its consequences see: Wiese 1999, 28-35. Tal 1975, 160ff. covers in detail the complex relations between liberal Judaism and Protestantism.
6   Hoffmann 1988, 8-20.
7   See: Meyer 1997, 172ff.

Hegelian; continuing through Nöldeke (1836–1930); and ending with Wellhausen and his school. At the same time, the political significance of biblical criticism was different than in earlier periods. At the turn of the century, biblical criticism (and Protestant liberalism) were closely tied to political liberalism; as the political reaction and its ally the Protestant orthodoxy gained in power, so biblical criticism was relegated to a defensive position at the margins of the academic discourse. The "New Era" saw the rise of political liberalism and the parallel increase in the power of Protestant liberalism. This political liberalization allowed biblical criticism to continue to develop with relative freedom and to return to and develop further some of the achievements that had been made before the conservative era (for example by de Wette). To engage in biblical criticism was no longer an act of political subversion, and while it remained primarily an undertaking of liberal Protestants, the overt ties that had previously existed between critical work and liberal political views were cut. It appears that the academics who engaged in biblical criticism during the final third of the 19th century, from the rise of Bismarck and of Prussian hegemony onward, were generally "apolitical" (in other words, conformists) like most German intellectuals of the time.[8] They were not among the critics of the German Empire, but belonged to either of the two other groups of intellectuals that Fritz Stern describes:[9]

> A larger group retreated to what was at the time called the a-political sphere and came to terms with its political impotence. A group even larger idealized the actual German state and its imperialist traditions and argued that the German culture, which was superior to Western culture, could also justify German might.

Typical in this respect was Julius Wellhausen. He was born to a conservative family, and as his rebelliousness against religious conservatism increased so did his political conservatism. He abstained from political activity, belonged to no party, seldom signed political petitions,[10] stringently distinguished between scholarly work and political activity, and objected to the haphazard and "journalistic" application of scholarship in general, and his own work in particular, to the political arena.[11] He carried out his academic work with complete freedom, taking no account of any religious dogma, and he even left the theological faculty for the faculty of philosophy in order to escape religious obligation; yet with regard to his political opinions he "always retained a certain

---

8   Dahrendorf 1961, 288; Tal 1975, 31.
9   Quoted in Dahrendorf 1961, 288.
10   Smend 1982, 272.
11   Liebeschütz 1967, 250.

fondness for anything of the Right,"[12] particularly Bismarck and German imperialism. Here is not the place to delve into the relationship between the eventual hegemony of the Wellhausen school and the anti-liberal and anti-Semitic atmosphere that reigned during the Second Reich;[13] but in the following pages we will see that the image of Jews in Wellhausen's work dovetails nicely with the spirit of the time, in which liberalism faded and made way for nationalism with anti-Semitic overtones.

The prominent public presence that biblical criticism enjoyed in Germany at the turn of the century diminished greatly by its close. The professionalization of the humanities occurred here as well: if at the start of the century biblical criticism attracted not only proper academics such as Michaelis and Eichhorn but also amateurs like Goethe, during the second half of the century it became almost exclusively the domain of academic theologians. If at the start of century scholars such as Semler, Michaelis, and Eichhorn were mentioned in popular works of literature by Goethe and Jean Paul,[14] even in 1889, at the pinnacle of Wellhausen's influence, Ludwig Philippson wrote that "Biblical criticism has long now been conducted in Germany with diligence and scientific gravity [...] but it remains within the domain of scholarship and only occasionally reaches the general public."[15] Even if it made its way into the public consciousness via various popularizers and agents, biblical criticism became first and foremost an autonomous academic occupation – a change which may also explain the decline of its political importance and the relative freedom it thus enjoyed.[16]

In contrast to the situation during the days of the Society for Jewish Culture and Science at the start of the century, it appears that Jews' attitude toward biblical criticism during this period can be explained not by the political opinions of Protestant biblical critics – opinions which were not always explicit and did not always align with those of the Jews – but by religious–political factors internal to the Jewish community (the struggles about reform and the definition of Judaism) and the theological–political content and implications of biblical criticism itself. The individual political opinions of non-Jewish biblical critics – to the extent that they held, expressed, and publicized them – had little

---

12   Schwartz 1918, 337; see also: Kusche 1991, 72; Krey 1991, 22.
13   See the (unpublished) master's thesis: Krey 1991.
14   See above, p. 31.
15   Philippson 1889, 559.
16   This situation would change only at the start of the twentieth century with the *Bibel-Babel* Dispute, which would achieve great public renown. See: Johanning 1988; Shavit and Eran 2007.

effect on Jewish attitudes toward the discipline. The present study therefore does not address questions such as whether or to what extent Julius Wellhausen was an anti-Semite.[17] It seems that Jews' reception of Wellhausen derived first and foremost from the content of his academic work and from its political use and abuse – whether in accordance with or in contradiction to his opinions – and not from Wellhausen's own political orientation (which he seldom expressed in public). In retrospect, Jews opposed to Wellhausen's approach would emphasize the anti-Jewish biases in his method, while his Jewish followers would attempt to downplay or amend them.

The Way to Wellhausen

The hypothesis that the legal parts of the Pentateuch postdated the others and were written after the Babylonian exile – the "Graf hypothesis" or the "Graf-Wellhausen hypothesis" – is considered the paramount achievement of biblical criticism at the end of the 19th century. It came to dominate biblical criticism in Germany and beyond; to this day it is by and large the basis for the prevailing views in the historical study of the formation of the Hebrew Bible. Because of its importance, the evolution from the critical position accepted during the mid-19th century to Wellhausen's historical revisionism has been relatively well-documented and studied; only the highlights will be presented in this chapter.[18]

Even during the period of conservative hegemony, several more or less critical scholars such as Ewald, Bleek, Hupfeld, Hitzig, and others studied the formation of the Pentateuch. Kuenen notes that as part of the campaign against criticism, "The defenders of the Pentateuch's 'authenticity' never tired of emphasizing the disagreements between their opponents."[19] Nonetheless around 1860, at the close of the con-

---

17 A question that provoked a bitter polemic during the 1980s between the two German giants of biblical criticism, Rolf Rendtorff (1980) and Rudolph Smend (1982). Rendtorff attributed to Wellhausen an anti-Jewish and even anti-Semitic orientation; Smend was pressed to defend Wellhausen by various arguments, for example that his anti-Jewish statements should be read against their historical context; that his criticism of Jews was no harsher than his criticism of Christians; and that his attitude toward Jews was highly complex and evolved over time.

18 For a summary with a personal touch by the scholar, who was a central participant in the development of the hypothesis, see: Kuenen 1886, xi-xl; for broader detail on the history of biblical criticism see: Kraus 1982; Houtman 1994. For our purposes, Thompson 1970 is particularly relevant; his focus is on the lateness of the Law.

19 Kuenen 1886, xi.

servative period, the critical biblical scholars were largely in consensus about how the Pentateuch came to be.[20]

According to this conventional critical view, Deuteronomy was composed during the seventh or sixth century BCE and underwent the Deuteronomistic redaction that resulted in the Pentateuch and Book of Joshua in the form we know today (with the exception of minor post-diasporal additions). About a hundred years before the Deuteronomist came the Yahwist, who was responsible for composing the books of Genesis through Numbers and the pre-Deuteronomistic version of the Book of Joshua. The Yahwist made use of an even earlier book – an "Elohistic" priestly text from (approximately) the 10th century BCE which contained the basic narrative of the Pentateuch from the first chapter of Genesis onward as well as the Levitical legislation found in the middle three books of the Pentateuch. Because of the fundamental nature of this latter work, which serves as a frame for most of the Pentateuch, many scholars (following Stähelin and Tuch) referred to it as the *Grundschrift*; Wellhausen called it Q;[21] but eventually Kuenen's term *Priestercodex* (P – the Priestly Code) took root.[22]

There was no consensus regarding questions such as how many Levite laws originated during the time of Moses; whether it was possible to divide the *Grundschrift* into earlier and later Elohistic sources; or whether the Elohistic and Yahwistic sources were complete or fragmentary. Yet there was general agreement regarding the four chronological stages involved in the redaction of the Pentateuch and Book of Joshua:

    (1) the Grundschrift;

    (2) the Yahwist (incorporating the Elohist);

    (3) the Jehovist (J), incorporating (1) and (2);

    (4) and finally the Deuteronomist (D), who redacted and added to J.

All of these stages, and the Pentateuch as we know it in its entirety, predated the Babylonian exile. The historical sequence was thus: Mosaism, Prophecy, Judaism.

It is customary to mention Graf's book of 1865 as a first stage in the revolutionary development of the Graf-Wellhausen hypothesis.[23] Graf cast doubt on the unity of the *Grundschrift*, separated it into narrative and legal sections, and determined that the legal sections postdated the Deuteronomist. He argued that the Deuteronomist's work amounted to

---

20   Rogerson 1984, 257f.; Kuenen 1886, xi ff.

21   *Quattuor*, after the four covenants – with Adam, Noah, Abraham, and Moses.

22   On the origin of the name P see: Thompson 1970, 49f.; see also therein about its exact scope and textual characteristics.

23   Graf 1866. According to Kuenen 1886, xix, the book was already published at the end of 1865. About Graf see: Houtman 1994, 99ff., including N.7 for a bibliography.

combining the narrative parts of the *Grundschrift* and the Yahwistic text together with Deuteronomy and Deuteronomistic material. The priestly material, he suggested, was composed in a style that *imitated* the narrative parts of the *Grundschrift* but was written later and inserted only after the Babylonian exile.

The next stage is considered Theodor Nöldeke's counterargument to Graf in 1869. Nöldeke attempted to defend the *Grundschrift*'s unity through a painstaking analysis of the Pentateuch. His view of the order in which the Pentateuch was composed was similar to the sequence generally accepted in criticism; as for the dates of composition, he admitted that it was impossible to prove that the *Grundschrift* was the earliest but nonetheless declared, in contrast to Graf, that it predated the Babylonian exile. It is interesting that a central reason for Nöldeke's opposition to dating the *Grundschrift* after the Babylonian exile was his view (his prejudice, as Kuenen noted) that the "uncreative" Jews who returned from Babylon were not capable of formulating such laws.[24]

The state of the research at the end of the 1860s[25] was thus undecided between two possibilities about the *Grundschrift*: (1) that the *Grundschrift* was a unity and in that case either was very early (from the 10th century) or postdated the Babylonian exile (à la Nöldeke); or, alternatively (2), that the *Grundschrift* was not a unity and its narrative parts were early while its legal sections postdated the Babylonian exile (à la Graf).

The possibility seldom discussed was that the *Grundschrift* was a unity and nonetheless postdated the Babylonian exile – and it is this hypothesis that would now emerge. While the list of suspects of full or partial responsibility for generating the hypothesis is extensive,[26] it is agreed that Kuenen proposed the hypothesis in a private letter to Graf

---

24 Nöldeke (1869, 127) writes: „Surely a period totally devoid of creative force would not have enacted such severe laws and executed them to the detriment of many – really to the detriment of the entire people, as far as it was at all possible. On the other hand, doing so would have been entirely characteristic of that restoration period, which clung fearfully to the written letter of the law, perceived it as the word of God, and obeyed it unconditionally." Kuenen (1886, xxix) replies critically: „That the Jewish people became dry and unfruitful as soon as it returned from Babylon must be accepted as soon as it is proved; but a mere traditional prejudice must not be allowed for a moment to protect an idea which is in itself equally mournful and astonishing." See also: Wellhausen 1878, 166.

25 Rogerson 1984, 259 (instead of "either early or post-exilic" read: "either early or pre-exilic").

26 It includes, at a minimum, George, Graf, Vatke, Kuenen, and Reuss; every scholar attributes it to a different source according to his considerations. Compare the following attributions: Rogerson 1984, 259; Thompson 1970, 55 N.2; Kuenen 1886, xi ff., xxxiv; Wellhausen 1878, 4; [Steinthal in:] Maybaum 1883b, 192 N.

in 1866; Graf accepted the proposal and in a short response to Nöldeke's book,[27] which appeared in 1869 (after Graf's death), he admitted that his attempt to divide the *Grundschrift* into separate sources had failed and that the *Grundschrift* had been composed in its entirety after the Babylonian exile.

At any rate Thompson, who lists several additional early supporters of this hypothesis, notes: "What would have been the fate of Grafianism if Wellhausen had not written, no one can really say."[28] It was Julius Wellhausen who succeeded in creating a comprehensive and convincing integration of all the critical work that had preceded him, from de Wette to Graf, thus initiating a paradigm shift in the field of biblical criticism and making his the dominant method in German biblical criticism (and beyond) within the space of a few years.[29]

Wellhausen's *History of Israel*

In his work on the Hebrew Bible and the biblical period[30] Wellhausen incorporated the conclusions and methodologies of all of his predecessors and proved that the *Grundschrift* – the priestly source, which Wellhausen called Q or the Law and is known today as P – appeared after the Babylonian exile. The basic principle in Wellhausen's reading is that texts serve as witnesses to the periods in which they were created and not to the periods they describe. His periodization is based on two central reference points: Josiah's reform (621 BCE) and the end of the Babylonian exile (444 BCE). He divides the history of religion and Scripture into three periods: the ancient period, before Josiah's reform; the brief intermediate period that followed it and lasted until the exile; and the late period beginning with the return from Babylon. In the custom of the discipline, the people of the first and second periods are called Israelites while after the return from Babylon they are called Jews. The central thesis of the book is that the Law was a Jewish rather than an Israelite creation. Wellhausen defines, orders chronologically, and dates the following main sources that appear in the first six books of the Bible, i.e. the Pentateuch and Joshua:

---

27   Graf 1869.

28   Thompson 1970, 58.

29   Rogerson 1984, 260.

30   This overview is based on the first edition, titled *Geschichte Israels* (Wellhausen 1878), due to its relevance for our purposes. Its later editions, titled *Prolegomena zur Geschichte Israels*, differ in certain details, but the overall framework remains unchanged.

(1) JE, a (complex) combination of J (Jehovist) and E (Elohist) from the days of the divided monarchy;

(2) D, the Deuteronomistic source, the platform of Josiah's reform;

(3) P, the priestly source or the Law, beginning at the return from Babylon.

The prophets operated for the most part during Wellhausen's first period, and their writings provide evidence about that time. Ezekiel, with his prophecy of religious revival after the exile (Ezekiel 40ff.), was active between D and P, and serves as a central anchor for dating the sources.

Wellhausen's historical narrative is highly convincing. Its power derives from the comprehensive analogy it offers between the division into sources and the development of the Israelite religion and cult. This development is described by means of several central elements, each of which is examined and compared in every source. Those elements are: the site of the cult, the sacrifices, the calendar and festivals, the priests and Levites, and the priestly economy.

The *ancient source* (JE), itself composed of even earlier sources, reflects the initial religious state of the Israelites, whose cult was characterized primarily by freedom. It was spontaneous, individualist, and anchored in nature, in the agricultural lifestyle, and in family or tribal life. Sacrifices could be carried out everywhere; JE sanctifies a multiplicity of cultic sites.[31] In this matter there was no distinction between laymen and professional priests: anyone could sacrifice as he liked. The priests depended for income on contributions by the sacrificers, there being no tax to ensure their livelihood (cf. 1 Samuel 2:12-16). Non-priests were not prohibited from approaching the sanctuary: Samuel, a member of the tribe of Ephraim, slept nightly alongside the Ark of Covenant; whereas according to P, only the high priest was allowed to access it, and even that only once a year after strict purification. Sacrifices were accorded great religious importance, yet they were not presented as a Mosaic innovation or fixed by special laws but were rather a living tradition extending from the dawn of history (Cain and Abel, Noah, the Patriarchs). The central distinction was between sacrifice to Jehovah and idolatrous sacrifice; any sacrifice offered to Jehovah was legitimate and there were no regulations regarding the sacrificial rites. The prophets who were active during this period, even when they de-

---

31 Exodus 20:24: "You need make for me only an altar of earth and sacrifice on it your burnt-offerings and your offerings of well-being, your sheep and your oxen; in every place where I cause my name to be remembered I will come to you and bless you."

cried the practice of sacrifice,[32] allowed that sacrifice was not a unique characteristic, commanded by Moses, of the cult of Jehovah; at times they claimed the exact opposite.[33]

The calendar had a cycle of festivals: the festival of ingathering, the festival of harvest, and the festival of unleavened bread (the main part of which was the sacrifice of First Fruits). All of the holidays were agricultural in nature and related to the dedication of the harvest to God. The books of Prophets contained a clear account only of the most important festival of unleavened bread; only faint signs existed of the other festivals. The Israelites still had no Law, and certainly no written one: Wellhausen even rejects the antiquity of the Decalogue, which was broadly in consensus during his time. There were only traditions and rules of behavior which were passed down orally. The prophets fought to advocate not the Law but "the priestly Torah, which, however, has nothing to do with cult, but only with justice and morality."[34]

The *Deuteronomistic source* (D) reflects the religious reform that took place during the days of Josiah (2 Kings 23), about a century after the destruction of the Northern Kingdom. The focus of the reform, which was carried out on the authority of the prophets and priests alike, was centralizing the cult at the Temple in Jerusalem and forbidding it at any other place. D was composed for this reform and presented as the Torah that had allegedly been found in the Temple; it was the reform's platform and law book. Though presented as though it had been handed down to Moses, it was in reality the first Israelite law, later to be succeeded by P.

The centralization of the cult – which D demands but which it clarifies has not yet occurred[35] – cut short the spontaneous, family–tribal sacrificial tradition and turned sacrifice into an institutionalized religious ritual conducted by the priests in Jerusalem and disconnected from its communal and agricultural contexts. Following the centralization of the cult, festivals became occasions for pilgrimage to the Temple and emphasis was placed on their historical rather than agricultural

---

32   E.g. Isaiah 1:11: "What to me is the multitude of your sacrifices? says the Lord; I have had enough of burnt-offerings of rams and the fat of fed beasts; I do not delight in the blood of bulls, or of lambs, or of goats."

33   As in the famous verse in Jeremiah 7:22: "For on the day that I brought your ancestors out of the land of Egypt, I did not speak to them or command them concerning burnt-offerings and sacrifices."

34   Wellhausen 1878, 60; here quoted from the English translation: Wellhausen 1885, 81.

35   Deuteronomy 12:5-8: "But you shall seek the place that the Lord your God will choose out of all your tribes as his habitation to put his name there. You shall go there [...] You shall not act as we are acting here today, all of us according to our own desires."

context. The festival of ingathering was now called the festival of booths, the festival of harvest was named the festival of weeks, and the festival of unleavened bread was now, for the first time, called Passover; its connection to the passing-over of the first-born Israelites during the Egyptian Exodus was an invention by D, as even before the Exodus Moses had pressed the Pharaoh for permission to celebrate the festival (Exodus 6:1).

Even earlier, with the establishment of the kingdom, a close relationship was formed between the king and the temples, and gradually the priests began to serve the king. There was not yet a tribe or set of families of clergymen – on the contrary, any man could become a priest; the only condition was that he cut his ties to his family and devote himself exclusively to serving God (e.g. Saul). Josiah's reform granted the priests an elevated status in society alongside the judges and the prophets; now there were priestly families that enjoyed royal privileges, and the term "Levite" in reference to the priests took root, as though it referred to a separate tribe (the precise relationship to the tribe of Levi – which now vanished, if it ever existed at all – remains a mystery). The priestly economy now relied on taxation rather than donation: one who came to sacrifice was required by law to give the priest "the shoulder, the two jowls, and the stomach" (Deuteronomy 18:3).

Josiah's reform, like the earlier, similar reform under Hezekiah, would have failed if not for the Babylonian exile, which severed the natural connection to the ancient cult of the *bamot* (high places). In the wake of this disconnection, on the return from the exile the centralization of the cult was already perceived as natural.

The *priestly source* (P) was the Law written after the exile, reflecting the religious conditions after the return from Babylon. The centralization of the cult, entirely unknown in JE but called for in D, in P became a matter of course and was presented as an ancient tradition originating in the days of Moses. At the center of its historical description P placed the Tabernacle – an invention that operated as the predecessor of the Jerusalem Temple – and projected it backward in time:

> The tabernacle is not narrative merely, but, like all the narratives in that book, law as well; it expresses the legal unity of the worship as an historical fact, which, from the very beginning, ever since the exodus, has held good in Israel.[36]

With the destruction of the Temple the sanctified rules of sacrifice became a subject of theoretical analysis and were now put in writing:

---

36   Wellhausen 1878, 36, quoted from Wellhausen 1885, 31.

Ezekiel (40–48) deals extensively with sacrificial practice, but in many places the prophet's description differs from that of P, which he could not have known. P itself expounds in great detail on the issue of sacrifice as a central element of religious life. Sacrifice became a fundament, a technique, and a practical implementation according to laws in which the "warm pulse of life no longer throbbed."[37] Sacrifices were the domain of priests alone; they were the central characteristic of the theocracy, in which the priesthood was the most important class. In the P version of ancient history (which is scattered throughout the books of Genesis and Exodus) there is no mention of sacrifice before Moses, and the entire meticulously detailed procedure of sacrifice (i.e., who was authorized to sacrifice where, when, what, and how) is presented as a unique characteristic of the Israelite religion that was given to Moses at Sinai, rather than as a continuation of an ancient cultic tradition. During ancient times sacrifice was spontaneous and carried out for personal or family reasons; after the exile, these reasons were replaced by the *sin* of the people, for which their sacrifices were meant to atone in an institutionalized manner. Instead of individual or family sacrifice, the sacrifice was carried out by the whole community.

The centralization of the cult also transformed the agricultural, popular, natural, private, and spontaneous festivals into religious, communal, legal, and fixed ones. The agricultural context was lost, and in its place historical context was emphasized: according to P the unleavened breads, for example, were not merely a *retroactive* symbol of the Exodus; the Israelites had been commanded about them *in advance*, even before the Exodus took place (Exodus 12:15ff.). The seventh day of Passover was transformed from a regular day of rest to a "solemn assembly," and as a result pilgrims to the Temple were obliged to remain in Jerusalem for an entire week. Josiah himself testified to this change, declaring that "No such passover had been kept since the days of the judges" (2 Kings 23:22). After the exile new holidays were added. New Year's day (holy convocation) reveals the change that took place in the calendar: according to Israelite tradition the year began in the fall, but the Jewish New Year was set at the start of the seventh (rather than the first) month; this shows the influence of the Assyrian–Babylonian culture, in which the year began in the spring. An additional new holiday was the Day of Atonement, and although P (and Judaism in general) declared it the most holy day of the year, it was mentioned nowhere in the other sources – not in the Prophets or even in Ezra or Nehemiah; its origin lay in the regular fasts that emerged during the exile, and it re-

---

37   Wellhausen 1878, 80, quoted from Wellhausen 1885, 62.

flected the new place of sin and atonement at the center of religious consciousness.

In P the status of the priesthood reaches its peak: now the counting of years was dictated by the high priest, where during the monarchy it followed the king. Similarly, with respect to taxation, P instructs that the priest be accorded an even greater portion: "the breast of the elevation-offering, and the thigh that is offered" (Leviticus 7:34). The status of the priesthood now became stratified, with the priests at the top and the Levites at the bottom. The explanation for these two ranks stems from the centralization of the cult: lest the provincial priests outside of Jerusalem become superfluous, P grants them permission to conduct sacrifices in Jerusalem, and the people are commanded to take them along when they travel to the Temple. But the Sadducee priests, who controlled the Temple in Jerusalem, were not enchanted by the idea of letting the priests of the *bamot* take part in the holy service and thus granted them only a marginal position; they preferred to entrust some lowly tasks to gentile workers (perhaps prisoners of war). Thus the two classes of religious officials – the priests and the Levites – took form. In his prophecy Ezekiel calls to punish the Levites, the priests of the *bamot*, and to employ them only in lowly tasks at the Temple, in place of the heathen workers.[38] P, in contrast, claims that the Levites have since the beginning of time been forbidden to serve at the Temple. Here, according to Wellhausen, is decisive evidence of the chronology of the sources: if P had been the earlier text and the Levites had indeed always been forbidden to officiate, Ezekiel could not have demanded such a punishment.

After the Babylonian exile the ancient Israelite people thus became a Jewish theocracy centered around the Law. Political matters were handled by a foreign rule, and the Jews were confined to a religious community led by the priesthood. During the Hellenistic period the high priest was the highest authority and the head of the Sanhedrin, and only by taking control of the high priesthood could the Hasmoneans take power.

Prophecy is not examined in detail in Wellhausen's book, which in general deals little with specific protagonists (its true protagonist is the Law). Wellhausen determines that the prophecy and the priesthood were originally one and the same – thus both vocations were attributed

---

38 Ezekiel 44:10ff: "But the Levites who went far from me [...] They shall be ministers in my sanctuary [...] They shall not come near to me, to serve me as priest [...] But the levitical priests, the descendants of Zadok, who kept the charge of my sanctuary when the people of Israel went astray from me, shall come near to me to minister to me."

to Moses – and only later did they diverge. At first there were no priests but rather advisers and arbitrators, whose entire authority derived from mutual consensus. The word "Torah," Wellhausen writes, was derived from the Hebrew root for "instruction" rather than cult or sacrifice. What made a man a priest in ancient times "was not knowing the technique of worship, which was still very simple and undeveloped, but being a man of God, standing on an intimate footing with God."[39] Later,

> After the spirit of the oldest men of God, Moses at the head of them, had been in a fashion laid to sleep in institutions, it sought and found in the prophets a new opening […]. They [i.e., the prophets] do not preach on set texts; they speak out of the spirit which judges all things and itself is judged of no man.[40]

The priests preserved tradition, while the importance of the prophets lay in their very individualism. The priests were like an ever-flowing spring; the prophets were like a spring erupting. Without them there could be no revelation; they were subjectivity at its highest, unconnected to any law and thus transformed into objective truth, "just as Jesus [transforms the law] in the Gospel of John."[41] It was folly to say that the prophets interpreted and applied the Law. In Isaiah the servant of Jehovah expresses his thoughts on the development of the prophecy: according to him, the mission of the people of Israel is to disseminate the Torah, not only among themselves but also among the Gentiles; "Torah" here does not mean Law, but rather *logos* as used by John. Here Wellhausen's Christology emerges prominently:

> As Jesus is the revelation of God made man, so the servant of Jehovah is the revelation of God made a people. The similarity of their nature and their significance involves the similarity of their work and of their sufferings, so that the Messianic interpretation of Isaiah 52:13–53:12 is in fact one which could not fail to suggest itself.[42]

The very emergence of the Law signified the death of prophecy. Jeremiah was in effect the last prophet. Not only the cult but also the religious spirit were fixed in the written word; Judaism's sacred constitution was an artificial construct, with P its comprehensive image. "The water which in old times rose from a spring, the Epigoni stored up in cisterns."[43] For this reason, on the eve of exile the struggle between the true and the false prophets was particularly bitter. Wellhausen most

---

39   Wellhausen 1878, 412, quoted from Wellhausen 1885, 270.
40   Wellhausen 1878, 413f., quoted from Wellhausen 1885, 271.
41   Wellhausen 1878, 414, quoted from Wellhausen 1885, 272.
42   Wellhausen 1878, 417, quoted from Wellhausen 1885, 274.
43   Wellhausen 1878, 426, quoted from Wellhausen 1885, 280.

detests Ezekiel, "the forerunner of the priestly legislator in the Pentateuch": "Ezekiel had swallowed a book and gave it out again"; he was a
"priest in prophet's mantle";[44] he deserved to be expelled from the canon as punishment for the contradictions between him and the laws of
P, which were composed a century and a half after him.

Wellhausen's *value judgments* about Jews and Judaism are already
evident in his first book from 1874, *Pharisees and Sadducees*.[45] In this
book, which covers the days of the Second Temple, Judaism is described as the creation of the Pharisee leaders, who turned the will of
God into 613 commandments. The Pharisees were "Jews in the superla-
tive, the true Israel." They vanquished nature with their laws, left no
room for conscience, acted as inquisitors, and inflicted a tyranny of the
educated. This was in contrast to the Sadducees, in whom Wellhausen
saw a continuation of the militant spirit of the original Israelite theocracy.

Increasingly judgmental views also stand out in this book the closer
Wellhausen approaches the Jewish era.[46] If his descriptions of the history of the cult and the history of the canon are relatively free of judgmental depictions, the first part, "Israel and Judaism," abounds in
them. Wellhausen's historical narrative is organized around a central
dichotomy – Israel versus Judaism – and the element that differentiated
them is the Law, which is, again, in effect the protagonist of the entire
story. This antinomy exists not only in the content but also in the value-
laden charge that Wellhausen reserves toward each side; the Israelite
religion is given a basically positive evaluation and Judaism a negative
one. All these – the dichotomy and the centrality of the Law – are expressed even in the first paragraph of the book:

> In the following pages it is proposed to discuss the place in history of the
> "law of Moses"; more precisely, the question to be considered is whether
> that law is the starting-point for the history of ancient Israel, or not rather
> for that of Judaism, i.e., of the religious communion which survived the de-
> struction of the nation by the Assyrians and Chaldaeans.[47]

From a religious–cultic perspective, Israel is identified with freedom
(i.e., the absence of law), originality, vitality, spontaneity, individualism, an organic connection to nature and agriculture, an unbroken tradition, and justice and morality (i.e., the role of the priests and prophets). From a political perspective Israel is identified with a sovereign

---

44 Wellhausen 1878, 62, 419, quoted from Wellhausen 1885, 48, 275.

45 See: Kusche 1991, 34-36.

46 On Judaism and the Jews in Wellhausen's work see: Kusche 1991, 30-74; Liebeschütz
1967, 245-268; as well as: Smend 1982; Rendtorff 1980.

47 Wellhausen 1878, 1, quoted from Wellhausen 1885, 11.

and independent monarchy. Judaism in contrast is identified, as in typical Hegelian and Christian tradition, with a sterile adherence to the dead letter of the Law which regulates all of life and leaves no room for individualism, and with an "artificial construction," barren ritual, a severed connection to nature and its exchange for rigid cult, the disruption of tradition due to Josiah's reform and the exile, and legal formalism (i.e., the role of the priests, scholars, and rabbis). Politically, Judaism is identified with a community or sect given to strict and cruel theocracy or hierocracy, derived from its lack of political independence and from its dependence on foreign rule. Wellhausen himself provides the explicit association of Judaism with the Catholic Church: "The Mosaic 'congregation' is the mother of the Christian church; the Jews were the creators of that idea"; "The Mosaic theocracy, the residuum of a ruined state, is itself not a state at all, but an unpolitical artificial product [...] and foreign rule is its necessary counterpart. In its nature it is intimately allied to the old Catholic church, which was in fact its child."[48]

If we apply Wellhausen's methodological principle to his own writings – that is, that texts testify to the period in which they were written more than to the period they describe – one can hardly avoid the impression that Wellhausen ultimately saw in ancient Israel a reflection of the Prussian kingdom – the enlightened Protestant monarchy – and in Judaism a reflection of all that was opposed to it. Here and there one can identify ambivalence toward the ritualization of the cult: the process stigmatized for the most part as petrification and decline is sometimes also described as spiritualization (*Vergeistlichung*), a positive concept in Protestant theology; and Wellhausen adds that the Law also preserved some prophetic influences. But overall it is apparent that alongside the complete anti-dogmatic freedom that Wellhausen allowed himself to employ in his description of ancient Israel, his depiction of Judaism was not only hostile but hostile in a very traditional Christian (and particularly Hegelian) manner. Wellhausen went against Christian tradition when he stripped the Israelites of the Law and attributed it instead to Judaism. But he adhered absolutely to both the negative Christian image of the Law and to the definition of the Law as the central, constitutive element of Judaism. The transfer of "copyright" on the Law from Israelite culture to Judaism preserved the overall Christological image of history, and in fact strengthened the opposition between Judaism on one side and Israel and (Protestant) Christianity on the other. There is thus truth in Hoheisel's statement that "ultimately,

---

48   Wellhausen 1878, 84, 439, quoted from Wellhausen 1885, 65, 288.

modern biblical scholarship conserved and softened the image of Jewish nomism because the Pauline depiction of salvation history authoritatively supported its background."[49] And Kusche's remark on this point, about the dialectic nature of the liberation from salvation history simultaneously with its preservation on another level, is very apt: "It is clear that Judaism is perceived in full accordance with the traditional salvation history, after ancient Israel was freed of the bonds of that history."[50]

It was not for nothing that, as an epigraph to the third part of his book, Wellhausen used the Pauline verse[51] "But Law entered in-between" – the negative attitude of (Pauline, Lutheran) Christianity toward the biblical Law (the Torah) and Judaism in a nutshell – and explained:

> It is true that in Romans 5:20 Paul did not employ this expression in the precise sense in which we have invoked it as an epigraph for the present section; but the change in meaning is very reasonable to one who hears in the verdict about Abraham in Genesis 15:6[52] the voice of prophecy (Habakkuk 2:4),[53] particularly since the Law which the Apostle wishes to uproot is for him also the Law of Judaism.[54]

In other words: Paul's statement meant to argue that the Law had been given to the Israelites during the days of Moses, in between the Lawless period before Moses and the Law-less period that Jesus ushered in. Wellhausen, on the other hand, argued that the Law – the same law, the Law of Judaism – entered *historically* (gradually) in the period after the exile, between the ancient Law-less period and that begun by Jesus (which would be perfected in Protestantism), and was inserted *historiographically* into that period, as though it had existed since the days of Moses. The similarity between his historical framework and the Christian salvation history, despite their greatly differing details, was clear to Wellhausen himself.

---

49 Hoheisel 1978, 179.

50 Kusche 1991, 39.

51 Romans 5:20 (Wellhausen 1878, 377). The verse continues: "with the result that the trespass multiplied; but where sin increased, grace abounded all the more, so that, just as sin exercised dominion in death, so grace might also exercise dominion through justification leading to eternal life through Jesus Christ our Lord." See p. 106 above.

52 "And he believed the Lord; and the Lord reckoned it to him as righteousness."

53 "But the righteous live by their faith."

54 Wellhausen 1878, 379 (omitted in later editions and in the English translation).

Paradigmatic Change

Here is not the place to investigate the reasons for the dizzying success of the Wellhausen school, which may also have to do with its political context.[55] For our purposes, what matters is its rapid ascendancy over nearly all of German academia in the field of biblical criticism, an ascendancy that constituted a real paradigmatic shift:

> The decade following the publication of the *Prolegomena*[56] saw the capitulation of almost every influential Old Testament scholar in Germany to the new teaching, with the exception of the powerful triumvirate Delitzsch, Dillmann and Kittel. Even these, however, went a long way towards it.[57]

These three scholars – Delitzsch, Dillmann, and Kittel – also supported a documentary hypothesis in one form or another, but they predated the legal parts (P) to the period before the Babylonian exile. The documentary hypothesis as an explanation for the formation of the Pentateuch thus achieved complete dominance, which even conservative scholars conceded.[58] Comprehensive opposition to the documentary hypothesis was heard only at the margins of academia and by conservative writers outside it.[59]

The Wellhausen school reigned supreme until the end of the 19th century – and not only in Germany – as well as during the start of the 20th century. Only then, little by little, did it become subject to criticism and doubt, both in the wake of archaeological discoveries from excavations in the Near East (these had already begun during the 19th century, but Wellhausen's method disregarded them) and the disciplines they inspired (Assyriology, Egyptology, etc.), and in the wake of new theoretical approaches. Thompson points to 1905 as the turning point in the rise of two new post-Grafian critical movements: form criticism, identified with Hermann Gunkel, and the tradition-historical method identified with Klostermann.[60]

---

55   See: Krey 1991, and for the broader (and contemporary political) context of the issue see also: the (problematic, in my opinion) Whitelam 1996.

56   From the second edition (1883) and onward, the name of Wellhausen's book was changed to *Prolegomena zur Geschichte Israels*.

57   Thompson 1970, 60.

58   Rogerson 1984, 271.

59   Thompson 1970, 62.

60   Thompson 1970, 109ff.

Chapter 8
Meeting Again: Popper versus Dozy

Beginning in the 1850s, glimmers of change began to appear in German Jews' attitude toward biblical criticism, in contrast to the almost complete estrangement described in the previous part. In 1854 David Einhorn, the radical reformist, published a book about "the essence of Judaism" that relied among other things on the hypothesis of the Pentateuchal sources and the division into an Elohistic and a Yahwistic source.[1] In January 1857, the central German-Jewish weekly *Allgemeine Zeitung des Judentums*, for the first time in its twenty years of existence, published a short article by the editor Ludwig Philippson that dealt with biblical exegesis and briefly mentioned biblical criticism.[2] As we have seen above in chapter 5, Philippson believed that "critical work has now more or less been exhausted" and that "despite two or three certain and unquestionable successes" it was possible to summarize its results "as worthless on the one hand and harmful on the other." This was biblical criticism's image on the eve of its great breakthrough. But the very fact of its mention is a testament that Philippson attributed importance to a discipline that "since the middle of the previous century has taken seniority in the field of exegesis." Geiger's *Urschrift* (1857) has also been mentioned above, and despite its caution it appears to be part of this trend. A few years later, in 1863, a character in a novel by the Reform rabbi Salomon Formstecher (1808–1889) is asked for her opinion about biblical criticism; she replies that it does greater harm than good and that its conclusions are dubious and volatile – a testimony to the subject's importance on the one hand, and the negativity with which it was viewed on the other:

> The conclusion that one scholar may today prove beyond all question will be exposed tomorrow as a lie by another scholar, with the same degree of certainty. One will show you that the first two chapters in Genesis are the earliest portions of the Bible, and the other will convince you just as clearly that they must be regarded as the least ancient.[3]

---

1   Einhorn 1854. On "Jehovah" vs. "Elohim" in Einhorn see: Greenberg 1994. About Einhorn see: Bechtoldt 1995, 90-194.

2   Philippson 1857.

3   Formstecher 1863, 137.

But if we had to determine a clear date from which a Jewish awareness of biblical criticism was evident, we might, surprisingly, settle on 1864: that year saw the publication of Reinhart Dozy's work *The Israelites in Mecca* – a problematic, insignificant book which nonetheless had an unprecedented resonance in the Jewish press, as we shall see in the following pages.

In order to place the reception of the non-Jewish Dozy's book in historical proportion, we will first examine another work of biblical criticism which was published only two years earlier during the "dead" period described above – namely, the Jewish author Julius Popper's book about the Tabernacle. We will then survey the reactions to Dozy's book, which varied greatly across the different streams of thought that consolidated during the second half of the century within the *Wissenschaft des Judentums*.

Popper's Book about the Tabernacle and its Reception

In 1862, for the first time, a book was published whose author was Jewish and explicitly wished to make a contribution to Pentateuch criticism: Julius Popper's *Der biblische Bericht über die Stifthütte. Ein Beitrag zur Geschichte der Composition und Diaskeue des Pentateuchs* (The Biblical Account of the Tabernacle: A Contribution to the History of the Composition and Redaction of the Pentateuch).[4] The book was printed in Leipzig and was 256 pages in length. Very little is known about Popper beyond the dates and locations of his birth and death (Hildesheim 1822 and Berlin 1884, respectively),[5] and that he was affiliated with the Reform community in Berlin. He also wrote a Bible for Jewish children;[6] at the time of its publication (1854) he preached and taught religion in Dessau.

In the book's preface, signs of the polemic of the reactionary period are still clearly recognizable: Popper writes against conservatives of all religions (in particular, it seems, "ecclesiastical" conservatives), and the primary goal of his book – the fruit of twenty years of research – is:

> [...] to prove – to Orthodoxy's stubborn adherence to its regular, old views; to the strict, blind dogmatism of educated and uneducated obscurants of all religions and all theological and ecclesiastical streams, colors, and hues – in short, to prove to all who oppose and disparage critical–scientific re-

---

4   Popper 1862.
5   Heuer 1982-1988 II, 178.
6   Popper 1854. For a full bibliographic description and brief overview see: Shavit et al. 1996, 839f.

search, by means of a truly conclusive dogma, the invalidity of the accepted, traditional views, as well as the truthfulness and necessity of the
results of criticism as a whole to an extent even greater than had been realized up till now; and so, when our respectable apologists are left with no
escape and no arguable excuse, all possibility of retreat will once and for all
be eliminated.[7]

Ardent declarations, to be sure. Did Popper's work warrant them?

His work concerned the description of the Tabernacle in Exodus.
With the exception of three chapters that deal with the golden calf (32–
34), the final sixteen chapters of Exodus are concerned with that topic
(25–40). Popper identified a repeated description in the text: the initial
chapters (25ff.) include *instructions* for collecting the required offerings,
for constructing of the ark, table, lampstand, mercy-seat, etc. ("Then
you shall make a mercy-seat of pure gold," Exodus 25:17), while in the
final chapters (35:4ff.) the very same actions and items appear again but
this time as the *implementation* of the instructions given previously ("He
made a mercy-seat of pure gold," Exodus 37:6). Popper compared the
two versions and discovered between them slight but systematic linguistic differences. On the basis of these differences, while broadly
relying on the Samaritan version of the Pentateuch and on the Septua-
gint (the latter greatly distorts the second part of the description), Popper proved that the second description was a later interpolation which
attempted to reproduce an older linguistic style at a time when such
linguistic sensitivity had been lost: it unconsciously contained linguistic
usages of a far later period. On the basis of philological considerations
and external evidence, Popper also managed to estimate the date of the
later redaction. His central thesis is:

> […] That even in the Hebrew text of our Masoretic Bible, not only were in-
> dividual phrases and sentences redacted and inserted, but so were 3–4 *en-*
> *tire chapters* in a very late period, after 260 BCE, as may be demonstrated
> with almost complete certainty.[8]

Recall that the book was published in 1862. As we have seen, the accepted view among critical scholars at the time was that after the Deuteronomistic redaction in the seventh or sixth century BCE, the Pentateuch had existed – with the exception of slight distortions and
corrections – in the version we know today. Popper's thesis delayed the
date of the essential redaction of (part of) the Pentateuch by at least 300
years, moved it from the period before the Babylonian exile to the period after, and was therefore, upon publication, radical and revolutio-

---

7   Popper 1862, iiif.
8   Popper 1862:7.

nary in the extreme. Popper's impassioned preface, quoted above, was thus warranted.

Moreover, the chapters Popper examined (Exodus 25–40, excluding 32–34) were considered legal sections and were included with the *Grundschrift*,[9] then considered the most ancient part of the Pentateuch. In moving the date of the redaction/composition of a significant portion of these chapters forward to the post-exilic period, Popper was ahead of his time: postdating the *Grundschrift* to the post-exilic period stands at the heart of the Graf-Wellhausen hypothesis, which would be published a few years after Popper's book. It is no exaggeration to say that Popper's work contains the ("Jewish"?) roots of the Graf-Wellhausen hypothesis. Furthermore, these roots were not buried or forgotten; they attracted the recognition of non-Jewish biblical scholars.

An important theological journal, *Protestantische Kirchenzeitung*, devoted to the book a glowing and expansive (twelve-column) review three years after its appearance, writing among other things that with regard to the later redaction of the Pentateuch,

> Mr. Popper can clearly claim to be the first to point definitively to this idea, which is of enormous importance to Pentateuch criticism as a whole. We recommend his book to all who hold critical scholarship dear to their hearts.[10]

An even more important testimony is found in the preface by the prominent Dutch biblical critic Abraham Kuenen to the English translation of his 1866 book, a preface that surveys the development of the Graf-Wellhausen hypothesis and is one of its chief accounts.[11] Kuenen addresses Popper explicitly, briefly summarizes his conclusions, notes that the revelation that parts of the *Grundschrift* were later even than Ezra was "a real discovery by Popper,"[12] and finds that:

> This book of Popper's is in more than one respect a tough piece of reading. The style is so diffused as to furnish an unbroken illustration of the well-known rule of *l'art d'ennuyer* [*consiste à tout dire*]. [...] A still greater difficulty, however, was, in the first instance, raised by the result of the investigation. It departed so widely from the traditional belief and seemed so far to overstep the limits of all legitimate hypothesis that it took some time to recover the calm and impartial frame of mind imperatively requisite for the fair consideration of the theses here maintained. [...] but from the first I was profoundly impressed by his argument, which gave a shock to the very generally accepted belief in the unity of the 'Grundschrift,' and introduced

---

9   Thompson 1970, 50.
10 Merx 1865. The article is unattributed. Its attribution to the biblical scholar Merx follows Thompson 1970, 34 N. 6.
11 Rogerson 1984, 257.
12 Kuenen 1886, xxi.

the idea of a 'continuous *Diaskeue* [redaction]' that was obviously destined to exercise a powerful influence upon future investigations.

With the exception of Geiger and Graf, the recognised German critics took no notice of this work,[13] brimful of suggestion though it was, and thereby they showed but too plainly how the 'dominant hypothesis' had established itself in their minds too firmly to allow them to see the importance or the truth of anything that conflicted with it.

It was by no means an accident that Graf, almost alone of German critics, did justice to Popper's word, for he had very largely shaken off the critical tradition which blinded the rest.[14]

In his account of the development of the "late Law" hypothesis Kuenen thus gave Popper's book respectable credit as one of the important sources of inspiration that influenced his own work and Graf's. Graf did accept the main points of Popper's conclusions and summarized them in a lengthy footnote in his book;[15] Wellhausen also mentioned Popper in a bibliographic note in the preface to his own book – in the same breath as the scholars Hupfeld and Nöldeke, and the critical Anglican bishop J. W. Colenso (1814–1883).[16]

Popper and his work were destined for an entirely different reception among Jewish scholars. Abraham Geiger, for one, recognized the scholar's greatness. In a letter written in October 1861 he urged his friend Rabbi B. Wechsler to purchase Popper's book "with all possible haste":

> This little book was apparently already complete in 1857 [...] The author is entirely independent in his work and in his method; he does not deal with my specific subject; and yet, despite this, in his basic thought, in his progress, and in his results he agrees with marvelous precision with my *Urschrift*. The book was written out of a profound internal compulsion and with all the vitality and daring that implies; aware of his innovation, the author often repeats himself [...] but the freshness and passion of his persuasion nonetheless make the reading interesting.

And Geiger encourages his "young, battle-fresh friend" Wechsler to "drill a hole in the heads of the stubborn, beat them obstinately, shout it loudly time and again in the ears of the deaf!"[17] So in a private letter. In public, Geiger devoted to Popper's book a very long (nineteen-page) review in his periodical. After a comprehensive summary of Popper's

---

13   Merx's review (see above) apparently weakens Kuenen's claim here, but it was
     published three years later.
14   Kuenen 1886: xviii-xix
15   Graf 1866, 86f., N. 1.
16   Wellhausen 1878, 8.
17   Geiger, A. 1875-1878 V, 253f.

hypothesis, Geiger admits that "it appears to us so convincing, that we do not expect well-founded objection to it from almost any quarter."[18] He even takes up Popper's method and promptly applies it to the story of Potiphar's wife, there too locating two verses which he identifies as a later interpolation on the basis of the same linguistic criteria that Popper applied to the description of the Tabernacle.[19] He concludes: "We leave this foundational work with great appreciation, and only express our wish that similar monographs be published by the author and by others."[20]

Yet apart from this favorable review the book inspired no reaction at all in the Jewish press; not a single word was devoted to it. Thus Popper – one of the heralds of the revolution in biblical criticism! – was destined to be forgotten entirely. To this day he remains unmentioned in any Jewish encyclopedia. Even Soloveitchik and Rubasheff, in their book on the history of Jewish and non-Jewish biblical criticism, made no mention of his book.[21] Entirely different was the fate of another, dubious book by a non-Jewish scholar, which appeared only two years after Popper's.

Dozy's *The Israelites in Mecca* and its reception

In 1864 the well-known Dutch Orientalist Reinhart Dozy published a short book in Dutch titled *De Israëlieten te Mekka, van Davids tijd tot in de vijfde eeuw onzer tijdrekening* (The Israelites in Mecca from the Time of David to the Fifth Century CE).[22] Dozy[23] was a professor of history and Oriental languages at the University of Leiden. His main field of research was Arabic and Islam, and he was known in Germany for several of his earlier works – catalogues and dictionaries on Islamic subjects, which he composed in Latin and French.[24] His book on the Israelites in Mecca was translated into German under the author's supervision[25] and appeared in the same year with the additional subtitle *Ein Beitrag zur alttestamentlichen Kritik und zur Erforschung des Ursprungs des Islams*

---

18 Geiger, A. 1862a, 129.
19 Genesis 39:7ff. Verses 14-15 are identified as a later insertion.
20 Geiger, A. 1862a, 140.
21 In a footnote they do mention Popper's second, less important book (Popper 1879) without any further comment (Soloveitchik and Rubasheff 1925, 135 N. 1).
22 Dozy 1864a.
23 Reinhart P.A. Dozy, 1820–1883. For a biography see: De Goeje 1883.
24 Later, in 1874, he published a book on the Spanish Moors; see: Wasserstein 1999.
25 De Goeje 1883, 31.

(A Contribution to Old Testament Criticism and to the Study of the Origins of Islam).[26]

Dozy was not a biblical scholar, nor was his book perceived as an important contribution to biblical criticism. Academic circles viewed it with derision; histories of the discipline[27] do not mention it at all. Nonetheless, Jewish periodicals of the time treated it as biblical criticism and their reaction to it was exceptional in its scope. This reception – not the importance of Dozy or his book on their own – allows us to examine the attitude of the *Wissenschaft des Judentums* to biblical criticism after its prolonged silence during the second third of the century.

Dozy summarized the central arguments of *The Israelites in Mecca* in three statements at the very start of his book:

1. The holy site at Mecca was established during the time of David by the Israelites, specifically by the tribe of Simeon. These Simeonites were known as Ishmaelites, whom Arabs also called the first *Gorhum*.

2. They established the Hajj to Mecca; the rituals it involved were illuminated by Israelite history, and many words used to describe it were of Hebrew origin.

3. During the Babylonian period, Jews escaping the Babylonian exile arrived in Mecca – a name which did not originally denote a city. These Jews were known by Arabs as the second *Gorhum*.[28]

Thus Dozy's was not a book of biblical criticism; it was rather a study of the history of the establishment of the Arab cult in Mecca before the Muslim period. But Dozy resorted to secondary arguments in several areas: the ancient Israelite religion (from which he derived the cult at Mecca), the history of the tribe of Simeon (which he claimed had vanished from Israelite history and made its way to the Arab world), and the history of Arab religion before Islam. His relevance to biblical criticism derived from his arguments about the first of these subjects– the history of the ancient Israelite religion. As a foundation for his claim, Dozy opened his book with a preface of about 40 pages[29] on the subject of biblical criticism. The remaining chapters of the book had little to do with biblical criticism and will not be discussed here.

Dozy describes himself as a critical and anti-dogmatic scholar: "Is Man correct in believing he possesses what he calls common sense, or is he mistaken?" he asks rhetorically. Like Popper, Dozy mentions the difficulties that confronted non-dogmatic scholars in the past and praises the tangible progress made in the study of the history and reli-

---

26   Dozy 1864b.
27   E.g. Kraus 1982; Houtman 1994.
28   Dozy 1864a, 17f. = Dozy 1864b, 15f.
29   Dozy 1864a, 1-44 = Dozy 1864b, 1-39. The book numbers about 200 pages.

gion of the ancient Israelites; but he regrets the divide between the study of the Hebrew language and literature and the study of Arabic language and literature – a divide he intends to bridge in his book.

Dozy bases his approach to the biblical text on textual criticism. In this discipline, he maintains, progress has been made only lately: until recent years distortions in the text were typically attributed only to copying errors. "Only in 1857 did the learned rabbi Dr. Geiger point out, in his wonderful work *Urschrift* […], the correct path, by demonstrating that the Jews intentionally altered the text in many places." His argument with respect to tendentious alterations in the biblical text, which he made in the name of Geiger and Popper, allowed Dozy to treat the biblical text with great freedom and to reconstruct the formation of the Pentateuch and the ancient Israelite religion.

First, Dozy declares that the Pentateuch was written by Ezra and his followers. For this purpose he cites Jewish, Muslim, and Christian "traditions"; with respect to the Jewish tradition he cites 4 Ezra, "a very ancient Jewish book" which points to Ezra as the author of the Pentateuch, as well as Talmudic statements that regard Ezra as a second Moses. Dozy then attempts to reconstruct the ancient Israelite religion as it existed before its post-exilic redaction by comparing our version of the Pentateuch to the version known by Ezekiel (who was a priest and as such familiar with the pre-exilic Pentateuch) and by comparing the older Book of Kings to the younger Book of Chronicles, which was written after Ezra's time. He concludes the following:

1. Abraham and Sarah were not historical figures at all; instead they were a large rock (Abraham) containing a cave (Sarah), which together were considered the mythological progenitors of the people of Israel. Only in Ezra's monotheistic purification were they anthropomorphized, at which time stories about them were created in order to grant them a human character.

2. The ancient Israelite religion was founded on the worship of certain stones and trees (this would assist Dozy in reconstructing the source of the cult of the Ka`ba in Mecca). Among his evidence: the prohibition on chiseling the stones of an altar (Exodus 20:25) and the verse "[…] who say to a tree, 'You are my father', and to a stone, 'You gave me birth.'" (Jeremiah 2:27).

3. The first and second generations after the Exodus from Egypt were pagan. This claim was made by Ezekiel; but Ezra polished their image with a tendentious redaction of the Pentateuch.

4. The ancient Israelite religion involved a widespread cult of the Baal (also known as Saturn or Shabtai), in honor of whom the seventh day was sanctified and the Tabernacle and Ark of the Covenant were

created. Only after the Babylonian exile did Ezra invent another justification for the sanctity of the Sabbath and consequently insert into the Pentateuch the Persian story of creation he had learned in exile. Ezra also invented the second Commandment, which forbade the creation of idols and visual representations of God, a commandment that could not have existed during the days of the ancient pagan cult.

5. The ancient Israelites also worshiped Jehovah in the form of a bull or a goat. Even Moses himself worshiped Jehovah in this form. Only later did Jehovah become an abstract God, though several of Baal's traits were preserved in Him.

6. The ancient Israelite cult included human sacrifice. Dozy derived this from the words of Ezekiel (20:25-26): "I gave them statutes that were not good and ordinances by which they could not live. I defiled them through their very gifts, in their offering up all their firstborn." Ezra objected to this law and consequently changed the first word of Exodus 13:12 from *ve-hiv'arta*, "you shall *burn*," to *ve-ha'varta*, "you shall *set apart* to the Lord all that first opens the womb."

7. The Day of Atonement, the most important Jewish holy day, was introduced only after the Babylonian exile. Ezekiel himself made no mention of it, nor did it appear in the list of festivals in the Pentateuch (Exodus 23:14ff., 34:18ff., Deuteronomy 16).

Dozy's conclusions were characterized more by daring and exaggeration than by innovation. His comparison of Kings and Chronicles was similar to that of de Wette. Spinoza had already pointed to Ezra as a possible author of the Pentateuch. As for his claims about Israelite paganism (3), the Baal–Saturn cult, the non-original nature of the second Commandment (4), and the pagan cult of Jehovah (5), we have already seen all these with Vatke. Accusing the Israelites of human sacrifice was a well-known ancient motif.[30] In effect, almost all of Dozy's claims had been raised before him by others; his innovation lay in the idea that Abraham and Sarah were rock and cave (1), and perhaps in his claim about the cult of stones (2).

The reception of Dozy's book by prominent Christian biblical scholars – important for our purposes both as a background for examining its Jewish reception and as a comparison to the reception of Popper's book – was not positive. Kuenen's preface mentions it only in a rather qualified footnote:

> The quasi-autobiographical character of this introduction justifies, and indeed almost demands, the mention of another work that might otherwise have been passed over. I refer to that startling and fascinating book of Dozy's, 'De Israëlieten te Mekka', Haarlem, 1864. Though I cannot indicate

---

30 See also p. 110 above.

any considerable obligations to this book on the field of Pentateuchal criticism, and am still less prepared to defend its dashing and brilliant hypotheses on the field of history, yet the awakening caused by Dozy's rare originality and freedom from traditional restraint produced an effect on my own studies none the less real and important for being entirely indirect.[31]

Graf devoted a lengthy review to the book in the prominent periodical of the German Orientalist Society. There he rejects Dozy's main claims outright: Ezra had a role in creating the Pentateuch, but he was not its author. There was no substance to the claim regarding the cult of stones or to the claims that Abraham was a stone, that the Ark of the Covenant was dedicated to Baal–Saturn, that Baal was a national god of the Israelite people, or that they worshiped Jehovah in the form of a bull. In effect Graf rejects all of Dozy's original claims and accepts only those proposed previously regarding paganism in the desert, human sacrifice, and the late appearance of the Day of Atonement. He describes the book as "a great disappointment" and wonders at "the daring, not to say the adventurousness" of Dozy's claims. In summary he writes:

> If in closing we ask how real, scientifically sound history has benefited from the author's work, a work in which such great acuity and learning are invested, we must regretfully reply: it really has not, not at all.[32]

No less scathing was the relatively conservative Heinrich Ewald, who remarked that the book's author

> [...] begins in error and falls into new and increasingly comprehensive errors in enormous numbers, until it is truly a coincidence if, in the course of his lengthy, deluded ramblings, we encounter something that is not entirely invalid.[33]

Dozy's book was thus given attention due to his standing as an Orientalist, but it was considered an embarrassing stumble by a renowned scholar in a field not his own. The German translation of the book was printed in a single edition, and there is no reason to suppose that it was particularly popular.

In contrast, Dozy met with an intensive reception in the Jewish press: the foremost German-Jewish periodicals published no fewer than seven reviews of the book, most in the year of its publication and the final one eleven years after. A prominent Jewish weekly in the Netherlands also dedicated a lengthy article to it which was published in in-

---

31   Kuenen 1886, xviii.
32   Graf 1865, 350.
33   *Göttingische gelehrte Anzeigen,* quoted in: Dünner 1865-1866.

stallments and would later be quoted in Germany as well.[34] The scope of this Jewish attention was certainly exceptional, a fact which was noted at the time.[35] To compare, Geiger's *Urschrift* – inestimably important, written by a prominent Jewish scholar – was published seven years before Dozy's book but greeted with only three reviews.[36] We have seen above the meager reaction to Popper's important book, which had appeared two years earlier: a single review by Geiger. No book on the subject of biblical criticism that appeared during the nineteenth century, whether before or after Dozy's book, was given so many reviews in the Jewish press – not even the work of Wellhausen.

The reviews themselves can serve as a measuring rod of German Jews' attitudes toward biblical criticism. They range along a spectrum beginning with firm opposition to biblical criticism, not to mention Dozy's book; through acceptance of biblical criticism alongside rejection of Dozy's dubious book; and at the other extreme to an attempt to find merit even in Dozy's book. A clear correlation is evident between the reviewer's position on the Orthodox/Reform spectrum and his position regarding Dozy.

It seems that the main intent of Marcus Jastrow's[37] review in Frankel's *Monatsschrift für Geschichte und Wissenschaft des Judenthums* – which was identified with the Positive–Historical stream – was to mock and deride Dozy's book, and with it the entire discipline of biblical criticism. He begins with a sweeping negative generalization: "Our time, with respect to biblical criticism, has truly not treated us kindly. It has already offered us so many confused and astonishing things that

---

34 The reviews in order of publication: Ludwig Philippson in *Allgemeine Zeitung des Judenthums*, September 1864 (Philippson 1864a); Marcus Jastrow in *Monatsschrift für Geschichte und Wissenschaft des Judenthums* 1864 (Jastrow 1864); a mention by Abraham Geiger in *Jüdische Zeitschrift für Wissenschaft und Leben*, September 1864 (Geiger, A. 1864); Moritz Steinschneider in *Ha-maskir*, September-October 1864 (Steinschneider 1864); a two-part review by Raphael Kirchheim in *Ben Chananja*, November 30 and December 14, 1864 (Kirchheim 1864); a lengthy review in seven installments in the Dutch weekly *Nieuw Israëlietisch Weekblad* published under the pseudonym "X + Y" (Dünner 1865-1866); in 1869 *Monatsschrift für Geschichte und Wissenschaft des Judenthums* published an article by the Dutch rabbi Dünner in which he quoted the aforementioned Dutch article and revealed that he was its author (Dünner 1869); in 1875 the Dutch rabbi Jacob Hoofiën (1846–1886) wrote "About Pentateuchal Criticism" in the same *Monatsschrift*, broadly summarizing Dünner's article (Hoofiën 1875).

35 See for example the start of Kirchheim's review.

36 In the periodicals *Ben Chananja, Jahrbuch für Israeliten* and *HeChalutz*. A list of references to Geiger's book can be found in its second edition: Geiger, A. 1928, 49-51.

37 1829, Posen – 1903, Philadelphia (Pennsylvania). Jastrow spent only a few years working in Germany. From 1866 he lived in America and was one of the founders of the conservative Jewish Theological Seminary.

we may rightfully wonder at the fact that people still marvel at any new development."[38] Jastrow sarcastically presents Dozy as a prattler. In response to Dozy's rhetorical question, "Is Man correct in believing he possesses what he calls common sense?," he replies: "Not every man is correct in believing that he possesses common sense."

Jastrow mockingly points out contradictions in the book. For instance, Dozy – who saw himself as a critical and anti-dogmatic scholar – argued that the Pentateuch had been redacted (or even forged) by Ezra, and in this context quoted Jeremiah 8:8: "in fact, the false pen of the scribes has made it into a lie." Jastrow remarks that he, though "dogmatic," finds no difficulty in believing that Jeremiah had indeed, via the Holy Spirit, prophesied what Ezra was destined to do long after his time, as the "critical" Dozy maintained.

Jastrow is reluctant to use any terminology of biblical criticism that might imply a non-divine origin of the Pentateuch. He consistently precedes critical terms such as "the Yahwistic documents" with "so-called." He ridicules Dozy's more arbitrary corrections to the biblical text (elekha, "to you," instead of derekh, "a way," in Amos 8:14), makes no effort at all to address the conventions of biblical criticism, and is content with specifically refuting some of Dozy's particularly half-baked claims. His greatest scorn is heaped on the idea that Abraham and Sarah were not human but rather rock and cave – indeed, Dozy's most ridiculous claim. Jastrow seizes on Dozy's most far-fetched claims in order to invalidate not only his book, but the field of biblical criticism in general.

By the time Joseph Hirsch Dünner,[39] an Orthodox rabbi, pseudonymously reviewed Dozy's book in a Dutch-Jewish weekly, Jastrow, Philippson, Kirchheim, and Steinschneider's reviews were already available to him, as were those of Graf and Ewald; in his review he surveys the lot. Above all he praises Graf's review and even relates an (unfulfilled) wish to translate it in its entirety into Dutch. Thus the irony of history gave the anti-critical Dünner an unlikely cause to embrace – the archetypically critical Graf, just a moment before the great revolution he would ignite!

Dünner's review is far more detailed and to-the-point than Jastrow's, but he too partakes in the strident objection to both Dozy himself and biblical criticism. His overall evaluation is similar: Dünner writes that Dozy would have done well to restrict his intelligence to

---

38   Jastrow 1864, 313f.
39   Joseph Hirsch Dünner, 1833, Krakow – 1911, Amsterdam. Studied at Bonn. Was since 1862 a leader of the Dutch Orthodoxy.

fields he was well versed in, and that the book was a great step – though not a step forward, as one review had it,[40] but backward.

Dünner's work reveals criticism and wariness of "scientific" scholarship in general as it was carried out in his day; he objects to the historical–philological orientation as opposed to enlightened–philosophical scholarship. This is clear from the following paragraph of his Dutch review:

> By the way, we need not attack Mr. Dozy too greatly on this account. For in our day this manner of critical work has become more or less a general phenomenon which is a necessary result of the direction the study of the classical languages has taken over the years. Rather than studying them philosophically, that is, in order to learn the art of rigorous thought from the great representative artists of antiquity, the philological element, which should have served as a means toward that goal, instead has managed to crown itself the sole ruler of the field.

Dünner places Dozy in the same league as "Ghillany, Daumer, Vatke, Nork, etc.,"[41] blurring the lines between academic scholarship and anti-Semitic propaganda. He puts Dozy's praise of Geiger in quotes and is clearly uncomfortable with it. He ridicules the idea of Abraham as a rock and Sarah as a cave at the very outset of his review; but he reserves most of his slings and arrows for the claim that the Pentateuch was composed (or forged) in the days of Ezra. Dozy relied on "Jewish, Christian, and Muslim traditions" which Dünner rejects, as well as on several familiar verses of the Prophets. From Jeremiah 7:22[42] Dozy derived that the sacrificial laws had not been given during the days of Moses;[43] from Jeremiah 8:8[44] he understood that the Pentateuch had already been forged in Jeremiah's time; and from Ezekiel 20:25-27[45] he

---

40 Namely M.J. de Goeje, a follower of Dozy and author of his biography (Goeje 1883); upon the book's publication he reviewed it with great enthusiasm in the prominent Dutch periodical *De Gids* (Goeje 1864).

41 About Daumer and Ghillany see p. 110 above. Nork was the pseudonym of the converted Jewish satirist and religious scholar Selig (Friedrich) Kohen Korn, 1803–1850. He argued that the origin of the Mosaic religion lay in Brahmanism via Persia and Egypt (EJ X, 333).

42 "For on the day that I brought your ancestors out of the land of Egypt, I did not speak to them or command them concerning burnt-offerings and sacrifices."

43 A fair reading of Dozy, in contrast to Jastrow's hostile reading above.

44 "How can you say, 'We are wise, and the law of the Lord is with us', when, in fact, the false pen of the scribes has made it into a lie?" (See already in: Spinoza 2007 <1670>, 163ff. [chapter 12]).

45 "Moreover, I gave them statutes that were not good and ordinances by which they could not live. I defiled them through their very gifts, in their offering up [Dozy's reading: in their burning] all their firstborn, in order that I might horrify them, so that they might know that I am the Lord" (See already: Spinoza 2007 <1670>, 208ff. [chapter 17]).

concluded the existence of human sacrifice. Dünner pits Dozy's interpretations against each other: the claim that the sacrificial laws were
nothing but a forged insertion contradicts the claim that the Pentateuch
commanded human sacrifice. As for Ezekiel 20:25, Dünner interprets it
as words placed by the prophet in the mouths of God's objectors, as
though God had said: "They claimed I have given them bad laws." This
seems to be an innovation on Dünner's part: Jewish exegetical tradition
interpreted the verse as "I delivered them into the hands of their temp-
tation to stumble over their iniquity"[46] or "Since they despised my
laws, I surrendered them to their enemies who would impose bad statutes on them."[47]

In 1869 Dünner republished a summary of his article in the *Monatsschrift für Geschichte und Wissenschaft des Judenthums*, and in 1875
Hoofiën reiterated Dünner's main claims in the same periodical. During that year Graetz published the (first part of the) second volume of
his great historical work; at the end of the sixth note, which dealt with
criticism of the Pentateuch, he repeated several of the arguments in
Dünner's 1869 article and expressed his own regret that a scholar as
celebrated as Dozy had joined the charlatans of biblical criticism.[48] Later we will see that Dünner's article was repeatedly invoked by the Positive–Historical stream.

Ludwig Philippson's response was quite cautious and characteristic
of the moderate Reform camp. In it he sweepingly rejects several of
Dozy's arguments: for example, in order to support the hypothesis that
Abraham and Sarah were not human, Dozy maintained that no other
characters in the Bible bore those names; Philippson responds that two
thirds of the names in the Bible appear only once, so that Dozy's argument is groundless. Yet Philippson's tone reveals an essentially positive
attitude to biblical criticism. Criticism is not invalid, but must be carried out wisely: "Experience has long since taught us that erudition and
acumen do not suffice for real critical work; a measure of reason is also
necessary." Dozy's approach was irresponsible and could lead only to
"baseless hypotheses, absurd arguments, and grotesque conclusions,"
but all these had nothing to do with "real scholarship." Furthermore,
such irresponsible criticism gave a bad name to real critical work: "Any
man will admit that in this way criticism's freedom (*Freiheit*) turns into
impertinence (*Frechheit*) and so it inflicts great harm to its own interests." Several years later Philippson reported the appearance of an English translation of Dozy's book. This time he was more concisely cate-

---

46   Rashi following Targum Jonathan.
47   David Kimhi's reading, and see a similar idea in Altschuler's *Metzudat David*.
48   Graetz 1902, 438f.

gorical: "Ancient Jewish history is treated here with great historical frivolity, and Daumer and Ghillany's forgotten accusations are served anew in, fortunately, an even more boring form."[49]

Moritz Steinschneider[50] wrote an exceptionally long review of the book in his bibliographical journal, which generally devoted only a few lines to any given book. After summarizing the book's contents, Steinschneider fiercely criticizes Dozy's method and many of his conclusions. Regarding the hypothesis of Abraham and Sarah as rock and cave, he supplies the ironical comment it demanded: "*mit obscönem Nebenbegriff*" ("with an obscene implication"). He likens the book to a building supported by unstable arches; "to our regret we must remark that informing us of the danger of such buildings is the greatest utility this book can provide." About Dozy's use of Geiger's book in order to reinforce his claim of the Jews' "forgery" of Scripture, Steinschneider remarks that he is convinced Geiger himself would object to the conclusions Dozy derived from his work. In his conclusion, Steinschneider too expresses concern about the damage Dozy's book will inflict on free scholarship:

> To this book, which was received with ridicule and scorn in many quarters, we have given our serious attention, which is what is owed to the vigorous search for truth, despite missteps, and to a man of so many other respectable accomplishments. [...] We are obliged to regret that his first major work in our field bears so little ripe fruit. It is likely to be harmful only in that it will contribute to the discrediting of free scholarship; but it appears the time has come to confront such supposedly historical work with a serious cry of "Stop!"

Raphael Kirchheim,[51] a clear reformist who wrote after Philippson and Jastrow, occupies the liberal end of the spectrum of reactions and actually attempts to find redeeming merit in Dozy's work. "You have listed the bad but not the good," he accuses his predecessors: Philippson wrote about the celebrated author in an altogether negative and disparaging tone, "as though he were one of the scholars of the *Mainzer Kladderdatsch*." Indeed, many of Dozy's conclusions were unacceptable *Absurditäten* – his rejection of the traditional stories of Abraham and Sarah, and his claims about the ancient Israelite cult of stones or of the bull, had already been proposed in the past and were groundless – but not all of Dozy's book was based on these; and Kirchheim was the only

---

49 Philippson 1868.

50 1836, Moravia – 1907, Berlin. One of the most prominent members of the *Wissenschaft des Judentums*, an Orientalist and father of Jewish bibliography.

51 1804–1889, Frankfurt am Main. Kirchheim started out as an Orthodox Jew, but under Geiger's influence he eventually became a radical Reformist (JL III, 717).

reviewer to devote a few pages to Dozy's findings about the Muslim cult at Mecca. In conclusion he writes:

> It is our duty to admit that the minimal weight the author gives to the Pentateuch's data, whose reliability he considers inferior to that of Joshua, frequently offends the Jewish reader, and not unjustifiably one might exclaim here and there "Don't let the complete Torah that is ours be like the idle chatter that is theirs";[52] but the author's serious, scientific approach and his fair criticism will surely leave no bitterness in even the most pious readers, and on the contrary they will contribute to the vitality of biblical criticism.[53]

Note Kirchheim's positive attitude toward the discipline of biblical criticism in general, which also influenced his very moderate reservations about Dozy's book.

As for Abraham Geiger, he let lie the glove Steinschneider tossed his way. Geiger maintained a correspondence with Dozy[54] and seems to have been fond of him even before the publication of his book. A year earlier[55] Geiger had complained that German scholars were ignoring his *Urschrift*, in contrast with the broad attention it received in other countries and the grand praise Dozy had heaped upon it in his own book on the history of Islam. Geiger then quoted, in his own newspaper (in Dutch!), about half a page's worth of Dozy's celebration of the "learned rabbi from Breslau" whose book, "a ripe fruit of rare wisdom and twenty-five years of research, has undoubtedly advanced biblical criticism far more than quite a few Introductions and Commentaries." Perhaps in consequence, when Dozy's *Israelites* was published and he once again mentioned Geiger and his work, the latter avoided expressing a real opinion of its contents. He remarked that Dozy "relies impartially on my critical conclusions," and even undertook to protect him from Ewald's stinging review, declaring that it stemmed from Ewald's dissatisfaction at the fact that Dozy had adopted "Jewish" opinions![56] Geiger's response to Dozy's work thus testifies primarily to his thirst for recognition by non-Jewish academics – recognition which in Germany, Geiger believed, was slow to arrive.

The great attention Dozy received among Jews seems to be the outcome of internal dynamics in the Jewish scholarly community. It may have been the very far-fetched nature of the book that roused the conservative Jastrow to seize upon it as easy prey and to use it as a means to discredit biblical criticism in general. In doing so, he may have pro-

---

52   Cf. Babylonian Talmud, *Baba Batra* 116A.
53   Kirchheim 1864, 1001.
54   Geiger, L. 1878, 289f.
55   Geiger, A. 1863.
56   Geiger, A. 1864, 300.

voked liberal representatives into launching a counterattack. A hint of this can be found in Kirchheim's review; more than a hint can be found in Steinschneider's. Despite the fact that a negative opinion of Dozy's book was shared by all its reviewers, there is a clear difference in how they applied that impression to biblical criticism. While the conservatives used Dozy's book in order to dismiss and slander biblical criticism as a whole, the liberals feared precisely that danger and sought to defend biblical criticism, whether by drawing a distinction between the discipline and Dozy or by searching for redeeming qualities in the book.

Either way, it appears that thanks to Dozy's book – or at least since its appearance – biblical criticism forged its way into the Jewish public consciousness. The next chapter will examine in greater detail the relationship of the various streams of thought to biblical criticism, in theory and in practice. As for Dozy himself, it seems that thanks to his dubious book he managed to enter the Jewish public consciousness and stay there; unlike Julius Popper, who was forgotten entirely, this Dutch Orientalist, to whom the Dutch *Grote Winkler Prins* encyclopedia today devotes scarcely fifty words,[57] has been rewarded with detailed entries in nearly every Jewish encyclopedia, from German-Jewish ones to the Israeli *Encyclopaedia Hebraica*.

---

57   GWP VII, 518.

Chapter 9
The Attitude of the Various Jewish Streams Toward Biblical Criticism

During the second half of the nineteenth century German Jewry increasingly organized into disparate camps – the Liberal camp on one side
and the Orthodox camp on the other. This split was accompanied by
the each camp's establishment of its own institutions – synagogues,
rabbinical seminaries, and at times even separate congregations. In
parallel, it is customary to categorize intellectual work in Jewish studies
into three main religious ideologies: the Reform movement, which
based Judaism primarily on moral monotheism and continuous development; the neo-Orthodoxy, which based it on the traditional oral law
and on the fulfillment of the practical commandments; and the Positive–Historical stream, which sought a middle path between the two
and emphasized the centrality of tradition. Each stream was identified
with ideological leaders, scholars, and journals, and while the differences and antinomies between the streams will naturally be emphasized below, it is important to remember that they had a great deal in
common. All three streams opposed the traditional Jewish Orthodoxy
(which to them was represented by the downtrodden image of Polish
Jewry). Each in its own way welcomed emancipation and saw a need to
prepare Judaism for the challenge it faced in the modern world; the
belief in Judaism's special mission was also shared by all three. Each of
the streams attempted to assimilate as Jews in non-Jewish society and
culture (literature, art, scholarship); they all spoke and wrote in German, not Yiddish (including for religious purposes), and sometimes
even used it as the language of worship. All of them accepted – in one
way or another – the ideology of modern scholarship, which characterized European society at the time, and they regarded *Wissenschaft* as a
foundation or at least a necessary support for a modern form of Judaism. Hence the term *Wissenschaft des Judentums*, which with certain
changes of emphasis was taken up even by the neo-Orthodoxy. Each
stream tried to dress Judaism in scientific clothing, or scholarship in
Jewish robes; as a result they found it difficult to ignore scholarship in
its overall context, primarily biblical scholarship as it was carried out in

the Christian academic establishment – that is, in the theological faculties.

As we have already seen in the reactions to Dozy's book, Jews' attitude toward biblical criticism was largely stream-dependent, and we now move to survey the relationship of each of the three streams biblical criticism. Before that, however, let us examine a short and illustrative testimony by a rabbi and scholar who crossed camp lines – a man who was educated as a strict Orthodox Jew and was an outstanding student of Samson Raphael Hirsch, and who as an adult became a disciple of Abraham Geiger. This was Kaufmann Kohler (1843, Fürth – 1926, New York), who would become one of the leaders of Reform Judaism in America, where he moved in 1869. In 1908, in a speech in honor of the hundredth anniversary of S.R. Hirsch's birth, Kohler related:

> "[Hirsch's] teachings were a bold attempt at a revival of Orthodoxy. [...] But no sooner is the scientific method of philological, historical, and psychological investigations applied to it, than the whole structure proves a fabric of cobwebs. This was my experience on entering the University, an enthusiastic follower of Hirsch. I soon found myself beset with doubts, which even my beloved teacher, to whom I poured out my whole heart, could no longer solve for me. The *historical perception* of things, which Hirsch lacked, had alienated Graetz, who became a follower of Ewald. My critical studies led me in the van of the new school, now known as the Kuenen–Wellhausen school – and I became a follower of Abraham Geiger [...] *Romanticism* misunderstands real life. We cannot live the dead past over again. Samson Raphael Hirsch had not the faintest idea of the *historical* growth of language and law, of custom and tradition, nor did he ever recognize the use or necessity of studying the various historical forces, or the strata of either Biblical, Talmudic or post-Talmudic Judaism [...] For us the issue is between Samson Raphael Hirsch, the romanticist, the advocate of uncompromising stability, and Abraham Geiger, the Reform leader, the inaugurator of historical research and of the progress of the *inner* life of Judaism."[1]

Beyond its anti-Orthodox rhetoric, this excerpt reveals how strongly the scientization and historicization of Judaism in general, and biblical criticism (Ewald, Wellhausen, and Kuenen) in particular, made an impression on a young Orthodox student exposed to the German academic world – and to what extent these were central factors both in his search for a personal path between Orthodoxy and Reform, Romanticism and rationalism, and in the self-definition of each of the three

---

1   Heller 1908, 210-214. Also excerpted in: Kohler, M. 1913, 3f. On the relationship between Kohler and his teacher S.R. Hirsch see: Haberman 1998.

streams of German Jewish thought: Orthodox (Hirsch), Positive–Historical (Graetz), and Reform (Geiger).

A. Orthodox Judaism

Orthodox (or neo-Orthodox) Judaism,[2] as it took form in Germany during the latter half of the nineteenth century, can be characterized by its relative position in the Jewish cultural system with respect to the two other central groups of interest: the old Orthodoxy and the Reform.

Like the old Orthodoxy, to the extent that it survived as a direct continuation of the pre-emancipation ideology and way of life, Orthodox Judaism saw itself as continuing the centuries-old faith of normative rabbinic Judaism. But in contrast to the old Orthodoxy, which demonstrated indifference and even opposition to emancipation (a position which can be found even in the work of Moses Mendelssohn), neo-Orthodoxy had a positive attitude toward emancipation and sought – and even believed it found – a way for Jews to integrate into German society while preserving their Jewish identity. In this it was similar to its older sibling, the Reform movement, which had been quick in welcoming emancipation and meeting the challenges it posed by searching for ways in which Jews could integrate as Jews into German society and culture. The essential difference between Orthodoxy and Reform hung on the way they viewed the answer to the challenge of emancipation: the Reform movement sought essential and explicit changes in the Jewish ideology and way of life – changes which it believed were necessary because of changing circumstances – while Orthodox Judaism rejected any essential or explicit change and specifically emphasized the aspect of continuity between it and traditional Judaism.

Even if in practice, especially in all related to the Halakhah, the German Orthodoxy did preserve a clearer continuity than did the Reform movement, still within its worldview, which served as a foundation for its lifestyle, it too required renewal and was profoundly affected by the philosophy and mentality of the modern age.[3] Orthodoxy viewed Jews in a non-national way; their ancient existence as a nation served only as a means to their spiritual goal, and since then the Bible had become their movable homeland. The essence and gist of Judaism –

---

2   Comprehensive studies of this topic are: Breuer 1987; Liberles 1985. On Orthodox biblical criticism see: Morgenstern 2000; Shavit and Eran 2007: 139-149.

3   On the influence of Kant's moral doctrine on S.R. Hirsch and the Orthodoxy in general see: Ellenson 1992, 15ff.

the only way to do God's will – was not spiritual, internal faith but the fulfillment of the Commandments; through its particular way of life the Jews became the bearers of a universal goal. The *Jissroel-Mensch*, the ideal Jew, was one who obeyed the word of God. Emancipation was welcomed as progress, as moral elevation for the Gentiles, and as an opportunity for Judaism to develop its true inner nature without disruption. The separation between the Jewish and general spheres was nullified, and the two must be integrated in theory and in practice.

If Orthodox Judaism's famous slogan for the Jewish way of life was *"Torah im Derech Eretz"* (Torah with worldly involvement), with respect to the issue of *revelation* it was "Torah from heaven." One might expect that the rise of the modern scholarly narrative would lead believers to constrict the non-rational element of revelation to a minimal core; this was not the case. As Harris has demonstrated,[4] revelation actually had a broader place in the German Orthodoxy in comparison to traditional Jewish views that had prevailed during the Middle Ages. This was a reaction to the Reform movement's attack on the oral law and its attempt to "return" to the Bible or to some moral core of it, as well as a reaction to the argument sounded by, for example, Zacharias Frankel, the leader of Positive–Historical stream of Judaism, that not all of the oral law had been given to Moses at Sinai.[5] In reaction, Orthodox Judaism – from its prominent speaker S.R. Hirsch and forward – chose to emphasize the unity of the Torah, including both the written and the oral law, and to apply the concept of revelation to it uniformly. For S.R. Hirsch, Harris writes, "There was one sweeping, comprehensive oral revelation of all the laws incumbent on Jews by divine command, a small number of which, usually exceptional or otherwise distinctive cases, were set to writing";[6] this was in contrast to traditional Jewish conceptions in the past, which were prepared, at least in part, to see the oral law as a man-made derivative (interpretation) of the written law. To borrow Shalom Rosenberg's terminology,[7] Orthodox Judaism preferred to adopt an intuitionist approach to the oral law (i.e., to see halakhic interpretation as a continuation of the process of revelation of God's teachings) instead of a logistical approach (which sees halakhic interpretation as a development of the written law by means of reason) or a constructivist one (which sees the Halakhah as a permanent and continuous construction shaped by rabbinical authority).

---

4   Harris 1992; 1995.
5   Ellenson 1992, 16f.
6   Harris 1995, 227; see also: Ellenson and Jacobs 1988; Wiese 1999, 74ff.
7   Rosenberg 1993, 171ff.

One must not conclude from the expansion of the applicability of revelation that Orthodox Judaism rejected modern scholarship. The strength of the scholarly narrative in nineteenth-century German society was so great that integration into that society without accepting it scarcely seemed a viable option. But at times endorsing that narrative meant little more than using the term "science" – *Wissenschaft* – to characterize any desirable intellectual activity. The actual substance of such activity was often traditional and quite "unscientific." The conflict with modern *Wissenschaft* in the accepted sense of the word was unavoidable, in light of the fundamental gap between the traditional Jewish reading of the Bible – essentially an exegetical–homiletical method – and the modern historical approach. Jacob Katz characterized this conflict (in a different context) as follows:

> The method of exegesis and homiletics is of course the exact opposite of the historical approach, which seeks to understand sources against the background in which they were created. The historical approach consciously ignores what later generations tended to read in the sources, and has no concern other than the original meaning intended by their owners and authors.[8]

Of the various branches of modern scholarship, Orthodox Judaism's approach to the *Wissenschaft des Judentums* was the most highly charged. On the one hand, as we have seen, Orthodox Judaism found it difficult to reject the application of the term *Wissenschaft* to Judaism but was at the same time unable to ignore it. On the other hand, it could not accept how Reform circles employed the term to justify abandonment of the traditional lifestyle or even as a replacement for it. Mordechai Breuer describes the attitude of Orthodox Judaism toward the *Wissenschaft des Judentums* as "a non-homogeneous position. It included a cooperative approach and a parallel approach, but also a fundamentally adversarial approach."[9] This complex relationship stemmed from the fact that the *Wissenschaft des Judentums* was a sort of junction where many of the fundamental problems of Orthodox Judaism intersected: *Wissenschaft* stood for the problematic place of non-Jewish culture in Orthodox life, while *Judentum* represented the difficulties in transforming the traditional way of life and thought into a modern identity that must find its place alongside other identities and at times even contend and compete with them, whether from "outside" (Germanness as a culture, as a Christian religion, and as a nationality) or from "inside" (the various strains of Jewish Reform).

---

8   Katz 1988, 20.
9   Breuer 1992, 175.

It is customary to distinguish between two Orthodox approaches to *Wissenschaft des Judentums*, which at times even came into conflict. The first approach was identified with S.R. Hirsch and the Frankfurt community and was relatively hostile to the *Wissenschaft des Judentums* – "adversarial," as Breuer would call it. The second was that taken by the Orthodox rabbinical seminary founded in Berlin in 1873, which was identified primarily with its prominent founders and teachers, Esriel Hildesheimer, David Hoffmann, and other members of their circle; this approach was more favorable – in the sense of "parallel" – to the Jewish *Wissenschaft*.[10] We will examine the Orthodox response to biblical criticism through two prominent attempts at dealing with it – an early one from Hirsch's circle and a second, later one by Hoffmann. It should be noted that another Orthodox scholar – Jakob Barth[11] – was condemned simply because he was suspected of supporting the division of Isaiah into two prophetic sources;[12] needless to say, all the Orthodox scholars who dealt with criticism of the Pentateuch itself rejected outright any deviation from the principle of "Torah from heaven," specifically in its Masoretic form.

Joseph Gugenheimer on the Commentary of S.R. Hirsch

Samson Raphael Hirsch, one of the founders and the uncrowned leader of German Orthodoxy,[13] once claimed that if he were forced to choose, then "Better a Jew without science than science without Judaism," (he was quick to add: "But thank God, this is not the case.")[14] He expressed his fierce objection to *Wissenschaft des Judentums* in a distinction between "so-called" and true *Wissenschaft des Judentums*, where the latter had for centuries accompanied the Jewish praxis, and was in fact, as Michael Meyer notes, "nothing other than a continuation of *talmud torah*, the reverent study of sacred texts."[15]

---

10   Breuer 1992, 184ff. About the two approaches see also: Ellenson and Jacobs 1988. On the Orthodox rabbinical seminary (*Rabbinerseminar*) in Berlin see: Eliav 1992.
11   Jakob Barth, 1851, Flehigen (Bavaria) – 1914, Berlin. An Orientalist and biblical exegete. He taught at the University of Berlin and the Orthodox rabbinical seminary.
12   On the controversy with and around Barth, see: Breuer 1987, 167-168; see also: Blau 1958.
13   1808, Hamburg – 1888, Frankfurt. See: Wiener 1933, 69-82; Breuer 1992; Michael 1993, 300-305.
14   Quoted in: Breuer 1992, 178.
15   Meyer 1992, 184. And in Katz's more delicate formulation: "'Science' does not mean critical science, as in the usage of the scholars of *Wissenschaft* des Judenthums Zunz,

Hirsch strictly associated the *Wissenschaft des Judentums* – both in terms of its content and because of its scholars – with vulgar Reform Judaism, an anti-rabbinical movement, and abandonment of the Commandments.[16] He considered it false science, irrelevant, full of anti-Orthodox prejudices, concerned with insignificant questions, a shabby replacement for vibrant Judaism, and an obstacle to the flourishing of true Jewish scholarship. The *Wissenschaft des Judentums* did nothing for true Judaism and the real Jewish life, Hirsch believed. In a lengthy and detailed missive about the young discipline he asked:[17]

> What has [*Wissenschaft des Judentums*] done, first and foremost, for the Law, the true core of the Jews' scholarship and mission – what has it done to allow its generation to grasp the Law in theory and in practice as the essence of the age, to convince them to sacrifice their heart and soul for this Law [...]? What has it done that they do not regard this Law, this core of the Jews' entire learning and destiny, as anything but a burdensome yoke, a tight, painful shoe [...], and rather than devoting themselves eagerly to the study of the Law [...] they consider it an anachronistic waste of time and strive to banish it from their and their children's sight?

How, then, should the Torah be studied? To explicate the correct method, Hirsch drew an analogy between scholarship and the Bible in a lengthy note in his first book, *Neunzehn Briefe über das Judentum* (Nineteen Letters on Judaism).[18] According to that analogy, the world contains two revelations – nature and Torah – and the two are very similar. In nature, phenomena are taken as facts, and only from them can the rules of nature be derived; proving or disproving those rules can be done on the basis of nature itself; one counterexample suffices to disprove a rule altogether, and thus as much data as possible must be collected in advance about a phenomenon in order to see it in its entirety; and the absence of a scientific explanation for a phenomenon does not negate its factual existence. Similarly in the Torah: "The Bible is given to us like the heavens and the earth";[19] the ultimate reason in the Torah, as in nature, is God; as in nature, no fact can be denied, even if the rules it obeys are still unknown; nor can any ruling be denied, even if it is not yet understood; as in nature, the Torah too must be scoured for divine wisdom; and rules must be formulated and validated only according to their harmony with the Torah.

Graetz, or Frankel [...] it referred to systematic and consistent explanation of the concept of Judaism" (Katz 1987, 23).

16   Breuer 1992, 178ff.
17   Hirsch 1904 <1861>. The citation is on p. 428.
18   Hirsch 1919 <1836>, 110f.
19   Hirsch 1919, 110.

Even Hirsch, who rejected out of hand the scientific–modern approach to the Bible, thus needed analogies and legitimization from the philosophy of modern science in order to ground his rejection. However, the analogy cannot conceal the fact that his approach was fundamentally dogmatic and anti-"scientific." Hirsch did not distinguish between revelation and its corporeal form, but instead granted the entire Bible the status of "natural phenomenon" entirely free of human involvement and judgment. Thus he rejected the basic premise of biblical criticism, which might not necessarily reject revelation but "put it in brackets" for the purposes of "scientific" study and assumed that, as Jost wrote, "every book laid before us is entirely the work of one or more human beings, and is subject to the events of its time just like any other human artifact."[20] Hirsch also rejected the methodological distinction between the realm of faith or dogma and the realm of science: "There is only one truth. What is true dogmatically must be true also scientifically, and what science reveals as falsehood and fraud cannot be resurrected as a dogmatic truth," he wrote in a separate context.[21]

In principle, once Hirsch rejected the basic premise of critical biblical scholarship, he was no longer required to address the conclusions that derived from it. Moreover, if he were to contend explicitly with the conclusions of biblical criticism, this might have implied some recognition of its premises. On the other hand, presumably many Orthodox Jews who were immersed in German intellectual life[22] encountered biblical criticism in one way or another; the work of reform Jews in that discipline also served as an open channel for Orthodox introduction to criticism. The fundamental rejection of biblical criticism, as Hirsch expressed it, made it difficult for him to follow explicitly the Talmudic injunction to "know what to say to an unbeliever." It seems that Hirsch therefore chose an indirect approach.

In 1867 publication began of Hirsch's Bible translation and commentary. Completed in 1878, this was Hirsch's most popular work and "stood in almost every educated Orthodox home."[23] The commentary itself made not a single mention of biblical criticism; but in that same year the first installment of an article by Rabbi Dr. J. Gugenheimer was published in the Orthodox journal *Jeschurun*[24] – across from an advertisement for Hirsch's just-published commentary on Genesis – under

---

20   Jost 1820-1828 IIIb, 203.
21   Hirsch 1912 <1860>.
22   Breuer 1992, 149ff.
23   Breuer 1992, 153. The vast popularity Hirsch achieved among the "common people" was met with derision from Zunz (Breuer 1992, 182).
24   *Jeschurun* 13 (1867), 292.

the title "Die Hypothesen der Bibelkritik und der Commentar von Herrn Rabbiner S. R. Hirsch" (The Hypotheses of Biblical Criticism and the Commentary of Rabbi S.R. Hirsch). Six more installments would follow by 1869; the continuation promised in the final installment was never printed.[25] Joseph Gugenheimer (1833–1896), who was married to Hirsch's daughter Sarah, presided at that point as the Orthodox rabbi of Kolin in Bohemia and had long conducted a close relationship with his father-in-law, who even assisted him in his struggle against Reform Judaism.[26] Hirsch himself was the editor of *Jeschurun* and there can be no doubt that he approved of the article and perhaps even assisted in its writing. Even though Hirsch did not address the subject of biblical criticism, Gugenheimer argued, he nonetheless refuted its hypotheses.[27]

Clearly, Gugenheimer's primary adversaries were not Christian biblical critics (who certainly did not read his paper) but rather Jews who accepted biblical criticism and its conclusions: "Citing these conclusions in this periodical seems particularly justified, because the hypotheses of biblical criticism gain acceptance on the Jewish side as well."[28] Gugenheimer develops his accusation against Jews who strayed from the right path by tracing the lineage of biblical criticism to Spinoza, and quotes a Christian biblical scholar (Peter von Bohlen) who argued – based on Bendavid, Jost, and Zunz – that "even Jewish scholars in the modern era" no longer attributed the authorship of the Pentateuch to Moses. Gugenheimer thus emphasizes the Jews' "sin" with respect to biblical criticism, draws a straight line from Spinoza to Jost and Zunz, and even claims that Jews' reservations about the authenticity of the Pentateuch nourished and strengthened non-Jewish criticism (a fairly dubious claim given German academia's general tendency to ignore Jewish scholars).[29]

Gugenheimer seeks to present Hirsch's commentary as a work of modern scholarship:

> The work at hand can also prove to biblical critics that, though the basic premise of biblical criticism hangs on rejecting revelation and transgresses the bounds of scientific discourse – since the truthfulness of revelation, like the truthfulness of any historical fact, is neither provable nor falsifiable by reason – there is no need to seek refuge in "credulous exegesis" in order to resolve the difficulties that biblical criticism raises to justify its claims; Rabbi Hirsch's commentary, though it circumvents biblical criticism [...] is able

---

25   Gugenheimer 1867-1869.
26   For a brief biography of Gugenheimer see: Klugman 1996.
27   Gugenheimer 1867-1869, 299.
28   Gugenheimer 1867-1869, 294.
29   Discussed in detail in: Wiese 1999.

to clear away the objections that biblical criticism raises in order to ground its premises by means of rational and accurate scientific interpretation.[30]

This is the background against which Gugenheimer debates the claims of biblical criticism – a background he defines as rational and "scientific." In a sort of *argumentum ad ignorantiam* (because it is impossible to prove that there was no revelation, it cannot be ruled out) he attacks the basic premise of biblical criticism, which rejected revelation.[31] In effect he argues that the historical–critical school is not "scientific," while hermeneutics immanent to the text is. This hermeneutics is derived from Hirsch's dogmatic approach, which regards the Pentateuch as a "natural phenomenon." The perfection and originality of the Pentateuch as part of revelation exist as an absolute axiom, and the role of scholarship is to resolve seeming contradictions in the text on the basis of this axiom.

Gugenheimer is familiar with the literature of biblical criticism: he mentions the "Belgian physician" Astruc,[32] Eichhorn, Ewald, Delitzsch, and others; he was not yet acquainted with Graf. His methodological principles are laid out at the very start of the article: the entire Pentateuch was given by God, and this may be proven by demonstrating through hermeneutical and linguistic means the "uniform spirit" that runs through it, as Hirsch writes in the preface to his commentary.[33] Gugenheimer not only refutes the division of the Pentateuch into different sources and the rejection of its attribution to Moses, but insists on its unadulterated divinity. Gugenheimer emphasizes this argument in a footnote about others' claims that Moses composed the Pentateuch on the basis of documents he had before him. Not so, Gugenheimer argues: Judaism does not consider Moses an author, but rather the first to introduce and record the Pentateuch in writing; according to the Talmud[34] anyone who admits the divinity of the entire Pentateuch, yet

---

30   Gugenheimer 1867-1869, 294.

31   In the twelfth century, in his *Dialogue Between a Philosopher, a Jew, and a Christian*, Peter Abelard provided the Jewish character with the following argument on the subject of the Law: "Even if we cannot convince you that it was given by God, you, for your part, cannot refute this." Quoted in Cohen 1999, 280; Cohen describes this as an "argument by default."

32   Astruc was French – a professor of anatomy in Paris – but his book was published in 1753 in Brussels; hence the anachronism (Belgium was founded in 1830).

33   Gugenheimer 1867-1869, 299f.

34   Babylonian Talmud, *Sanhedrin* 90A: "And these are the ones who have no portion in the world to come: He who says, the resurrection of the dead is a teaching which does not derive from the Torah, and the Torah does not come from Heaven; and an Epicurean." Ibid. 99A: "And even if he had said, 'The entire Torah comes from heaven, except for this one verse, which the Holy One, blessed be he, did not say, but which Moses said on his own.'"

believes that even a single word of it was inserted by Moses and not dictated by God, denies revelation.[35]

Gugenheimer's hermeneutics – which relies on Hirsch's commentary – can be demonstrated by his contention with the arguments proposed about the two narratives of creation (Genesis 1:1–2:3 versus 2:4–24). Biblical criticism dissected the text into two separate accounts based on their different names for God (Elohim versus Jehovah); on the heading "These are the generations of the heavens and the earth when they were created" (2:4), which begins the second account; and on the contradictions between the two: in the first account it is God who names the various creatures, while in the second Adam names them; in the first Man is created in God's image while in the second he is made of the dust of the ground; in the first the animals are created by the Word of God, while in the second He forms them out of the ground. Gugenheimer resolves the use of different names by arguing that even biblical critics admitted that the attribution of names to different sources was not always consistent. Furthermore, each of the two names of God emphasizes a different aspect of Him: "Elohim" is the unifier, ruling over and directing a multitude of phenomena, and so this name takes the plural form; He is regularity, law, justice, and stringency. Jehovah is the giver of life or existence, and so this name derives from the Hebrew root H-Y-H, "to be"; He is a guide, an instructor, a dispenser of mercy. The development of the world depends on both aspects in concert; together they form the combination "Jehovah Elohim." Regarding the heading above, the problematic word "*toladot*" (translated as "generations" in the NRSV) does not mean "becoming" (*Entstehung*) but rather "progeny" or "consequences" (*Erzeugnisse*). This may be understood by comparing the term's usage in other verses. The heading thus introduces the description of the *continuation* of the history of the heavens and earth *after* their creation: there are not two separate accounts, but rather a single account of creation and its aftermath. As for the contradictions, in the second account (2:7) it is not Man's creation that is described, but rather his development as a moral creature. The contradiction regarding the creation of animals is also resolved by means of a philological distinction:[36] the root Y-TS-R in the second narrative does not signify *creation* but rather subjugation or compulsion (as in *matsor*, siege).

The overall trend is clear and persists throughout the article, in which Gugenheimer continues similarly to examine and refute the divi-

---

35   Gugenheimer 1867-1869, 297f.
36   Already found in the Midrash (Genesis Raba 17).

sion of Genesis 3–6 into separate sources. His is a fundamentally dogmatic approach, and in order to prove the dogma he relies on modern
rhetoric that combines traditional arguments from the Talmud and
medieval exegesis with original philological arguments by Hirsch. The
discussion focuses on biblical source criticism and does not deal with
cosmogony, but it does insist that the biblical narrative is a reliable
historical account. Thus Gugenheimer – following Hirsch and Ibn Ezra
– maintains that the speaking serpent in the Garden of Eden was not a
miraculous phenomenon: before the Fall, animals existed at a higher
level of development than they do today and really did possess the gift
of speech. This is a surprising use of a rationalist, anti-miracle argument in support of irrational and unscientific belief.

Gugenheimer engages in an explicit polemic with the reformist David Einhorn. An illuminating example is his criticism of Einhorn's reading of the story of the forbidden fruit in the Garden of Eden.[37] Einhorn
accepted the distinction between the Elohistic and Yahwistic parts of
the Pentateuch, differentiated between the two accounts of the creation
of Man, and argued that according to the second, Yahwistic narrative,
Man was imbued from the outset with a "breath of life" that was little
different than that of the animals; he became a godlike creature – a
moral creature who could distinguish between good and evil – only
through eating the fruit of the tree of knowledge, an act which Einhorn
compared to Prometheus' theft of fire in Greek mythology.[38] This interpretation of the biblical story and its comparison to the Promethean
myth appear to have been favorites of the Reform movement; Kaufmann Kohler would employ them similarly.[39] Gugenheimer reveals
that Einhorn "borrowed" the Promethean comparison from Peter von
Bohlen, and accuses Einhorn of imitation and deterioration into "a bog
of crude materialism devoid of all morality" because his exegesis not
only rejected Man's creation in the image of God but also turned what
the Bible described as a clear sin into an exemplary act.

Here, then, behind the interpretation of a single biblical episode, lie
the many fronts of the debate between Reform and Orthodoxy: a typical Orthodox accusation that the Reform movement is eager to follow
Christian practices in the fashion of epigoni and imitators; an Orthodox
objection to the universalist comparison between biblical "history" and
Greek myth, a comparison that places the Jewish God on a par with the

---

37   Gugenheimer 1867-1869, 188f.
38   Einhorn 1854, 30f.
39   For an illustration of the claim that "each step humanity has advanced on its path to
      civilization has required provocation and struggle against divinity or against the re-
      ligious principle of which it was captive," see: Kohler 1868, 151.

gods of ancient Greece; and an Orthodox critique of the conception that sides with the rebellious Man against God (a rebellion that in this context was also aimed at tradition) and which sees the doctrine of morality as an autonomous human development rather than (exclusively) the image of God. Recall that the Promethean myth is one of the founding myths of modernity, which regards Man as a creature who has the power to control the world and his own destiny, to create an autonomous moral philosophy and so on. On top of all these, Gugenheimer also translates the disagreement to the level of concrete religious practice (the Law, *Halakhah*): he recalls that at a Reform conference, Einhorn was elected by a wide margin to the committee on repealing the dietary laws, and this explains his interest in presenting the sin in the Garden of Eden as a positive act – the prohibition on eating of the tree of knowledge was the first dietary law and the basis for all that followed.

David Hoffmann versus the Graf-Wellhausen Hypothesis

The Berlin Orthodoxy's attitude toward *Wissenschaft* was somewhat different: there was no fundamental objection to critical historical scholarship, so long as it did not displace the old style of Torah study. In place of Hirsch's ambition to unite and merge Torah and *Wissenschaft*, Esriel Hildesheimer and his circle preferred to let the two exist side by side as separate fields. Both fields were devoted to the search for truth, and this search gave them positive value. While Hirsch's method proposed to transform biblical scholarship itself into a modern, scientific form of worship – hence its attraction to Frankfurt's Jewish bourgeoisie – the Berlin approach proposed to integrate modern scholarship alongside religious life and better suited the educated Orthodox Jews of Berlin.[40]

This approach was represented by David Hoffmann.[41] Hoffmann studied at the University of Vienna, moved to Berlin, and was one of the founding teachers – since 1873 – of the city's Orthodox rabbinical seminary led by Esriel Hildesheimer, where he taught for forty-seven years. In a series of articles written from the mid-1870s until World War I, Hoffmann attempted to disprove the Graf-Wellhausen hypothesis

---

40   Breuer 1992, 181ff.
41   1844, Verbo (Hungary) – 1921, Berlin. See: Wachsman 1958; Ellenson and Jacobs 1988; Bechtold 1995, 363-438; Morgenstern 2000.

through an exacting refutation of its arguments.[42] He based this effort on contradictions he identified in Wellhausen's theory and evidence.

Hoffmann's basic premises were laid out in detail in his other writings: Moses was the author of the Pentateuch; the entire Masoretic Torah was true, sacred, and divine in its origin, which no man had the right to question; and the written and oral laws were a unity that must not be separated.[43] This was the source of his wishful thinking: as early as 1876 he predicted that Wellhausen and Graf's hypothesis that most of the legal parts of the Pentateuch were written after the Babylonian exile had "no chance to ever become dominant";[44] more than forty years later, in 1918, the Orthodox periodical *Jeschurun*, which published his articles, declared that Hoffmann had made away with Wellhausen.[45] "One of many such prophecies, with the wish apparently the father to the thought," Thompson remarks.

Hoffmann's method can also be illustrated through his argument against the division into two sources of the creation story. Hoffmann explains[46] that the second account, which biblical criticism attributed to the earlier source J, could not be read on its own as an independent story but relied on the first account, which was attributed to the later source P. The opening verse of the second account, "These are the generations of the heavens and the earth when they were created" (2:4), is in his opinion a heading that evokes the creation of the heavens and the earth related in the first narrative; he rejects both the idea that this is a heading for a creation account in itself and the proposals of Christian critics who considered it a conclusion to the first account,[47] or moved it to the latter's beginning. The use of the paired divine name (Jehovah Elohim) in the second narrative also points to the creative divinity (Elohim) of the first; Hoffmann rejects the hypothesis that it was the redactor who inserted the second name, "Elohim," arguing that it is not the habit of a redactor who views his texts with holy awe to interpolate the name of God twenty times as an act of interpretation. Such a redactor would have inserted it just once. Furthermore, the second account is incomplete; it omits not only the creation of the heavenly bodies but also the creation of many entities it itself mentions: "In the day that the

---

42   Hoffmann 1876; 1877; 1879-1880; 1914-1919. Some of these articles were later collected in a two-volume book: Hoffmann 1904 (a Hebrew translation followed in 1928) and Hoffmann 1916.

43   Ellenson and Jacobs 1988, 31f.

44   Hoffmann 1876, 2.

45   Quoted in: Thompson 1970, 81 N. 3.

46   Hoffmann 1916, 1-6; Hoffmann 1914-1919, 114-119, 272-280, 390-396.

47   Like the conservative Oehler, who will be mentioned again in reference to Zunz.

Lord God made the earth and the heavens" (2:4) assumes the creation of the earth and the heavens, and "no plant of the field was yet in the earth" (2:5) raises an expectation of details about the creation of flora (in particular in light of 3:18, "and you shall eat the plants of the field") – but no such details appear in the story and there is no evidence to support critics' claims that the description was omitted by the redactor.

Hoffmann's arguments are convincing at times, less so at others. In the first creation story (1:11) Adam is created after the flora. According to Hoffmann, the second story is meant to emphasize that Adam was formed of the virgin soil of Eden, which had not yet yielded any plant life; without the information from the first story, the second is meaningless. And so, in a vicious circle, Hoffmann transforms the contradiction between the two accounts into the glue that binds them; from his resolution of the contradiction between the stories (his assumption that the second narrative refers solely to Eden's soil) he concludes that the contradiction is imperative and necessary, since without the contradiction the resolution could not stand.

Similarly – in ways that sometimes point to real contradictions in the critical hypotheses but at times suggest that his method is defined by his own predetermined conclusions – Hoffmann argues against Wellhausen's chronological arrangement of the Pentateuchal sources: P and D are contemporary and preceded the Babylonian exile; Ezekiel is based on P and not vice versa. In short, wherever Wellhausen proposed a chronological order, Hoffmann demonstrates that the earlier source refers to the later one; wherever Wellhausen identified multiple sources, Hoffmann finds a unified text.[48] A contemporary Orthodox reviewer was correct in writing that Hoffmann "proves how every verse belongs to its context; how various parts, described as separate sources, complement and presuppose each other's existence; and how on their own they were incomplete and impossible to understand correctly."[49]

Hoffmann's style is dry and to the point, but his sentiments are clear: he does not accuse biblical criticism of Christian or anti-Jewish biases and has no interest in making a general statement about biblical criticism; all he wants is to contradict the historical picture presented by Wellhausen's school and thus to prove the validity – by way of elimination, as it were – of the traditional approach to the text. The extent to which Hoffmann's work was directed at Wellhausen and Wellhausen alone is demonstrated by his attitude toward the prominent biblical

---

48   For a short survey see: Thompson 1970, 80f.; for more detail see: Bechtold 1995, 406-438.

49   Serber 1916, 589.

scholar August Dillmann. Dillmann rejected Wellhausen's historiography and centered his historical description around the concept of holiness, which he believed made Israel unique among the nations. Hoffmann adopted Dillmann's approach and frequently relied on him as a supporter of his claims against Wellhausen. But he turned a blind eye to the fact that Dillmann had developed his own documentary hypothesis[50] and believed in the antiquity of the legal source P.[51] Hoffmann, who was not interested in an earlier or later dating of the Law but only in rejecting Wellhausen's specific historiography, thus relied on a scholar who himself espoused a documentary hypothesis which Hoffmann did not even mention, let alone refute.

A prevalent accusation against biblical criticism before the Graf-Wellhausen revolution was that it was fundamentally negative: it cast doubt on the unity and attribution of the biblical text but did not offer a constructive alternative theory of its creation. Ironically, this criticism can also be applied to Hoffmann's work. He refuted the critics' arguments but offered no alternative of his own; instead he implicitly represented the traditional argument that the entire Pentateuch had been divinely dictated to Moses. The Hebrew writer Rav Tza'ir (i.e. Chaim Tschernowitz, 1870–1950) was correct in writing that Hoffmann "demonstrates the weakness of his opponent's assumptions, but does not propose any positive proofs for the antiquity of the Torah," and that his implicit assumption was that "the burden of proof lies on the one who departs from tradition."[52] Hoffmann's image of modern scholarship was naturally very different than the one Thomas Kuhn would offer much later, according to which scholars did not treat exceptions as counter-examples and a theory was "declared invalid only if an alternate candidate is available to take its place";[53] Hoffmann made no attempt to supply such a theory, and for modern biblical criticism the road back from Wellhausen's hypothesis to the traditional approach of revelation at Sinai was entirely blocked. Hoffmann's work is an exhausting read, and although it is considered a serious attack on Wellhausen's method[54] it has little value for cultural analysis. In order to maintain an appearance of "scientific" scholarship, Hoffmann avoided debates concerned with imagery or the socio-cultural sphere; but his scholarly façade falls away altogether in light of the very dogmatic

---

50   Ellenson and Jacobs 1988, 32.
51   Thompson 1970, 61; Kraus 1982, 375.
52   In *HaTekufah* 13 (1931), quoted in the translator's preface, Hoffmann 1928, xix-xx.
53   Kuhn 1970, 77.
54   "His work is well done and remains one of the best statements of scientific Conservatism" (Thompson 1970, 81).

premises that guide it. In evaluating his work in the field of biblical studies Ellenson and Jacobs concur with Alexander Altmann, who wrote that "Hoffmann's learned and skillful rebuttal of Wellhausen was more in the nature of apologetics than of modern scholarship, no matter how justified were his strictures in details,"[55] and they declare (in contrast to their far more positive evaluation of Hoffmann's work on rabbinic literature) that "he completely accommodated this scholarship to the demands of his Orthodox Jewish faith."[56]

Conclusion and Evaluation

The German Orthodoxy unanimously rejected biblical criticism, a reaction not at all surprising given the dogmatic Orthodox positions on revelation. It focused its struggle against biblical criticism not on exposing criticism's image of Jews and Judaism or developing an alternative historiography, but on stubbornly defending the principle of "Torah from heaven" in its most literal sense. S.R. Hirsch accomplished this defense via philological exegesis. Ignoring biblical criticism was consistent with his proposal to effectively circumvent modern scholarship and replace it with "truly" Jewish scholarship, an approach that Gugenheimer elaborated in his article about Hirsch's commentary. David Hoffmann skillfully penetrated the critical discourse, but his extensive efforts were aimed at a very narrow goal: discovering contradictions and inconsistencies in the Graf-Wellhausen hypothesis. He did not contradict the documentary hypothesis in its own right, nor did he attempt to propose a modern scholarly alternative to it; he refrained from any cultural or theological analysis of Wellhausen's work and did not transcend the level of specific details. His premise – that the contradictions he found in Wellhausen's work would destroy it, prompting a return to traditional dogmatics – seems naïve to the expert and almost impenetrable to the layman. This negatory attitude of Orthodox Judaism toward modern biblical criticism would essentially continue during the twentieth century, and not only in Germany; "In general, Orthodox Jews in America, Israel and elsewhere have remained on the periphery of biblical scholarship."[57]

---

55   Altmann 1956, 210f.
56   Ellenson and Jacobs 1988, 34.
57   Sperling 1980, 39.

B. Positive–Historical Judaism

In between Orthodox and Reform Judaism stood the Positive–
Historical stream of Judaism.[58] This was first and foremost an intellectual stream which did not establish the variety of institutions that
turned Orthodoxy and Reform into influential camps among German
Jews. The importance of the stream – the primary figures associated
with it being the rabbi Zacharias Frankel, its leader, and the historian
Heinrich Graetz – derives from its later developments (conservative
Judaism, especially in the United States) and from the significant influence of Graetz's writings and historiographical approach on Jewish
nationalism.

While Orthodox Judaism singled out a particular point in history –
the revelation at Sinai – as the basis for its understanding of Judaism,
both Reform and Positive–Historical Judaism emphasized historical
continuity. But while Reform Judaism placed theological and moral
elements at the center of this continuity, the Positive–Historical stream
placed faith and the Halakhah at the center. Some see a Romantic element in the importance that stream attributed to tradition and the collective Jewish consciousness; its emphasis on faith and emotion reveals
some resemblance to German Pietism.[59] The *positive* aspect of Judaism,
according to Frankel, was manifested in faith that ranked Judaism
above history and was anchored in the revelation at Sinai, as well as in
the Halakhah, which paralleled Christianity's dogmas. The *historical*
aspect was tradition formed over the course of generations; while
guided by providence, it had nonetheless been created by Man and was
therefore open to change, albeit in an organic, slow, and cautious manner. In his studies on the development of the Law Frankel declared,
provoking Orthodox fury, that the laws classified in the Talmud as
"Halakhah to Moses from Sinai" did not really originate at Sinai but
rather in later generations.[60] But Frankel preferred to speak of development and evolution rather than revolutions and innovation. In this
approach he attempted to find the golden mean that would avoid both
militant Orthodoxy and radical Reform, in the hope of preserving the
cohesion of German Jewry.

The Positive–Historical concern with biblical criticism was minimal.
Thompson somewhat exaggerates in his estimate[61] that the movement's

---

58   On Positive–Historical Judaism see: Wiener 1933, 100ff.; Horwitz 1984, 11-41; Roten-
     streich 1987 I, 107ff.; Meyer 1988, 84ff.
59   Meyer 1997, 150.
60   Ellenson 1992, 16.
61   Thompson 1970, 80 N. 3.

important monthly, the *Monatsschrift für Geschichte und Wissenschaft des Judenthums*, was silent on the subject of biblical criticism until 1907, but its reaction was indeed quite limited in frequency and scope. We have already encountered Jastrow's derisive review of Dozy's book in that monthly in 1864, as well as Dünner's 1869 article in the same periodical,[62] which dealt with Ezekiel 20:25ff.[63] In that article Dünner accused biblical criticism of failing to rise above hypothetical arbitrariness and of bias in the sense that it identified in the Bible what it set out to find from the start, and thus was guilty of the same anachronism of which scholars accused traditional Jewish exegesis. As we have seen, in 1875 the Dutch rabbi Jacob Hoofiën[64] once again, in an article in the same periodical, summarized Dünner's main arguments in his Dutch review of Dozy. Dünner's initial reaction to Dozy's article thus ran as a common thread through the publications of Positive–Historical critics, even in the work of Heinrich Graetz. Indeed, Dünner in his response attempted to contradict the Pentateuchal critics' claims through "scientific" arguments and by pointing out their bias. Both approaches were adopted in greater scope and depth by Graetz.

Heinrich Graetz

Heinrich Graetz[65] was born and educated in a traditional Jewish community in a Polish *shtetl* (under Prussian rule) and studied for a few years with Samson Raphael Hirsch; in 1842 he began to study at the University of Breslau. Graetz viewed himself first and foremost as a historian – not as a religious leader or a theologian. He searched for the essence of Judaism in its "totality," that is, in its history; in doing so he placed himself in opposition on the one hand to the a-historical Orthodox approach, and on the other to the Reform approach, which reduced Judaism solely to its philosophical and moral content. The concept of

---

62   See p. 146ff. above.

63   "I gave them statutes that were not good and ordinances by which they could not live," etc. Dünner interpreted the perplexing verses as indirect speech in which the prophet presents the arguments of the opponents of the Torah. Graetz also pointed out this solution (in the tenth volume, 1868, p. 191), but Dünner recalled that he had anticipated him in his anonymously published Dutch article (Dünner 1869, 460).

64   See p. 148 above.

65   1817, Posen – 1891, Munich. Graetz has been subject of intensive research. His attitude toward the Bible, the biblical period, and biblical criticism has been thoroughly studied, particularly in Michael 1993, 306-365; Shavit and Eran 2007, 133-139; only a general overview of the main points will be provided here, with certain changes in emphasis. See also: Liebeschütz 1967, 132-156; Ettinger 1969; Wiener 1933, 217ff.; and as biblical commentator also: Porges 1917.

Judaism descended into the world through the will of Providence (here
Graetz was influenced by Steinheim); Judaism was eternal and meta-
physical but embodied in the tribe that sustained it, which was itself
eternal; and the transformations of the concept and the tribe were the
very history of Judaism. In a continuing polemic with the Reform
movement, Graetz emphasized the importance of the national aspect of
Judaism in all its historical stages and objected to its abstraction away
from that aspect – an abstraction that in his opinion rendered Judaism a
shadow of itself. Here he departed from the view shared by both Jost
(whose abrupt break between the Israelite and Jewish periods was
vehemently rejected by Graetz) and Wellhausen (as well as other Christian scholars), who saw post-biblical Judaism as a sect or religious
community with no national dimension. Graetz emphasized that "in
Judaism, nation and religion have a single root,"[66] and he even had
positive regard for the role of the Halakhah in preserving barriers between the Jewish people and its environment.

Graetz's periodization of Jewish history was threefold, following
the Hegelian pattern: it was divided into the periods of the First Temple, the Second Temple, and the Diaspora, and each period was itself
divided into three stages. Unlike Hegel's method, however, this
framework did not follow a structure of thesis, antithesis, and synthesis. Jewish history did not develop toward a specific goal, and certainly
was not in a state of decline or degeneration. Here Graetz's critique of
Christian historiography is also evident. Graetz rejected the claim that
after the destruction of the Temple the Jews had no history, and explicitly addressed the Christian prejudice that was expressed in this approach as well as its hidden motivations: "one thereby avoids the difficulty which would loom before any strictly Christian construction of
world history."[67] Graetz was the first Jewish historian to make such a
critique.[68] The whole of his work is characterized by a fine sensitivity to
anti-Semitic prejudice and a strong tendency toward polemic.

Graetz stated that theoretical contemplation – a common pursuit of
the Jewish people throughout the world – and scholarship stood at the
center of the current period of Jewish history. Graetz thus also adopted
the ideology of *Wissenschaft* which was so central in his time: "The
course of history in this period is distinguished by the organization of
schools and systems: Judaism becomes scientific scholarship," he wrote
in "The Structure of Jewish History."[69] To Graetz, "scientific scholar-

---

66   Quoted in Michael 1993, 313.
67   Graetz 1975 <1846>, 94.
68   Michael 1993, 311.
69   Graetz 1975 <1846>, 95.

ship" meant first and foremost the systematic study of history; he had little interest in theology and regarded it with suspicion and even hostility. He fiercely attacked the prominent conservative theologian of the early century, Schleiermacher, and accused him of anti-Jewish bias.[70] In an 1854 critique, Graetz rejoiced over the fact that the strict criteria that prevailed in historical scholarship were applied to ancient Israelite history, and praised two contemporary historians – Menzel and Duncker – who were "very far from theology and thus from prejudice against Judaism." Consequently, he added, they were able to free Jewish history from the obfuscation and certain Christological elements that pervaded it in Ewald's work.[71] Although Graetz was unable to accept all the conclusions of these historians – such as their postdating of the Pentateuch to the time of Jeremiah – his preference for history over theology is nonetheless clear.

Graetz's work frequently dealt with the Bible; it included articles about several biblical books and the volumes of his history that examined the biblical period. Porges has already written extensively about his work as a biblical exegete.[72] Importantly, Graetz postponed dealing with the Bible until the final decades of his life, beginning approximately in 1870. In 1853 he began writing his great work of history, starting at the fourth volume, which covered the Talmudic period, and proceeding forward in history until the eleventh volume, which reached his own era and was published in 1870. Only then, in 1874 – twenty years after launching his great undertaking – did he publish the first volume, which dealt with the biblical period, and the remaining volumes were published over the following years. Graetz attributed this delay to the abundance of material about the period, to its being in the hands of theologians, and to the fact that as a historian he was obliged to examine the sources himself, and this required him to "read the books of the Bible in their land of origin, or to tour the biblical setting with the book in hand";[73] his visit to Palestine took place only in 1872.

In an article in the London-based *Jewish Chronicle* in 1887 Graetz assured his readers that Judaism had nothing to fear from biblical criticism: the "negative" criticism was fundamentally unsound, because those responsible for it – Reuß, Colenso, Wellhausen, and Kuenen – lacked even basic knowledge of Hebrew and their claims were thus groundless. In contrast "positive" criticism was healthy and welcome and could only contribute to strengthening Judaism, because unlike

---

70   Michael 1993, 339-340.
71   Graetz 1854 (the quote is on p. 69).
72   Porges 1917; see also briefly: Soloveitchik and Rubasheff 1925, 139ff.
73   Michael 1993, 348.

Christianity, whose foundation would collapse without the Gospel, Judaism was established on a firm and unshakable foundation – the books of Prophets, Psalms, Proverbs, and others – and because it was not a dogmatic faith:

> If all the miraculous stories in the Old Testament were put down as the legendary creations of imagination or to conscious poetical fancy, still much, very much, would remain that can be regarded as truth. The essential fact remains of the recognition of the unity and the lofty holiness of God; from this follows the demand for a holy life for His servants, for the love of our neighbours, and care for the stranger, the widow, and the orphan; in short, for the lofty ethics which Judaism posits as its ideal, and of which the Ten Commandments offer only a short summary. This essential germ of Judaism cannot be affected by doubts as to the historic reality of the narratives in which it is embodied.[74]

Here and elsewhere Graetz expressed a favorable approach toward biblical criticism and objected to dogmatic attitudes that rejected it at the outset: on the contrary, he believed that critical scholarship could only strengthen Judaism. This approach is understandable given his self-perception as a historian in the modern sense of the word, trained in the critical research methods of his time. Indeed, in his studies of the books of Prophets and Writings, which relied on the full range of contemporary non-Jewish scholarship, Graetz arrived at independent and far-reaching conclusions: he divided Isaiah into six separate books and Hosea into two; he determined that Obadiah was written after and the books of Writings during the days of the Second Temple; he believed that most of the Psalms were written after the return from Babylon, some even during the Hasmonean period, and similarly the epilogue and prologue of Job and the first and final chapters of Proverbs; Daniel and Chronicles, Ezra, Nehemiah, and the Song of Songs were composed in the Hellenistic period; and Ecclesiastes did not appear until the reign of Herod. Yet behind Graetz's favorable approach and radical conclusions lay a rigid distinction, which was already noticed in his time, between the Pentateuch and the other books of the Bible:[75]

> In his critical studies of the Writings, Graetz's work is fearless and fairly radical; likewise in his treatment of the books of Prophets he is revealed as unrestrained by dogmatic ties beyond a deep appreciation for the spirit of these books. But when it comes to the Pentateuch as a book of law, Graetz must be included among the conservative biblical scholars who firmly ob-

---

74   Graetz 1887.
75   Note that Ben Ze'ev (1810), similarly, translated and adapted Eichhorn's critical introduction to cover only the Prophets and Writings, but not the Pentateuch.

jected to the Wellhausen hypothesis regarding its multiple authors and redactors.[76]

This does not mean that Graetz regarded the stories in Genesis as historical evidence: on the contrary, he saw them as myths or fables subject to the Pentateuch's moral views and containing at most certain
kernels of historical truth; but he vigorously rejected the lateness of the
Pentateuch and the retraction of its attribution to Moses, and he did his
best to disprove these claims through academic arguments.

Graetz referred to Pentateuch criticism in two places: in the sixth
note ("The Composition of the Torah or the Pentateuch") to the first
half of the second volume of his Jewish history, which was published in
1875,[77] and in an article published in his own monthly in 1886 dealing
with the "most recent" biblical criticism, particularly Wellhausen's.[78] In
a second, revised edition of the above-mentioned half-volume, edited
by Markus Brann after Graetz's death, the article was included and
printed in full after the sixth note;[79] but in the following we will distinguish between the two reactions, as one predated Wellhausen's work
and the other addressed it.

At the start of the sixth note – written before Wellhausen's
groundbreaking book – Graetz seeks the origin of Pentateuch criticism,
"because all the mistakes and pretensions found in that discipline stem
from its source." Here in effect Graetz constructs a brief history of Pentateuch criticism, whose central actors were actually Jews. The first
critic of the Pentateuch, Graetz claimed, was the Jewish scholar Isaac
Ibn Castar Ben Yashush, known as Yitzchaki, in the eleventh century:
"Yitzchaki said in his book that this section was written during the
days of Jehoshaphat [...] Heaven forbid that such a thing be true, and
his book deserves to be burned," Graetz writes, quoting Ibn Ezra's
commentary on Genesis 36:30. Next came the "trickster" Ibn Ezra himself, who wrote: "If you understand the mystery of the twelve and of
'Moses wrote the Law' and 'the Canaanite was then in the land' and 'it
will be revealed on the mountain of God' and 'behold this bed, a bed of
iron,' then you will know the truth,"[80] thus revealing his opinion that
not all of the Pentateuch was written by Moses. His position served as a
starting point for Spinoza – who was "a first-rate and original philosopher, but understood very little of history and literary criticism." From

---

76 Porges 1917, 54.
77 Graetz 1875, 452-475.
78 Graetz 1886.
79 Graetz 1886 = Graetz 1902, 426-436.
80 Ibn Ezra on Deuteronomy 1:1; see p. 21 above.

there Graetz's history continues with Christian scholars such as Richard Simon and Astruc.

Graetz thus identified Jewish roots in Pentateuch criticism and constructed a sort of Jewish history of it. He did this not out of agreement with Pentateuch criticism (in order to draw legitimacy from earlier Jewish involvement in the discipline, as Reform scholars did) nor in order to malign the critics (as Gugenheimer did), but out of reasoned objection. This makes his attempt to create a Jewish history of the discipline especially interesting: it appears that Graetz tried to deny Christianity a monopoly on criticism, which he perceived as negative. Note the similarity to the anti-eurocentric argument that would emerge at the end of the twentieth century against the "West's outlandish claim to have invented everything, including Evil," in the words of the African-American cultural critic Barbara Christian.[81] According to Graetz even respectable Jews like Ibn Ezra had sinned by engaging in Pentateuch criticism.

Graetz begins his note by summarizing the attempts to divide the Pentateuch into sources based on the various names of God, and points to the fact that while this criterion of Astruc's may have been suitable for the first chapters of Genesis, it was of no benefit in the parts of the Pentateuch dealing with Law. Graetz thus immediately delves into the importance of the Law. Unlike Reform approaches, which considered morality the essential substance of the Pentateuch, Graetz actually places the Law at the center: at the very least, the story of Noah marks the beginning of "the divine education of the human race by means of the Law," and the Patriarchs were "rational law come to life," in Philo's words.[82] Among the non-Jewish critical scholars, Graetz praises Nöldeke for noticing that the legal, not the historical sections form the central part of the Pentateuch. In his praise he also includes Graf – both[83] were the only ones to delve into the legal parts of the Pentateuch; but he rejects their conclusion regarding a later redactor. In contrast, Graetz frequently references the work of older biblical scholars. Not coincidentally these were scholars who belonged to the conservative, "positive" streams, who were at least a generation older than Wellhausen (b. 1844) and found themselves marginalized by the hegemony his method attained. Thus with respect to the division and internal structure of the Pentateuchal laws Graetz refers to Ernst Bertheau (1812–1888), who was part of the exegetical approach to Old Testament criti-

---

81   Quoted in Shohat 1994, 3.
82   Graetz 1875, 462f.
83   Graetz explicitly mentions Nöldeke 1869; it is unclear which of Graf's works he was acquainted with.

cism, which developed out of opposition to historical criticism.[84] In refuting the division of the Pentateuch according to the names of God, Graetz cites Gustav Friedrich Oehler (1812–1872), a professor at Tübingen who belonged to Hengstenberg's conservative school.[85] To argue against the stylistic criterion for dividing the Pentateuch, Graetz relies on the prominent theologian Karl Friedrich Keil (1807–1888), who espoused "criticism that believes in revelation" (*offenbarungsgläubige Kritik*), objected to "negative" criticism, and emphasized the unity of Scripture.[86]

Graetz does not adopt criticism's terminology or its division of the sources. After rejecting the accepted criteria for dividing the beginning of the Pentateuch, he arrives at the conclusion that the narrative portions of Genesis and Exodus are a unity; henceforth he attempts to demonstrate the coherence of the Pentateuch's internal structure, which is built around the legal sections. Graetz does not ignore the repetitions and divergences in those sections, nor does he argue that the Pentateuch was revealed as a whole to Moses at Sinai. He assumes a number of occasions on which different parts of the Law were revealed and finds support for this approach in the text itself, which describes how the laws were given at various times and places. The historical events are the organizing framework that explain the parts of the Law and its contents. For example, the laws in Exodus (23:14-19) concerning festivals were given immediately after the Decalogue; but later, after the sin of the golden calf, with which the Israelites broke the first Commandment, it was necessary to repeat them with particular emphasis on the prohibition of idolatry (Exodus 34:18-26). Thus literal repetition does not testify to the existence of different sources, but is the result of additional revelation, for which the historical circumstances given in the text provide a justification. In this way Graetz demonstrates the unity of the entire Book of Exodus (making no mention of Popper's study on the Tabernacle). Leviticus was related in its content to Exodus: after the creation of the Tabernacle and the relevant laws at the end of Exodus, the sacrificial laws in Leviticus were required (1–7) and thereafter the consecration of the Tabernacle (8–9). After this Aaron's sons committed their sin (10:1-5), and that event explains the need for laws of purity and impurity, which follow immediately. Only Leviticus 27, Graetz admits, cannot be explained according to his method. By similar means he demonstrates the connection between Numbers and its predecessors (again with very few exceptions that Graetz can not resolve).

---

84   Kraus 1982, 169.
85   Rogerson 1984, 139; BBK IV, 1122ff.
86   BBK III, 1293ff.

Thus the first four books of the Pentateuch are shown to be a single work of ongoing revelation, with an internal logic that does not require any assumption of documents, sources, completions, or later redaction, whereas Deuteronomy is evidently a complete, later compilation. The question, Graetz writes, is not who composed each of those two texts, but at what point they became widely known. Here Graetz is willing to distinguish between revelation, through which Scripture came into being, and Scripture's public dissemination. Either way, the second Hosea (Hosea 4–14 in Graetz's method) said "Though I write for him the multitude of my instructions, they are regarded as a strange thing" (8:12), which Graetz corrects to "I write for him the words of my instructions, they are regarded as a strange thing" and interprets as "I wrote down the words of my instructions for it (i.e., for the people), but they were considered alien," meaning that during the prophet's time – during the reign of Ahaz – the Pentateuch was known not only in Judah but also in the Northern Kingdom; and Graetz cites additional verses from the second Hosea and his contemporary Micah[87] which, he claims, prove their familiarity with the first four books of the Pentateuch. As for the date of Deuteronomy, that was mentioned at the start of the book itself – "These are the words that Moses spoke to all Israel beyond the Jordan," and consequently this was the text that was discovered in the Temple during the days of Josiah (2 Kings 23:2).

In short, Graetz uses three main tools to demonstrate the antiquity and unity of the Pentateuch: an argument for multiple events of revelation, which explain repetitions and changes in wording and emphasis; internal evidence about the dates at which laws were revealed, which he accepts as reliable; and a few verses from Hosea and Micah, which testify to a familiarity with the Pentateuch even at this early stage, during the days of the Divided Monarchy. The Pentateuch, according to Graetz, was not revealed in its entirety at Sinai, but rather – as evident from the text itself – at various points during Moses' life.

This was Graetz's approach before the Wellhausen revolution. It seems that during the mid-1870s, members of the Positive–Historical stream really believed that the dangerous form of biblical criticism had reached a dead end. In 1874 Zacharias Frankel published in the stream's monthly an article about "Misunderstood Verses in Genesis," in which he cheerfully announced the death of the "patchwork hypo-

---

87 "In the womb he tried to supplant his brother, and in his manhood he strove with God. He strove with the angel and prevailed, he wept and sought his favour" (Hosea 12:3-4); "Jacob fled to the land of Aram; there Israel served for a wife, and for a wife he guarded sheep" (Hosea 12:12); "O my people, remember now what King Balak of Moab devised, what Balaam son of Beor answered him" (Micah 6:5).

thesis" (*Flickwerk-Hypothese*) that rejected the unity of the Pentateuch. He described it as a "childhood illness" and maintained that no serious scholar would dare argue that the Pentateuch had been composed or redacted during Ezra's time or that Deuteronomy predated the rest of the Pentateuch.[88] Nonetheless – because not every futile critical claim had been discredited as it deserved – he would take the effort to interpret a verse that had been problematic since Ibn Ezra and Spinoza, namely "At that time the Canaanites were in the land" (Genesis 12:6): "At that time," he believed, should be read as "already" rather than "during that time."

The rise of the Graf-Wellhausen hypothesis during the 1880s seems to have embarrassed Positive–Historical scholars. Though the Orthodox Hoffmann had already begun to publish his critique of biblical criticism in the 1870s, and Reform scholars were active all the while, until the mid-1880s the Positive–Historical monthly refrained from engaging in a real discussion of Pentateuch criticism and only sporadically published a few short reviews and articles. A clear sign of this embarrassment is provided by an editorial note on an 1881 review by Hermann Vogelstein about the books of the Reform scholar Siegmund Maybaum. That Vogelstein of all people, who was affiliated with the Reform, was commissioned to review the work of Maybaum, a follower of the Graf-Wellhausen school, is in itself evidence of a certain discomfort, and as one might expect, his favorable review provided no comfort to the editors. Consequently they inserted the following editorial comment:[89]

> Following the principle adhered to in these pages, to grant full freedom to scientific inquiry, this review is published with an explicit condition: to illuminate with counter-notes the groundlessness, frivolity, and hypercritical character of the Graf-Wellhausen theory, upon which Maybaum's book generally relies. Because of the absence of the editor at the time of printing, these notes and corrections were not inserted. They will be published at a later date.

The absent editor of the journal was none other than Heinrich Graetz; but his promised counter-arguments were never published.

Only five years later did Graetz publish his article against Wellhausen, which was printed in two installments in the same monthly.[90] The article begins with a lengthy and detailed attempt to resolve the con-

---

88   Frankel 1874a. (Wishful) assessments regarding the approaching death of biblical criticism were sounded more than once by its opponents before the Wellhausen revolution: cf. above, p. ###.

89   Vogelstein 1881. The editorial comment is on p. 192.

90   Graetz 1886.

tradiction between "For six days you shall continue to eat unleavened bread" (Deuteronomy 16:8) and "Seven days you shall eat unleavened bread" (Exodus 12:15 among others), which served Wellhausen in his description of the development of the cult. Graetz explains that the difference was due to different definitions of the festival that were provided at the different points at which the laws were announced; the Pentateuch itself refers to this in its statements that the first books were revealed at Sinai (Leviticus 27:34) while Deuteronomy was revealed in the land of Moab (Deuteronomy 28:69). Thus, and using his own interpretation of the verse "in every place where I cause my name to be remembered I will come to you and bless you" (Exodus 20:24) – not "everywhere" (*an jedem Orte*) but "at some place" (*an irgend welchem Orte*) – Graetz does away with Wellhausen's theory of the lateness of the legal sections and the centralization of the cult.

In the second part of the article Graetz provides a further list of inconsistencies and difficulties with Wellhausen's theory regarding the lateness of the legal sections: if it was composed in Ezra's time, why does Leviticus (18:3), in its warning against incest, specifically mention the deeds of the Canaanites and the Egyptians, which were irrelevant to the Israelites returning from Babylon? Why provide agrarian and slavery laws to the few returning Israelites, whom Nehemiah describes as slaves of the Babylonian kings? What was the point of the story of Zelophehad's daughters (Numbers 36), the entire moral of which is preserving the tribal territorial laws, if the tribes no longer existed? And most of all: how could Ezra, whose Hebrew was clearly of a later style, write in the style of ancient times? Regarding the rituals of atonement and purification of the Temple – the very essence of the allegedly late Day of Atonement – Graetz also finds evidence in what Wellhausen considered the earliest parts of the Pentateuch (Exodus 29:36-37) and in Prophets (Ezekiel 43:20-22); and in general, if Ezra and his circle acted as a gang of forgers, why did they leave behind incriminating evidence – why did they edit some verses instead of simply deleting them altogether? How did this reconcile with the careful instructions (like *Kri* and *Ktiv*) in their redactions? Graetz also contended with Dozy and other scholars' arguments, and was aided by Dünner's article against Dozy.[91]

But the more interesting section of the second part of the article[92] is Graetz's ideological critique of Wellhausen's approach. Why was Wellhausen so eager to postdate the legal parts of the Pentateuch, Graetz

---

91   The aforementioned Dünner 1869; Graetz 1875, 474.
92   Graetz 1886, 233ff.

wonders; after all the priestly Torah contains, among other things, moral laws of the first order which became the cornerstone of Jewish culture; what does it matter if this part of the Pentateuch is a few centuries younger? Graetz's answer is here translated almost in full:

> But Wellhausen's intent in postdating this part is obvious. It has the pungent scent of bias. This great portion of the Pentateuch is meant to derive not from the context of vibrant national life, but from the circles of an anemic small sect. Beginning in Ezra's time this sect went about its own business for a while, making use of the strict Levitical laws, until it became irrelevant and now "a vessel no one wants";[93] this is the bias of [Wellhausen's] *Prolegomena to the History of Israel*. One can guess in advance how this story will end. Wellhausen swims in a stream created by the great German historians of our time, in the stream of subjective historiography that worships success and glorifies power. A cult of heroes. [...] Imperators, legions and divisions, the gleam of weaponry and diplomatic victories are once again at the forefront of world history. Anything that is weak, that is trampled by the victors' Titanic stride merits disdain from this school of historical thought. *Vae victis!* The fallen are counted only to illuminate the great victory of the strong. And here is a people, who despite its repeated defeats nonetheless remains strong in its weakness and has achieved universal historical importance. The history of Israel is thus an undeniable exception to the rule. It has carried out a cultural mission without violent means. The mighty stream of civilizatory deeds in Judea must drain into the manger at Bethlehem, or – as Wellhausen wishes to describe it – perhaps it was no stream, but just a trickle which would have been lost in the sands had not a mystical messianism made it flow. Wellhausen's history of Israel, as we could say from the outset, is far more tendentious than Ewald's. He will now surely find in Germany a most favorable climate for the pragmatism, albeit concealed, of his Israelite history.[94]

The article concludes with the following remark:

> David Strauss once noted that it was always possible to judge the political climate among the ten thousand most privileged people in Germany by the dominant theological stream, because both tended to be on the same level. Well, then, theology or biblical criticism in the hands of some daring critics has truly reached the edge of nihilism. It will be most unfortunate if the political climate follows along in lockstep.[95]

More than any other Jewish scholar in this study, Graetz placed Wellhausen's method in its broader critical context. In it Graetz identified an anti-Jewish bias which saw the Jewish Law as a later product of an "anemic, small" sect that existed for just a short period, and not as the product of a healthy, independent nation (according to the Romantic,

---

93   Originally in Hebrew; cf. Jeremiah 22:28.
94   Graetz 1886, 234f.
95   Graetz 1886, 251.

nationalist perception of Herder's *Spirit of Hebrew Poetry*), and thus minimizing the value of both the Law and its Jewish creators and preservers. Graetz saw this as a continuation of the Christological bias in that it shrank the essence of Judaism into a tiny kernel that was only saved from oblivion by Christianity, and he pointed to the similarity between this Christological bias and the Christian bias in general, which diverted all of Judaism into "the manger at Bethlehem." Graetz also placed his argument in a more overarching context of power relations – of power-worship and history written by the victors: Judaism posed a paradox for historians precisely because its political weakness contradicted its success in terms of the history of ideas. Christian historians, who stood on the victors' side, tried to overcome this paradox by creating a division between Judaism, on the defeated side, and its contents, which became the spoils of victorious Christianity. In addition to all this Graetz hinted at historiography's contemporary bias – the fact that theology represented the dominant mood in Germany and was tightly bound to political developments there; undoubtedly he was referring in part to the rise of anti-Semitism. One year later, in his article in the *Jewish Chronicle*, he explicitly wrote of Wellhausen that "his criticism is largely influenced by his anti-Semitism which he takes no pains to disguise. He vents his antipathy against a Jewish nose on Abraham, Moses, and Ezra."[96]

Conclusion and Evaluation

The Positive–Historical engagement with biblical criticism in the nineteenth century was minimal: for many years Dünner's minor article against Dozy filled that need, and later it was expressed primarily in the work of Graetz. There are signs of embarrassment and avoidance of the subject, which may even explain why Graetz postponed his own biblical studies to the final decades of his life. While criticism of the Prophets and Writings did not pose particular difficulties for him and he took it up without hesitation, Graetz did not address the Pentateuch until a much later stage and ultimately did so from a clearly conservative position. Unlike Orthodox Judaism, Graetz rejected the historicity of the early stories in Genesis and read them as fables with a moral or legal message; but with regard to the division of the Pentateuch into sources he adopted a wholly conservative stance and viewed the entire Pentateuch as a divine revelation of God to Moses. Graetz did not re-

---

96   Graetz 1887.

quire the Pentateuch to be given all at once in a single act of revelation; he believed the Pentateuch was revealed bit by bit in Moses' day, and if it contained repetitions, redactions, and even contradictions, the solution to these could be found only in the specific historical context of the brief time between the revelation at Sinai and Moses' death. Nothing was composed or redacted during Josiah's reform; rather, the book that was found in the Temple was rediscovered and read in public. In each of these arguments Graetz adhered to the literal reading of the biblical text and rejected any attempt to question it. In discounting the Christological element, Graetz's approach resembled that of the non-Jewish "positive criticism," which also admitted the contradictions in the text but tried to resolve them in systematic ways that would prompt no religious difficulties; indeed, Graetz was aided by the findings of that approach.

Such attempts – to settle the difficulties raised in one verse by means of another – occupied Graetz before the rise of the Wellhausen school. After Wellhausen's hypothesis was published, in the mid-1880s, Graetz transferred at least part of the struggle to a new battlefield: the meta-disciplinary, ideological, and political field of biblical criticism. In Wellhausen's approach Graetz identified Christian and anti-Jewish biases, and he considered it an example of the power-worshiping historical approach of the rising anti-Semitic trends in Germany. In these articles Graetz broke through the barriers of engagement with biblical criticism and demonstrated that such engagement was part of the overarching struggle over the image of Judaism and the ideology of modern Western historiography.

C. Reform Judaism

The challenge that biblical criticism posed to Reform Judaism was perhaps the greatest of all. On the one hand, Reform Judaism had a very close relationship with liberal Protestant Christianity. On a philosophical–ideological level this closeness, which has been covered in detail by Uriel Tal,[97] stemmed from the fact that both camps derived from rationalist schools and were to a great extent continuations – perhaps the last remaining ones – of the Enlightenment. At the end of the nine-

---

97 Tal 1975, 160-222, whose use of the term "liberal Judaism" I follow: "[...] the groups, whether organized or amorphous, that did not belong to the Orthodoxy or did not identify with it, but which nevertheless defined their Judaism as a religion and wished to maintain some kind of a tie with the Jewish public or religion" (Tal 1975, 164).

teenth century the two camps turned to the discipline of history, and in that context to Protestant biblical criticism, in an attempt to find in them positive content that could be of use in the modern reality. Reform Judaism had a firm obligation to *Wissenschaft*: "the general sphere in which Judaism must be placed," as Wiener put it,[98] was demarcated among other things by rationalism and the scholarly ethos. Reform Judaism's attraction to biblical criticism was thus inevitable. On the other hand, as we have already seen, the historical narrative of Christian biblical criticism included a sharp criticism of Judaism and a negative image of it as a "religion of Law." According to this image, Judaism – no later than the Return from Babylon and in effect even earlier – replaced Israelitism, and prophecy and its values were displaced by adherence to the dead letter of the Law in a process described as one of decay and petrification. This depiction was doubly problematic for Reform Judaism. On the one hand, the Reform movement itself relied on elements of that negative depiction in its struggle with the conservative streams within Judaism. Popper, for example, in his aforementioned book, used typical anti-rabbinical terminology such as "religion of Law," "rabbinism," "adherence to the written letter" and so on,[99] and this scathing critical attitude was characteristic of Reform Judaism, particularly in its early stages.[100] A central goal of the Reform movement was to reduce, simplify, and limit the practical commandments – "the Law" – and to define a small number of fundamental commandments that would "suit the modern world." On the other hand, fully accepting the negative image of the Law was impossible, and was even liable to become a double-edged sword that would injure the Reform movement itself. Consequently Reform Judaism had an ambivalent approach to biblical criticism. There was also a difference between the attitude of typical scholars – Abraham Geiger and others – and that of a typical popularizer such as Ludwig Philippson.

---

98   Wiener 1933, 240.

99   For example: "Let us imagine ourselves in those times, in the centuries following the exile, when people began more and more to cling fearfully and firmly to the written letter of the Law, when the literal, exact being of the written word became an expression of the most lofty thing one must aspire to in religion – in short, when the Jewish spirit delved deeply into the direction that we know as 'legalism,' as the perspective of the *nomos*, on whose basis the entire gigantic structure of rabbinism was later constructed [...] this ambition of the redactors, sickly and distorted as it might seem to us [...]" (Popper 1862, 81).

100 Schorsch 1994, 317.

Abraham Geiger

Let us first examine Abraham Geiger (1810–1874), the "father of the Reform" even if he did not initiate it. Geiger was both a rabbi and a scholar, but when the two vocations conflicted he always preferred the scholarly approach; he once even expressed regret that he had chosen the rabbinical profession.[101] He certainly would have preferred to study Judaism in an academic setting, an ambition he tried in vain to realize at a German university.

The primary goal of Geiger's great scholarly project was to historicize Judaism, which would once again enable the Reform movement to utilize a significant part of normative Judaism's inalienable assets. Traditional Judaism's self-image was static: Judaism existed in a sort of continual present in which every generation preserved the heritage of its predecessors, or at least developed it in accordance with fixed, eternal laws. Geiger took it upon himself to historicize the entire Jewish canon. For Geiger, every text reflected an understanding of its own time and the reasons for which it was created, including the struggles that took place during that period. No text was immune to historical criticism; the validity of every element in the history of the Jewish religion was relative, subject to the test of time and likely to change or be overturned by the course of history. Thus every element was dependent on the judgment of the present day. In such an approach the traditional texts were no longer an eternal norm but rather sources of the Jewish spirit, and it was that spirit which connected the different periods of Jewish history into a single whole. Geiger's approach stood in contrast to the Orthodox one of consecrating each and every text (and Geiger was caught in bitter struggles with Orthodox Judaism); but his approach also opposed the demands of some radical reformists to comprehensively reject all the traditional texts and create a new Judaism, a "Mosaic faith" that would be founded on enlightened principles alone.[102]

This was the ideological backdrop to Geiger's extensive and varied work, which pointed to a fundamental rift between the oral and written laws and between the Talmud (particularly the Babylonian) and the Mishna, questioned the principles of *midrash halakhah*, and more. Already in his great work on the Bible and its translations (the *Urschrift*, 1857) Geiger declared the existence of an ancient Sadducee Halakhah which was cast aside by the Pharisee Halakhah only after the suppres-

---

101 Geiger L. 1878, 29.
102 Meyer 1988, 94.

sion of the Bar Kokhba revolt (132–136 CE); he also subordinated the biblical text itself to its historical context and the internal conflicts that accompanied its transmission.

Michael Meyer has distinguished between Geiger's activity as a scholar and that as a rabbi and preacher: "Neither historical criticism nor agitation for ritual reforms was the substance of Geiger's sermons."[103] As a preacher he adopted an a-historical approach; he called the Judaism he preached in his sermons "prophetic Judaism," and its most important element became the prophets' moral message, which he perceived as universal and applicable beyond its original contexts. Geiger presented these ideals – concern for the poor and oppressed, the ideal of world peace, derision for literal cult – as the eternal foundations of Judaism. In this too he represented and even defined a typical stance for the Reform movement as a whole.

Geiger's approach to the Bible and biblical criticism has already been the subject of a number of studies; here, a general overview will suffice.[104] Geiger became familiar with the work of Herder and Eichhorn at an early age; later he was profoundly influenced by Strauss's *Life of Jesus* and de Wette's autobiography. He knew Vatke, George, and Hitzig personally, and met and corresponded with Nöldeke.[105] Throughout his active years he maintained a very positive attitude toward biblical criticism, even when it was taboo among Jews. This is abundantly documented. Already in 1847 he insisted on including biblical exegesis and even biblical criticism in the "Jewish *Wissenschaft*" and expected Jews to once again achieve a respectable place in biblical scholarship as a counterbalance to its Christian biases.[106] He attacked Jews who feared criticism;[107] in his journal he frequently reviewed works dealing with criticism and biblical history.[108] As we have seen, he enthusiastically welcomed Popper's 1862 book. In reviewing it he distinguished between two types of belief: external–dogmatic (*äusserlich*

---

103 Meyer 1988, 95.
104 Perles 1910; Liebeschütz 1967, 113-132; Wiener 1933, 239-253 and more; Meyer 1975; Sarna 1975; Meyer 1988, 89-99; Michael 1993, 279-300; Bechtoldt 1995, 195-288; Schorsch 1994, 311-319.
105 Eichhorn: Sarna 1975, 18; de Wette: Geiger, L. 1878, 26; Vatke and George: Geiger, L. et al. 1910, 67; Hitzig and Nöldeke: Geiger, L. 1878, 259, 321.
106 Geiger, A. 1847.
107 Geiger, L. 1878, 183.
108 For example, a review of Hupfeld's article on the theology and exegesis of Scripture (Geiger, A. 1862b); on Graf, Kohler, Derenburg, and many others (Geiger, A. 1867); on Hausrath and Hupfeld's writings on biblical historiography (Geiger, A. 1869a); on Ewald's monograph (Geiger, A. 1869b); on Lagarde's book on Pentateuchal criticism (Geiger, A. 1860c); on Kuenen's Dutch study about the Masoretic version (Geiger, A. 1875); and more.

dogmatisch) faith that relied on facts, scriptures, and personalities and disappeared when they did – a faith typical of the Sadducees and Samaritans; and internal–vital (*innerlich lebendig*) faith, characteristic of the Pharisees and rabbinic Judaism, which relied on the doctrine of revelation and used it as a measuring rod for evaluating facts, scriptures, and personalities. Revelation in Judaism was stripped of any concrete aspect and remained as revelation in spirit only; no longer was it exposed to external subversion. As a result, Geiger declared, not only did Judaism have no reason to fear criticism, but on the contrary: "Knowing the true Judaism is possible through, and only through, criticism of the Talmud and the Bible."[109] Already in 1863 Geiger published in his journal a very radical article by B. Wechsler, who declared – à la George – that the Day of Atonement was invented at a late date and that neither the prophets nor the ancient laws of Exodus and Deuteronomy were familiar with it.[110] Years later he praised Zunz's radical work.[111] During his final years in Berlin, Geiger was the first to introduce biblical criticism into the curriculum of the rabbinical Seminary.[112]

This enthusiastic support in principle, which characterized Geiger throughout his life, contrasts sharply with the fact that in practice his work rarely dealt with biblical criticism. Again, the *Urschrift* refrains altogether from dealing with "the most ticklish subject of all"[113] – the history of Israel during the days of the First Temple; Geiger himself, in his sympathetic review of Popper's book, clarified that in the *Urschrift* he did not address the formation or redaction of the text but only its transmission.[114] In his final days, during the 1873-1874 academic year, he gave a seminar at the *Hochschule für die Wissenschaft des Judenthums* in Berlin that did address biblical criticism. This was probably a daring act in itself, but the findings of his research were limited in scope: they involved primarily the division of Genesis into an Elohistic and a Yahwistic source and an attempt to trace the socio-geographical origins of those sources.[115]

Why did Geiger engage so little in biblical criticism? The question has been asked in the past and answered in various ways. It was first raised by Max Wiener:

---

109 Geiger, A. 1862a, 124.
110 Wechsler 1863.
111 Geiger, A. 1875.
112 Perles 1910, 326; Sarna 1975, 22.
113 In the words of Meyer 1988, 93.
114 Geiger, A. 1862a.
115 Geiger, A. 1875-1878 IV, 222-279.

It is almost impossible to understand the fact that the critical investigation into the most ancient history of Israel's literature and religion [...] passed over him without stirring intense interest. At the same time, the prophets' moral monotheism increasingly became an essential positive part of his theology, and a critical examination of the formation and status of the biblical laws would have been likely to shed light on his concept of historical development.[116]

Nahum Sarna attempted to resolve the difficulty as follows: "If we wonder, then, why Geiger neglected the study of the Pentateuch, the answer is not embarrassment or cowardice, but that Protestant scholars had already largely preempted the field and had produced the conclusions he needed."[117] Sarna's effort is not particularly convincing: indeed, embarrassment and cowardice were probably not an issue, and while it was true that Protestant scholars had thoroughly investigated the field, Geiger was well aware of the fact that their conclusions were not the ones he needed. On the contrary, shortly before his death he wrote in his periodical that "Despite my esteem for Christian scholarship on the topic, its work has consisted only of preliminary attempts that are usually quite insufficient and have arrived at no real findings, whether positive or even negative";[118] similarly, in one of his final letters to Nöldeke he implicitly criticized the fact that a scholarly discipline so important to Judaism remained entirely in Christian hands.[119]

A more complex answer to the same question has been proposed by Liebeschütz.[120] In his opinion, Geiger retained something of the traditional Jewish concept of revelation that he considered similar to the natural religion of reason (*Naturreligion der Vernunft*) and which was the eternal legacy of Judaism to the world. Historicization allowed Geiger to separate between the kernel and shell of Judaism in general and biblical law in particular by means of this revelation, which was both the origin of Judaism and its final destination. Liebeschütz believes that Geiger was afraid lest historicizing the Pentateuch would drive the holiness of the ancient biblical world from the modern world and would thwart his identification – which combined both enlightened and traditional Jewish a-historicity – between the original kernel of revelation at Sinai and the religion of reason.

Is this answer convincing? I find it doubtful. First of all, it does not sit well with the unqualified support that Geiger demonstrated toward

---

116 Wiener 1933, 252.
117 Sarna 1975, 23.
118 Geiger, A. 1871, 274.
119 A letter to Nöldeke from July 13, 1874 (some three months before Geiger's sudden death). Quoted in Liebeschütz 1967, 131.
120 Liebeschütz 1967, 132.

biblical criticism and Pentateuch criticism in particular. Secondly, if Geiger required any sort of revelation as the basis of his own Judaism it seems he would surely have insisted on the revelation to the prophets rather than the revelation at Sinai. In my opinion the most convincing answer to the question is still Wiener's, which claims that "the rabbinic literature was what served as a starting point for Geiger even from a scientific perspective," and that "his theoretical interests were always influenced by practical motivations, and the aim of these interests was changing rabbinic Judaism."[121] His answer also accords with Geiger's own admittedly early remark that "Only when we have finally done with the Talmud will biblical criticism have its turn."[122]

But this too is only a partial answer; it must be filled in with what emerges from Geiger's great studies on post-biblical subjects, which dealt with the question "what did Mohammed borrow from Judaism," with the Sadducees and the Pharisees, with Jesus' Judaism, and so on. In a typical post-colonialist step Geiger chose to reverse the perspective, and instead of dealing with the Christian view of Judaism (by engaging with biblical criticism) he preferred to examine Christianity (and Islam) through Jewish eyes. Geiger moved from a politics of "blackness" to a politics of "whiteness": instead of contending with the claims that Jews were alien to European culture by reconstructing Jewish history, he preferred to do so by creating a revision and counter-history precisely of Christian Europe and demonstrating to what extent the Jewish legacy stood at the center of European Christianity. This fascinating tactic is explored in detail by Susannah Heschel.[123]

Ludwig Philippson

Not all of Reform Judaism shared Geiger's unambiguous esteem for biblical criticism. Although throughout his life he remained close to the community and his preacher's pulpit, Geiger represented the intellectual end of the spectrum – the scholar at the forefront of Reform; and as we have seen, from his pulpit Geiger played slightly different tunes. In contrast we have Liebeschütz's remark that Ludwig Philippson largely represented the position of average Jewish intellectuals;[124] it is therefore interesting to examine his views, which are rather different than Geiger's. Philippson was not a great scholar. He was mostly a journalist,

---

121 Wiener 1933, 253.
122 Letter to Jacob Auerbach, January 13, 1846 (Geiger, A. 1875-1878 V, 188).
123 Heschel 1998; 1999.
124 Liebeschütz 1978, 5; see similar sentiments in: Wiener 1933, 167f.

writer, and popularizer; he published most of his articles in his own journal. He was considered a moderate reformist, and his popular weekly, the *Allgemeine Zeitung des Judentums*, reflected the moods of the Jewish community at large. Tracing Philippson's own articles published in his journal throughout the period can illustrate those moods. Philippson appears to have attempted to find the golden mean between the Orthodoxy, which rejected biblical criticism out of hand, and many Reform scholars, such as Geiger and others, who greeted it favorably.

Philippson's first article, which was published in the *Allgemeine Zeitung des Judenthums* in January 1857 and briefly touched on biblical criticism, has been mentioned above. In it Philippson declares that "Critical activity has now more or less been exhausted." He distinguishes between three forms of biblical exegesis: literal exegesis, which views the words of the text as sacred and wishes to derive from them rules of conduct (*halakhah*), mystical meanings (*kabbalah*), or religious or moral ideas (*aggadah*); the critical approach, which was, again, exhausted; and a third form proposed by Philippson which would "attempt to identify and revive the moral–religious conception; which would strive to judge the content and significance of the Bible from a universal historical perspective, determine its importance to human culture as a whole and increase its influence." Philippson also proposes to apply this new approach to the biblical law: if the first, literal, form of exegesis wishes to address the specific content of the Law, while the second, critical, approach scatters the laws over hundreds of years and questions their validity, the third approach seeks "the general content of specific teachings" and thus "generalize[s] the discrete, specific judgments to general and basic rules that express a universal truth." For example, the biblical prohibition on plowing simultaneously with a bull and a mule[125] is not restricted only to those two animals but contains a general teaching prohibiting unnatural combinations.

A few years later – in the issue published August 23, 1864, a week before the review of Dozy's book – the top article in the *Allgemeine Zeitung des Judenthums* again reflected the Jewish community's current atmosphere, which in the meantime had changed significantly.[126] This time Philippson was called on to defend Judaism's very right to exist, which some believed was being questioned by biblical criticism. Were the critics correct in claiming that the floor was collapsing beneath Judaism's feet, that an axe was aimed at its roots or lodged deep within its flesh? Now criticism was not perceived as a phase whose time had

---

125 Deuteronomy 22:10
126 Philippson 1864a.

passed but rather – in spite of its contradictions and confusion – as a tangible threat to Judaism. Philippson grounded Judaism in its history and on moral–religious principles, and thus inoculated it from biblical criticism: "Whoever is convinced that the Sabbath is necessary, will not let its sanctity hang on investigations of the various sources of Exodus and Deuteronomy." Judaism was the teachings of God, the Creator, the unique – teachings of the equality and unity of all mankind, of mankind's moral and religious mission; Judaism was these ideas clothed in a 4000-year-old history, an effort to sanctify life and custom according to these ideas. What, Philippson asked, did such a Judaism have to fear or hope from studies about the authorship or date of Scripture? Biblical criticism should therefore be accepted and evaluated without prejudice. Not only did it pose no danger, but on the contrary it was possible that it of all things would encourage study of the Bible and thus increase the power of its eternal truths. While in 1857 Philippson had announced the death of biblical criticism and attempted to rescue the Bible for the sake of (Reform) Judaism, seven years later he already felt a clear need to protect Judaism from biblical criticism.

The rest of Philippson's engagement with biblical criticism was essentially a development and refinement of these principles.[127] His attitude toward biblical criticism became more negative over the years: to his regular claims that criticism was dubious, confused, and unstable he added an accusation that the goal of criticism – "in part consciously, in part unconsciously" – was to question the basis of any positive religion, a basis that could be found in the Bible. By deconstructing Scripture, Philippson admitted in 1879, criticism achieved that goal, and this negative achievement dwarfed all its benefits.

What could be done against such criticism? Strictly refuting the critical hypotheses was indeed necessary, but it could not keep the danger at bay. The only effective method was to find a solid basis for faith that would stand strong in spite of criticism. "The Unity of the Ideas in Israel's Holy Scripture" – the title of Philippson's main article on the subject[128] – is the solid basis that he proposes therein. Even if Scripture itself were deconstructed and dissolved, throughout the biblical books there is still a strand of conceptual unity. Once that unity is demonstrated, the questions raised by criticism about the development of those ideas will naturally be relevant to both history and literature; but criticism will not have the power to disrupt faith, because it is founded on the basis of the overarching conceptual unity expressed in the He-

---

127 Philippson 1871-1872; Philippson 1879; Philippson 1885a; Philippson 1885b.
128 "Die Einheit der Ideen in der heiligen Schrift Israels," Philippson 1879 (= Philippson 1911 II, 91-160).

brew Bible. Philippson even insists that "biblical criticism start again from the beginning on the basis that we are attempting to establish and construct for it – that is, departing from the spirit, from reflection."[129] Incidentally, Philippson already emphasized the internal conceptual unity of the Pentateuch and the unity of the Bible in the introduction to his Bible translation.[130] On this point, it is surprising to discover that Philippson shared a real similarity with S.R. Hirsch and his "uniform spirit" of the Bible.

In his article Philippson attempts to prove the existence of the conceptual unity of Scripture by constructing a sort of theology and philosophy of the ideas that form the basis of the biblical conception. Their unity is demonstrated by searching through all the books of the Bible, from Genesis to Chronicles, for supporting verses. Among the ideas Philippson enumerates:[131] God as the Creator of the world; His absolute unity, spirituality, omnipotence, wisdom, and goodness; revelation, the dietary laws, the Sabbath, circumcision, the Law (as an idea and an institution), sacrifice, and more. In this way Philippson avoids a direct confrontation with any particular biblical critic, and merely provides proof (supporting verses) from the Bible for each of these central ideas. The insight at the basis of Philippson's engagement with biblical criticism in this article seems similar to Jost's (see above, chapter 3), though his formulations fall short of the latter's. His rescue of the conceptual unity of the Bible as Judaism's foundational literary work resembles Jost's claim that the Jews were shaped not by their history but by the account of that history presented in the Bible itself.

A few years later[132] Philippson would distinguish between "biblical science" and "biblical criticism": The former (biblische Wissenschaft) aimed to study and describe the overarching unity of the Bible (in the spirit of his suggestions above), while the latter was merely one of the disciplines auxiliary to or within that "scientific" framework, and not necessarily the most important one. Philippson admitted that many Jewish scholars avoided biblical criticism – although he distinguished between its concrete findings, such as the division of Isaiah, which even these scholars accepted,[133] and Pentateuch criticism – but in his opinion

---

129 Philippson 1879, 419.
130 Philippson 1858, i-xxx.
131 Philippson 1879.
132 Philippson 1885a.
133 E.g. David Cassel, whose book about the history of Jewish literature indeed skirted the subject of biblical criticism entirely, but accepted the division of Isaiah (Cassel 1872 II, 130). The book was published through the Institut zur Förderung der israelitischen Literatur (Institute for the Promotion of the Israelite Literature), of which Philippson was a member.

this made them worthy of praise rather than condemnation. What was truly deplorable was the meager Jewish involvement in "biblical science."

Philippson perceived himself as a sort of happy medium between Orthodoxy and "extreme" Reform. The former was unwilling to accept any criticism and took refuge in dogmatism; in contrast, Reformist scholars were overly eager to join in criticism's labor of destruction. Philippson wished to remain loyal to scholarship in the "pure" sense of the word, despite his objection to the actual form "biblical science" took:[134] "Regarding scientific, truly scientific truth, liberal prejudice is as invalid as Orthodox prejudice." Radical Reform sought to base Judaism on the prophets' morality alone and to reject Mosaism; Philippson wished to prove that the prophets were a continuation, a second stage in the development of Mosaism,[135] and he devoted two articles to demonstrating that the prophets were familiar with the Pentateuch even before the days of Josiah.[136]

Philippson the popularizer did not pretend to delve deeply into biblical criticism, nor did he present it in particular detail to his readers. The issues that arose from biblical criticism and penetrated the consciousness of the greater Jewish community were twofold: first, the division of the Pentateuch into numerous sources written or edited in various periods; secondly, the claim that the Pentateuch was a late composition unknown to the prophets. The first claim was an old one, and Philippson contended with it by identifying the conceptual unity of the Bible. The second was new and derived from the Graf-Wellhausen hypothesis, and Philippson attempted to disprove it with the aid of relevant quotations. In effect Philippson accepted the fundamental academic approach to the study of Scripture. He made no pronouncements regarding divine inspiration or sacrilege on the part of academic scholarship, but he did attempt to divert the focus of its interest in the Bible from questions of composition and dating to a conceptual discussion of the Bible's overall theology and philosophy. Consequently he spoke for the traditional, pre-Wellhausen historical view according to which prophecy developed from the Pentateuch and Judaism developed from both. Yet this historical picture was not presented with any pretensions of religious sanctity but as a measured and objective truth that avoided any extremism – whether critical–scientific or dogmatic. Philippson refrained from listing the names of scholars who agreed with his position, just as he refrained from engaging in a

---

134 Philippson 1879, 419.
135 Philippson 1885b, 766.
136 Philippson 1871-1872; Philippson 1885b.

polemic with the scholars he opposed. Thus he gave the impression of representing a realistic approach based on common sense and simple logic, rather than any Jewish or Christian school whose position could be accepted or rejected.

Kaufmann Kohler, Leopold Zunz, and Others

Jewish scholars of a liberal orientation did not in effect refrain from accepting the conclusions of biblical criticism and studying the Bible, or even the Pentateuch, with a critical–historical approach; a sort of tradition emerged of Reform Jewish scholars who accepted biblical criticism to a greater or lesser degree and even referred to each other's work. Let us briefly survey a few of these. We have already encountered David Einhorn, the radical reformist who emigrated in 1855 to the United States of America, and his 1854 book which relied on the documentary hypothesis of the Pentateuch, as well as Julius Popper's important book about the Tabernacle.[137] Julius Fürst[138] – who studied with Gesenius – published in 1867 the first volume of his book about the history of biblical literature,[139] in which he adopted premises accepted in the more radical stream of biblical criticism at the time, on the eve of the Graf-Wellhausen revolution.[140] He relied on a long list of Christian scholars, beginning with Herder and Michaelis, through de Wette, Vatke, and George, and culminating with Ewald, Gesenius, and Hupfeld; among the Jewish scholars he mentioned were Geiger, Steinthal, and Luzzatto. Fürst attributed parts of the Pentateuch to Moses himself but identified earlier layers dating to the time of the Patriarchs (2000–1710 BCE) and divided the text between the narrator (*Erzähler*) and the supplementer (*Ergänzer*). In the legal sections of the Pentateuch he distinguished between three sources – laws that predated the revelation at Sinai, laws given during that revelation, and later laws – but attributed all of them to the work of Moses; Moses' national constitution, like Solon's constitution which was written 500 years later, included justice, religion, and morality and was deeper and more comprehensive than the laws of

---

137 Einhorn 1854 (see p. 135 above); Popper 1862 (p. 136 above).

138 Fürst (1805, Posen – 1873, Leipzig) was the first Jew to be appointed a professor; he taught Semitic languages and Biblical studies at the University of Leipzig. He studied with Hegel and Gesenius and worked with Zunz; the conservative Franz Delitzsch was one of his students (Kraus 1982, 163).

139 Fürst 1867.

140 About Gesenius see for example: Rogerson 1984, 50ff.

Athens or Rome.[141] In his preface he noted that the Bible (including the New Testament!) should be treated as the national literature of the people of Israel and studied like the literature of any other nation, while refraining both from religious dogmatism and any "obsessive desire for rationalist skepticism" (*rationalistische Zweifelsucht*), and from attempting to deny any uniqueness to the people of Israel.[142]

In 1867 Kaufmann Kohler published a study of Jacob's blessing which earned him the doctorate at the University of Erlangen. Relying among others on his teacher Geiger and on his method, he analyzed Genesis 49 and determined that the chapter had been composed during the period of Judges. In Kohler's opinion the Pentateuch was the product of the prophetic and priestly activity then in development. It was the fruit of the prophets' endless labor; prophecy was preferable to the Law and had shaped it. "The alpha and omega of Judaism is not the Law, but the eternal moral concept," he wrote, characteristically, in his introduction.[143] A year later Kohler published an article about the death penalty in the Bible; this was written for the purposes of a German polemic – in order to refute the argument that appeared in Hengstenberg's journal about "the shameful injury to the Word of God by the abolishment of the death penalty in Saxony" – but provides an illustrative example of Kohler's attitude toward the Law. Kohler argues that the biblical laws were tailored to their cultural environment and to the inferior moral stature of the ancient Israelites. These laws – whether relating to slavery, polygamy, or the death penalty – should not be approached in a literal or dogmatic manner; instead, their moral essence should be extracted and adapted to the moral level of the universal Judeo-Christian culture (*die jüdisch-christliche Weltkultur*) which developed in the intervening millennia.[144]

Kohler's stance toward biblical criticism was considered very radical in its time. This does not mean that he was blind to its Christian biases; later he would even claim: "All our Bible critics, Old Testament critics like Reuss and Wellhausen [...] with very few exceptions [...] are Christians only in so far as they hate whatever is Jewish."[145] But it became clear to him that because of his positions he would be unable to obtain a position as a rabbi in Germany, though he was ordained as

---

141 Fürst 1867, 288, 470ff.
142 Fürst 1867, V-VII.
143 Kohler, K. 1867. The quote is on p. vii. On Kohler's biblical criticism – including his work in that field during his American period – see: Bechtoldt 1995, 289-362.
144 Kohler, K. 1868.
145 Kohler, K. 1902, 417.

one.[146] In 1869, shortly after the publication of his two studies, David Einhorn – whose daughter would eventually marry Kohler – invited him to serve as a rabbi in Detroit. That both Einhorn and Kohler settled in America is no coincidence: the United States were perceived as far more advanced than Germany with respect to religious freedom. In a lecture in New York in 1887, Kohler spoke of the radical critical positions he had held in his youth and said: "I would in all likelihood not breathe the free air of America to-day, had I not many years ago been one of the first to publicly voice them."[147]

Aaron Bernstein based his critical study *Ursprung der Sagen von Abraham, Isaak und Jakob* (The Origin of the Legends of Abraham, Isaac, and Jacob), which was published in 1871, on the premise that the Pentateuch was not written by a single author but compiled from earlier texts which were since lost.[148] Bernstein identified three separate parts in the accounts of the Patriarchs, each of which revolved around a separate religious center: Abraham in Hebron, Isaac in Beer-sheba, and Jacob in Bethel; only after the exile were these stories consolidated and the three made Patriarchs of Israel. Zunz read the book and wrote him: "Forget the Orthodox and all the other stubborn bulls; I also do not think of the characters in Genesis – except perhaps for Nimrod – as historical figures."[149]

Indeed, a particularly radical contribution to the field belongs to Leopold Zunz himself, who, on reaching 80 in 1873 and after a long silence on the subject, published the results of his studies in biblical criticism. The first part of the study was published in the *Zeitschrift der deutschen morgenländischen Gesellschaft*, a central non-Jewish periodi-

---

146 Kohler, M. 1913, 4f.

147 Kohler, K. 1916. In this lecture – which, because of its American context, is beyond the scope of this book – Kohler emphasized that only a liberal approach to the Bible provided a broad and solid base for Reform Judaism: "The Bible is holy, *not because it is inspired, but because, and in so far as it does still, inspire*" (Kohler, K. 1916, 179). Kohler limited divine inspiration to the moral laws of the Pentateuch, while the rest – circumcision, dietary, and sacrificial laws – were not Jewish in origin, even though the divine legislator imbued them with moral content (Haberman 1998, 90). The Pittsburgh Platform of 1885, which Kohler authored, would include the following text: "[...] to-day we accept as binding only [the] moral laws [...] We hold that all such Mosaic and rabbinical laws as regulate diet, priestly purity and dress originated in ages and under the influence of ideas entirely foreign to our present mental and spiritual state" (quoted in Meyer 1988, 388).

148 Bernstein (1812, Danzig – 1884, Berlin) was a popular writer on politics and natural sciences and one of the founders of the Reform community in Berlin. See also: Schoeps 1992.

149 Bernstein 1893, 90.

cal;[150] it dealt with Deuteronomy, Ezekiel, Leviticus, and Esther. The second part of the study was not published in the same periodical;[151] the two parts were published together in Zunz's collected writings two years later.[152] Of his Jewish predecessors Zunz mentions Geiger, Popper (1862), and Bernstein (1871) in footnotes. Among his conclusions: Deuteronomy consists of three sources; Deuteronomy and Ezekiel do not mention the death penalty for working on the Sabbath; Deuteronomy is not familiar with Passover, the Day of Atonement, the high priest, or the classification of sacrifices, which were known to the author of Kings; the poem attributed to Moses in Deuteronomy 32:1-43 was composed only during the exile; Ezekiel is composed of two parts and was written from 440–400 BCE; Leviticus postdates Moses by about a thousand years; concrete evidence of the existence of the Pentateuch dates back only to 300 years after the reign of Josiah; the New Year festival, the Day of Atonement, and the Purim festival were unknown to ancient Judaism and their origin was late and foreign. Zunz writes in an entirely matter-of-fact style, dry and technical; only in the conclusion does he allow himself a meta-critical comment: "As long as poets and priests work toward results, historians and philosophers must never tire of looking for reasons."[153]

Even if Zunz was not "Grafian before Graf"[154] – since these works were published several years after Graf's death – he did precede Wellhausen in some of his conclusions. It is no wonder that when such a central figure in the *Wissenschaft des Judentums* tried his hand at biblical criticism, he stirred the ire of the conservatives: "Not all of the Jewish scholars, not even all of Zunz's admirers, welcomed these works. Some even could not forgive the Jubilee committee for not shelving Zunz's work";[155] Zacharias Frankel devoted an article to refuting his conclusions about Ezekiel.[156] Indeed, "No Jew in his time approached biblical research with such freedom and loyalty to its results as he did, and few in his generation expressed and proved their conclusions so clearly."[157] There is little doubt that Zunz's independence derived from the dis-

---

150 "Even now he did not find the Hebrew audience sufficiently mature for his needs [...] and found that he must move [...] to the foreign press" (Soloveitchik and Rubasheff 1925, 136). See also: Bechtoldt 1995, 84-88.
151 The reason for this is unclear. The second part was also meant to be published; see: Geiger, A. 1875, 248.
152 Zunz 1875.
153 Zunz 1875, 242.
154 As Thompson 1970, 78 believes.
155 Soloveitchik and Rubasheff 1925, 138.
156 Frankel 1874b.
157 Soloveitchik and Rubasheff 1925, 138.

tance he kept from the activity of any religious movement;[158] Geiger, who in public enthusiastically greeted the aging Zunz's work and printed his conclusions in their entirety in his journal,[159] noted in a personal letter to Nöldeke[160] that while it contained no great innovations, it was a good thing that it was written by someone "outside of the movement."

Also worth a brief mention are Julius Popper's second book on the origins of monotheism and the patriarchal stories,[161] which stirred little interest and in which Abraham, Isaac, and Jacob were described not as historical figures but as stages in the development of religion from nature worship to monotheism; Siegmund Maybaum's two books from the early 1880s about the history of the priesthood and prophecy; Hermann Vogelstein's book[162] about the history of the struggle between the priests and the Levites from the days of Ezekiel to the fall of the Monarchy; Moritz Lazarus's book on the prophet Jeremiah, whose Hebrew translation was published in numerous editions;[163] and Heymann Steinthal's work on the psychology of nations (*Völkerpsychologie*), which occasionally overlapped with biblical criticism.[164]

Conclusion and Evaluation

Geiger's claim at the start of the 1870s that "There is no doubt that useful works in biblical criticism have lately been written almost entirely

---

158 On the distance between scholarship and religious practice, which with Zunz increased over the years, see: Meyer 1971.

159 Geiger, A. 1875, 248-250 = Zunz 1875, 240-242.

160 Geiger, L. 1878, 363.

161 Popper 1879.

162 Vogelstein 1889. The book – which relies on Wellhausen's approach – had an exceedingly hostile reception ("from a purely scientific perspective") from the Orthodox David Hoffmann in the journal he co-edited with Abraham (Adolf) Berliner (Hoffmann 1890). Vogelstein was allowed to respond, but his response was accompanied by copious "editorial footnotes" that made a mockery of his words (Vogelstein 1890).

163 Lazarus 1894. Soloveitchik and Rubasheff (1925, 141) declare emphatically that Lazarus based his work on Maybaum; their conclusion is based on the Hebrew translation of the book (Lazarus 1897, 11). The prominent reference to Maybaum in the translation was, in the original German, a general reference to "any book of Jewish history" (Lazarus 1894, 5). It appears that the reference in the Hebrew translation was adapted for a Jewish readership, while the original was intended for a broader audience of German readers.

164 See: Shavit and Eran 2007, 328f.

by Jews,"[165] was a baseless exaggeration or perhaps an ironical comment on the work of non-Jewish scholars; yet during the final third of the century it was indeed possible to identify a non-trivial group of Reform Jews who engaged in biblical criticism. None of them devoted himself exclusively to biblical scholarship, and for all of them it was more or less a peripheral interest: they included professional clergymen like Geiger or Vogelstein (a rabbi in Stettin); independent scholars primarily interested in Jewish studies like Zunz; and Jews engaged in overlapping disciplines in German academia such as Fürst and Goldziher. In general these scholars did not, on the one hand, refrain from adopting even the most radical conclusions of contemporary Christian biblical scholars; on the other hand, we may assume that like Geiger and Kohler they were also aware of the biases of Christian scholarship. Most of the work that Jewish scholars published addressed partial and specific – albeit central – issues in biblical criticism; none of them attempted a comprehensive historiographical synthesis based on the findings of that discipline. An exception is Siegmund Maybaum, whose work – a sort of Jewish variation on Wellhausen – will be examined in detail in the next chapter.

The openness that Reform Jewish scholars displayed toward biblical criticism was apparently greater than that demonstrated by the average liberal Jew toward the discipline, as Philippson's skeptical articles imply. Evidence corroborating the existence of a rift between the intellectual elite and the broader community was provided by the Reform Synod that gathered in Leipzig in June 1869; among the eighty-three participants were Philippson and Geiger. The Synod discussed the subject of teaching "biblical criticism" to children – "biblical criticism" purely in the very narrow sense of providing rationalist explanations for miraculous events in the Bible, "without denying their existence, of course." With the support of the majority of the participants it was decided that religious instruction should avoid the critical approach, for fear that by raising doubts it might do harm to the students' idealistic outlook; at the same time, the Synod expected teachers to act with care and not to ignore critical findings but "to anticipate and prevent the conflict that might later erupt in the souls of our youth between religion and the accepted scientific views."[166] This ambiguous decision illuminates the problem far more than its solution.

---

165 Bernstein 1893, 70. Geiger included Popper's book on the Tabernacle in this context, as well as Kohler's *Der Segen Jacobs* (Jacob's Blessing, 1867), Bernstein's book (Bernstein 1871), and his own *Urschrift*.

166 About the Synod see: Philipson 1967, 284-307; the quote is on p. 300.

Chapter 10
The Graf-Wellhausen Hypothesis in Reformist Dress: Siegmund Maybaum

A Jewish scholar who engaged extensively with the Graf-Wellhausen hypothesis was Siegmund Maybaum,[1] a prominent preacher of the Reform Jewish community in Berlin and a lecturer at the city's *Hochschule für die Wissenschaft des Judentums*. Maybaum had received a traditional education in his birthplace in Hungary. From age fourteen he was a student at Esriel Hildesheimer's school in Eisenstadt, where he also studied classical languages; he was accepted into the evangelical gymnasium at Pressburg (Bratislava) and afterward spent several semesters at the University of Vienna studying philosophy, philology, and history, and simultaneously studied at the city's *bet midrash*. In 1868 he moved to Breslau where he studied at the Jewish Theological Seminary and the University (Oriental studies); two years later he received his PhD from the University of Halle and was employed as a rabbi in Hungary, Bohemia, and ultimately (1881) in Berlin, where he gained great renown for his sermons.

Maybaum published two books at the beginning of the 1880s that provide a fascinating example of a threefold undertaking: first, he accepted the basic premises and essential conclusions of biblical criticism, operated within its framework, and attempted to contribute to it; secondly, he criticized Christian biblical criticism for the anti-Jewish elements he identified therein, and drew a modified historiographical picture that depicted Judaism in a positive light; finally, he constructed that picture in such a way as to support Reform Judaism against the more conservative Jewish streams. This was thus a counter-history that took up non-Jewish historiography, amended it into a different historical picture, and applied it to the needs of the present.

---

1   1844, Miskolcz (Hungary) – 1919, Berlin. The research literature on Maybaum is quite meager. In addition to the various encyclopedias, see: Geiger, L. 1910; Salomonski 1919.

The Priesthood and the Prophecy

Maybaum published his books in 1880 and 1883: Geiger had already passed away, and Zunz had published his contribution to biblical criticism a few years earlier. At that stage, Reform Jewish involvement in biblical criticism required little justification. A short time earlier Wellhausen had published his central book,[2] and the hypothesis of the lateness of the Law became increasingly dominant. Maybaum operated within this framework, and in his books he refers to all the major biblical critics who preceded him – from Vatke and George to Nöldeke and Bleek. Wellhausen appears throughout Maybaum's books, though the claim that Maybaum was "an old disciple of Wellhausen's"[3] is inaccurate (and chronologically unlikely): Maybaum comes across as an old disciple of Graf's, "in whose footsteps our description follows," as he explains in the very first footnote.[4] Of the Jewish scholars, he frequently mentions Geiger and debates with Graetz; Julius Popper also appears in a footnote.[5]

Maybaum did not conceal his admiration for Graf's work. In an article published in 1883 he compared the "revolution" in Pentateuch source criticism to the Copernican revolution in astronomy and Kant's revolution in epistemology.[6] In the same article he also expressed his confidence that despite objections, Graf's theory would become the unquestioned foundation of biblical scholarship (in hindsight, he was an astute prophet).

Not for nothing does Maybaum begin his book about the prophecy with a quotation from Geiger, who wrote that "The Levite class is the most precise marker of all of the books of the Pentateuch":[7] the family resemblance between Maybaum's work and Geiger's *Urschrift* is evident. "Geiger's whole book," as Soloveitchik and Rubasheff wrote, "is nothing but commentary on this great principle":

> Every generation, every spiritual movement, and every person inserted into the Bible something of themselves and of their outlook [...] Each generation's national and religious consciousness merged completely with this

---

2   Wellhausen 1878, see chapter 7. The second edition appeared in 1883, after Maybaum's books.
3   Soloveitchik and Rubasheff 1925, 141.
4   Maybaum 1880, 1 N. 1. The reference is to Graf 1866.
5   Maybaum 1880, 81 N. 3.
6   Maybaum 1883b, 191f.
7   Geiger, A. 1875-1878 IV, 262, quoted in Maybaum 1880, 4. Geiger is also quoted in the preface to Maybaum's second book: Maybaum 1883, 6.

sacred treasure, and in doing so adapted it to its own needs, assimilated it and reformed it in its own image.[8]

But while in his book Geiger applied this principle to the books of Writings and to the transmission of the biblical canon, Maybaum applies it to the formation of the Pentateuch itself. Just like Geiger, Maybaum constructs his narrative of historical development around an internal struggle between two Israelite camps: in Geiger's case these were the Pharisees and the Sadducees, whose struggle shaped the Hebrew Bible, while Maybaum identifies the struggle between the priesthood and the prophecy as the defining issue in the formation of the Pentateuch.

Maybaum's first book is titled *Die Entwicklung des altisraelitischen Priesterthums* (The Development of the Ancient Israelite Priesthood); his second is *Die Entwicklung des israelitischen Prophetenthums* (The Development of Israelite Prophecy).[9] Steinthal, in his highly favorable review of the books, remarked that the two could be considered a single work and that they had been published separately simply because of the author's numerous occupations.[10] Taken together, the two books form a history of the biblical period from its beginnings to beyond the Babylonian exile, organized around the history of the priesthood and the prophets, the struggle between them, and the resulting formation of the Pentateuch.

As evident even from his choice of chapter names – "The Pre-Deuteronomic Period," "Deuteronomy," "Ezekiel's Theocratic Order" – Maybaum fully adopts the periodization and terminology of the Graf-Wellhausen hypothesis. He accepts with minor reservations the division into sources,[11] the process of the Pentateuch's formation,[12] and the central milestones in the development of Israelite religion as presented by the hypothesis: the ancient period (JE); Josiah's reform (D); the Babylonian exile; Ezekiel's prophecy; the Return to Palestine; and the Law (P). But within this framework he is able to construct an alternative

---

8   Geiger, A. 1857, 72; Soloveitchik and Rubasheff 1925, 130.

9   Maybaum 1880; Maybaum 1883. The orphaned references below refer to these works.

10 Steinthal 1886, 362.

11 A central reservation of Maybaum's about Wellhausen's hypothesis is that the narrative (Elohistic) parts are not part of P. Consequently Maybaum rejects the existence of the so-called *Grundschrift*, or the Elohistic source. He argues that P included only laws, and that the narrative parts were added to it later by the redactor (Ezra). In this he explicitly accepts and expands on Graf's initial position from 1865 (to which Maybaum 1883b is devoted; see also: 1880, 107ff.)

12 "In our composition of the Pentateuch one may observe the following main stages: (1) the Elohistic narrative (of Israelite origin); (2) the Jehovistic narrative, which used (1) as a source; (3) the Deuteronomist; (4) the post-Deuteronomistic redaction; (5) the Priestly Code; (6) the final redaction (Ezra)" (1880, 120).

historical narrative that purges the hypothesis of elements problematic for Jewish self-conception and the perception of Jewish history, exchanging them for positive elements, vital in particular for Reform Judaism. His books were not written as polemics; they present an independent narrative that borrows from Christian biblical critics and only occasionally disagrees with them outright, particularly in the footnotes.

Maybaum describes the ancient period in the history of the Israelite religion as a period of the cult of *bamot* (high places), as was commonly accepted. He adopts Wellhausen's conjecture that the prophets emerged from among the priesthood,[13] but he has a different idea of their role: the priests conducted the cult and did so according to laws – written or otherwise – that regulated the sacrificial rituals. These laws – with some regional varieties – were called the "priestly law." The priests maintained that their law originated with the revelation to Moses at Sinai, and therefore they considered themselves "wise."[14] The people recognized them in that role and held the priestly ritual as highly sacred; they identified it with the Law of Jehovah.

This period of the priesthood (1880: 5-20) was paralleled by three stages in the development of the prophecy (1883: 7-84). The first stage was prior to Samuel, when the prophets operated within the priesthood, engaged in fortune-telling, and were called magicians, soothsayers, diviners, and so forth. The priests were associated with the *bamot*, and each *bamah* had its own circle of prophets – a sort of school of its own. In the second stage, during the time of Samuel, the oracles, the diviners, and the cult of Baal were banished and replaced by spiritual revelation; the tribes of Israel were united through a national religion as "the people of Jehovah," a unification that was a precondition for a national monarchy. In the third stage, the "the age of the heroic prophecy," the prophets of the various *Bamot* fought against the cult of Baal led by Ahab. Elijah introduced the model of a wandering prophet, persecuted (by Jezebel) and independent of any school.

Throughout this period the prophets did not object to the cult of the *Bamot* itself, but only to idolatry. They did not perceive the cult as a unique element of the Israelite worship (which was precisely Wellhausen's claim); consequently they approached it as something of secondary importance and rejected the priests' claim that the source of their Law was the revelation at Sinai. In its place they offered their own law, the true "Law of Jehovah Zebaot": this was comprised of short, clear,

---

13   1880, 12 N. 12, which refers to Wellhausen 1878, 12.
14   Isaiah 5:21: "Ah, you who are wise in your own eyes"; Jeremiah 8:8: "We are wise, and the law of the Lord is with us."

monotheistic laws that were already present in the Jehovistic narrative and ancient book of law in Exodus 20–24.

The origin of the war between prophets and priests is hazy. Nonetheless it was well underway during the days of the second Jeroboam, at the peak of the prophets' power:

> I hate, I despise your festivals, and I take no delight in your solemn assemblies. Even though you offer me your burnt-offerings and grain-offerings, I will not accept them; and the offerings of well-being of your fatted animals I will not look upon. Take away from me the noise of your songs; I will not listen to the melody of your harps. But let justice roll down like waters, and righteousness like an ever-flowing stream. Did you bring to me sacrifices and offerings the forty years in the wilderness, O house of Israel? (Amos 5:21-25).

Amos, the prophet, preached against the priests in Judah; likewise Hosea in the Northern Kingdom, who called for an end to idolatry and for a transfer of emphasis from sacrificial practice to the true "Law of the Lord."[15]

But the prophets' efforts were in vain. They were unable to uproot pagan religion, and the latter reached its apogee in the days of Ahaz, who sacrificed his son by fire to Molekh. With time, after many failed efforts to uproot it, the prophets understood that correcting the religious situation would be possible only if all the *Bamot* were destroyed and the cult were centralized at a single site. The idea of centralizing the cult ripened among the prophets and awaited an opportunity to be brought into practice.

The first opportunity arrived in Judah during the days of Hezekiah (2 Kings 18). The conflict with the priesthood was then at its peak, led by Isaiah (1880: 64):

> What to me is the multitude of your sacrifices? [...] who asked this from your hand? Trample my courts no more [...] your hands are full of blood [...] remove the evil of your doings from before my eyes; cease to do evil, learn to do good; seek justice, rescue the oppressed, defend the orphan, plead for the widow (Isaiah 1:10-17).

Under the influence of the prophets – perhaps of Isaiah himself – Hezekiah ordered the centralization of the cult and the destruction of the *Bamot*. But this first reform, imposed by force, was unsuccessful. After Isaiah's death and during the days of Manasseh the people reverted to worshiping at the *Bamot*.

The prophets' protests increased, and the struggle became violent. This period in the history of the priesthood – the centralization of the

---

15 Hosea 8:11: "When Ephraim multiplied altars to expiate sin, they became to him altars for sinning."

cult (1880: 21-37) – paralleled the period of war between the true and false prophets (1883: 85-130). For many reasons the true prophets stepped out of the main school of the false prophets, who were loyal to the authorities alone. They held themselves apart from them ("I am no prophet," Amos 7:14), scorned them and fought against them. Jeremiah heightened the polemic and warned: "I am going to bring disaster on this people, the fruit of their schemes, because they have not given heed to my words; and as for my teaching, they have rejected it" (Jeremiah 6:19). In response, the priests placed even more emphasis on the divinity of their Law – "We are wise, and the law of the Lord is with us" (Jeremiah 8:8) – and Jeremiah in turn claimed: "in fact, the false pen of the scribes has made it into a lie" (ibid.). But the priests had the upper hand; the prophets were persecuted and silenced for fifty years.

The prophets learned from their failure. Their reform had collapsed for two reasons: first of all, it could not be anchored in the ancient Mosaic laws and was therefore perceived by the people as arbitrary and groundless; the second reason was the objection of the priests, who found themselves stripped of their profession with no sufficient compensation. Consequently, during the days of Manasseh the prophets decided to compose the Deuteronomistic source (D). This source was written as a law book and presented as though it had been revealed to Moses at Sinai; in this way it was meant to overcome the first obstacle to the reform. The second problem – the economy of the provincial priesthood which the reform would destroy – was to be solved by the license priests would be given to conduct sacrifices at the Temple in Jerusalem, as well as by a tax for their benefit as part of the taxation provided for the rest of the "proletariat" (strangers, orphans, and widows).

In Josiah's days the prophets were able to enact the Deuteronomistic reform by a royal order (2 Kings 22). It was presented not as an arbitrary decision on the king's part but as ancient Mosaic law. The *Bamot* were desecrated with the bones of the dead, to ensure they would not be used again. This time the reform was more successful, but the House of Zadok, which controlled the Temple in Jerusalem, prevented the provincial priests from sacrificing in the Temple. After Josiah's death, when Jehoiakim came into power as a vassal of the king of Egypt, the provincial priests (the Levites) once again carried out sacrifices at the *Bamot*, now to Egyptian gods – the gods of the victors – despite the protests of Jeremiah, Habakkuk, and other prophets; the Egyptian religion included a cult of the dead, and so the desecration of the *Bamot* with the bones of the dead was no obstacle. Like Wellhausen,

Maybaum seems to have believed that were it not for the Babylonian exile, the reform would have failed once more.

In formulating D, the prophets also attempted to define criteria for distinguishing between true and false prophets: prophecy in the name of Jehovah and the fulfillment of the prophecies (Deuteronomy 13:2ff.). But these criteria impressed neither the people nor the false prophets, who continued to satisfy their masters and their audience, and the true prophets themselves understood that the very institution of prophecy must come to an end; this was evident in the vision of the anonymous prophet in Zechariah as well as in Jeremiah.[16]

The sudden break that occurred with the destruction of the Temple and the Babylonian exile changed the situation. Their optimistic prophecies disproven, the false prophets saw their status decline, and the destruction of the Temple destroyed both their occupation and most of their livelihood (they had been supported by the priestly tax); once more they became magicians rather than prophets. In contrast, the stature of the true prophets rose greatly because they had correctly predicted the calamity.

Now the very nature of prophecy underwent a transformation. Its audience was no longer a nation but a religious community, and thus its contents were different than those of the classical prophecy in the days of Hezekiah: it dealt less with political matters and more with internal religious ones. The prophets now wrote more often and rarely preached in public. They lacked the concentrated audience they had had in Jerusalem, and it was easier to reach the scattered communities in exile by means of written missives. This was a natural development: from the start the spoken word had existed only in the service of the written (1883: 138). The prophets' literary activity increased, as did their occupation with the ancient texts that were preserved, including legal texts. Therefore the prophets' attention was directed toward the ritual laws; even more than to the prophets' laws, they devoted their efforts to compiling and arranging the sacrificial, priestly laws, adapting them to suit their own perspective.

The change in the prophets' attitude toward the priestly law is understandable in its historical context. The exile had brought a sudden end to monarchy and softened and reconciled the conflict between the two camps. The past, including the sacrificial practice, now appeared to the prophets – as it did to everyone else – as an illustrious period. From

---

16 Zechariah 13:3: "And if any prophets appear again, their fathers and mothers who bore them will say to them, 'You shall not live, for you speak lies in the name of the Lord'; and their fathers and their mothers who bore them shall pierce them through when they prophesy." Maybaum also refers to Jeremiah 31:33.

the outset the prophets had objected not to sacrificial practice in its own right but only to the religious and moral implications of the priests' focus on it: in exile, the resurrection of the cult of the *Bamot* was clearly no longer an option, and since after the destruction of the Temple and the cessation of sacrificial practice their importance had lessened anyway, the prophets could now view the priests in a more positive light and allow them a place in the new religious order.

> What Maimonides argues about the sacrifices, not out of any critical examination of their historical development but only from a philosophical recognition of the antinomy between sacrifices and pure monotheism – namely: that they were simply a concession to the concept of piety that reigned during the days of Moses – is in effect true only for the period of exile, when the prophets turned to shape the future on the basis of past historical development: the sacrifices were indispensable! (1880: 67, referring to *Guide for the Perplexed* 3:32).

Hence developed the theocratic order of the final chapters of Ezekiel (1880: 38-60), the most important prophet of his time, who also belonged to a priestly family. His was not a fantasy, but an operative plan to renew the cult and the theocracy: in exile it was evident that the remaining people must become the "people of Jehovah." On all matters – the grounding of sacrificial practice in Law, priestly taxation, the festivals, etc. – Ezekiel stood between D and P, and this enables us to determine the order of their composition. The contradictions between Ezekiel's regulations and P, Maybaum writes, are in themselves sufficient proof of Graf's hypothesis that P was post-exilic. Thus the Levites, for example, whose objection to the centralization of the cult Ezekiel still remembered, were punished in his vision and demoted to the status of lowly servants in the future Temple.

The Return from Babylon saw the composition of P, the Priestly Code. As evident from its prophetic style, its religious outlook, and its resemblance in form to Ezekiel's vision, its author apparently belonged to the circle of Ezekiel's disciples; Maybaum justifies this claim in detail and argues with Graf and Wellhausen about the attribution of several chapters in Leviticus (1880: 73ff.). The work of composition comprised two parts: independent composition and compilation. The former included the fiction of the "Tent of Meeting" and the description of all of P's regulations as though they were already customary during the Israelites' time in the desert, including the difference in status between the priests and Levites which Ezekiel still presented in his prophecy as a future punishment. Compilation involved collecting and editing the written and unwritten sources that contained the priestly law and incorporating the Jehovistic historical narratives into the Code.

Ezekiel presented his theocratic order as a vision that had been revealed to him; the composers of P, in contrast, preferred for the purposes of legitimacy to present their order as though it had been revealed to Moses at Sinai (just like the composers of D before them). In
this way the priests' historical claim that their law came to them from
Moses was accepted. In effect P integrated the law of the priests and the
law of the prophets: its composer divided the priestly law and scattered
the fragments into the Jehovistic narrative that had already been expanded by D. This was a wise and calculated step: it seemingly ac-
quiesced to the priests but in fact granted victory to the prophets' law.
For generations the people had identified the Law of Jehovah with the
priestly law, which was the familiar and dominant aspect of the cult;
now, thanks to this integration, it was possible to disseminate the law
of the prophets to the entire people. P was thus a creation of the prophets which entirely assimilated the priestly law.

Despite, and perhaps because of, the prophets' triumph, this period
saw the decline of prophecy (1883: 131-146). The prophets had achieved
their goal and completed their mission (as they had already foreseen):
the written word brought their mission to its conclusion. The Law of
Jehovah was now a written document – the "Torah of Moses" – which
was far more eternal than oral tradition. Ezra's final redaction and the
sealing of the canon concluded the prophets' work: the scribe (*sofer*)
and his commentary replaced the prophet and his revelation.

In his review, Steinthal provided a table summarizing the structure
of Maybaum's two books side by side:

Priesthood	Prophecy
	1. Before Samuel: prophecy within the framework of the priesthood.
	2. Samuel and the prophetic school: the separation of the prophecy from the priest-hood.
1. Before Deuteronomy: the ancient priesthood.	3. The age of heroic prophe-cy: the war against Baal and the purer conception of Jeho-vah. Opposition to the priest-hood.

2. Deuteronomy: the prophets enact reform of the priesthood during the days of Hezekiah and Josiah.

3. Ezekiel's theocratic order.

4. The true and false prophets: full development of the conception of Jehovah. Beginning of the decline of prophecy.

5. The decline of prophecy: exile, reconciliation between prophets and priests.

4. The Priestly Code: the final stage of prophecy.

5. The post-exilic period: redaction of the Pentateuch. The establishment of the high priesthood and the separation between priests and Levites.[17]

As this table illustrates, the final stages – i.e., the Law and Judaism – are a synthesis of prophecy and priesthood under prophetic hegemony. If the central subject of Wellhausen's narrative was the Law, Maybaum transferred the focus of discussion to the forces and interests that stood behind the Law and its development, placing at the center two subjects – the priests and the prophets – and examining history through the lens of their relationship. The struggle between the prophets and priests ended (at least in this stage) in reconciliation and in the triumph of the law of the prophets, which assimilated the priestly law.

Maybaum as Alternative Historical Narrative

By means of "amendments" to the concept of Law / Torah and its history, Maybaum was able to adopt Graf-Wellhausen's narrative framework, peel away its Christological layers, and dress it anew in a Jewish "skin."

Wellhausen's Christological narrative was built around the gradual development of the Law. The absence of laws during ancient times enabled him to set up a contrast between a law-less, original, and natural Israelite spontaneity and the later, artificial Jewish legal rigidity. The Law developed gradually from stage to stage: Wellhausen described D, the second stage of religious development, as the first Israelite law.

---

17   The table is translated from: Steinthal 1886, 363.

Ezekiel was a negative intermediate link; his law was even more developed than D's, and it heralded the arrival of P – the full-fledged Jewish Law, a degenerate, artificial creation from the period of decline that followed the exile. Christianity (especially Protestantism) was identified with liberation from the Law and with a return to the ancient spontaneity that Judaism had lost at the end of a long process of decline.

Simultaneously, this narrative was based on a gradual increase in the power of the priests, who were identified with the Law. During the ancient period the priests and prophets had shared a single Torah which included not laws but advice and moral principles. D was a shared creation of the two groups in which the Law was already central. Ezekiel was "a priest in a prophet's robes," a Trojan horse that the priests had sent to infiltrate the prophets and implant the Law; while P was described as a creation entirely of the priests – appropriately named the *Priestercodex*, it was the manifestation of the Jewish "religion of Law." The free spirit and individualism of the prophets were vanquished by the priestly law, which grew more dominant with every passing stage. At the end of this process of degeneration, after the return from exile, the Law became the defining characteristic of Judaism while prophecy vanished. Christianity (with Jesus) was destined to be a return to the universalism, freedom, and individualism of the prophets.

Maybaum begins his "amendment" already in his description of the ancient period; he requires some early seeds of the Law in order to hamper Wellhausen's developmental framework (from the absence of law to a proliferation of laws, from spontaneous to rigid, etc.).

In a footnote Maybaum comes out explicitly against Wellhausen's interpretation of Isaiah 29:13: "The Lord said: Because these people draw near with their mouths and honour me with their lips, while their hearts are far from me, and their worship of me is a human commandment learned by rote." Wellhausen declared that sacrifices during the pre-Deuteronomistic period had not been regulated, and that the role of the priests was to advise, arbitrate, and judge; the word Torah meant advice or guidance,[18] which the prophets took part in providing. They objected not to the sacrificial laws (which did not yet exist) but to the sacrificial practice. Thus, "a human commandment learned by rote" conveyed Isaiah's displeasure not with the sacrificial laws but with the people's inability to understand and attend to his warnings.[19]

Maybaum, in contrast, claims that the ancient priestly law "included nothing but ritual laws, instructions for carrying out various

---

18   Wellhausen 1878, 409f.
19   Wellhausen 1878, 60 N. 1.

sacrifices, and rites of purification for people and objects" (1880: 62). This was Deuteronomy's as well as Haggai's[20] description of the priestly law, and Maybaum maintains that

> Wellhausen is unable to explain away this expression, which according to the full meaning of the verse clearly refers to a sacred tradition of a venerated cult; and from here it is already proven that there is no basis for his claim that the prophets did not come out against the priests' "Torah," whether it was written or only orally transmitted, but only against the sacrifices themselves (1880: 65 N. 1).

Maybaum thus dates the Law back to the ancient period. With respect to the division of labor between priests and prophets, he differentiates from the start between two kinds of law, that of the priests and that of the prophets: the priests' law consisted of ritual law, while the prophets' law comprised monotheism, justice, and morality; in this he is not far from Wellhausen. But in order to account for later history he would require some link, albeit minimal, between the prophets and the Law, and therefore he is careful not to overemphasize the dichotomy between the two kinds of law and declares that the prophets' law also included ritual regulations. In this he agrees with Wellhausen, who argued that in ancient times the prophets adhered to the priestly law.

Regarding D, which Wellhausen described as a shared work of priests and prophets, Maybaum specifically emphasizes its prophetic aspects and thus interrupts Wellhausen's description of continuous "priestification," linking the prophets to the Law. Maybaum's Ezekiel is not a negative figure – a "priest in a prophet's robes" that Wellhausen would have been pleased to see banished from the canon – but rather a prominent positive leader of the prophets' circle who was the first to synthesize between the prophetic law with which he was familiar as a prophet and the priestly law he studied as a child in a family of priests. At the same time, P is transformed in Maybaum's work from a priestly to a prophetic work; Maybaum would presumably have preferred to call it *Prophetencodex* rather than *Priestercodex*.

In this way Maybaum interrupts the development Wellhausen described – from absence of Law to fixation on the Law – and shook off the negative label as a "religion of Law" that was applied to later Judaism. The Law had existed in Israelite religion even in ancient times; it was not a late creation. As for prophecy, Maybaum turns the ancient

---

20 Deuteronomy 17:8-9: "If a judicial decision is too difficult for you to make between one kind of bloodshed and another, one kind of legal right and another, or one kind of assault and another—any such matters of dispute in your towns—then you shall [...] consult with the levitical priests"; Haggai 2:11-12: "Ask the priests for a ruling: If one carries consecrated meat in the fold of one's garment, and with the fold touches bread, or stew, or wine, or oil, or any kind of food, does it become holy?"

history into a process of gradual victory for the prophets' law, albeit through certain concessions to the priestly law. Prophecy ceased not because it failed and was vanquished but precisely because it accomplished its goal. From the start, the prophets' intent was not to destroy the priestly law but to unify the two laws into a single one (1883: 137), and this goal was fully realized during the days of Ezra.

In Maybaum's narrative the course of Israelite history becomes one of progress rather than decline. Before the exile, the great majority of the people perceived the worship of Jehovah syncretically; the prophets were an insignificant minority that was hundreds of years ahead of its time. But the definitive criterion for evaluating a religious period is not the cultural level of individuals but that of society as a whole; only through the Law and by replacing the prophets with sages (*Schriftgelehrte*) was the religion of Jehovah able to strike root among the people as a whole, to withstand Hellenistic paganism and flourish in the days of the Maccabees. The Law was therefore necessary from a religious–historical perspective in order to fulfill the prophets' vision (1883: 144).

Unsurprisingly, Maybaum rejects Wellhausen' claim regarding the Law's "lack of vitality" in P: the festivals and other rituals did not entirely lose their joy of life, as Wellhausen claimed, and testimony to this exists in both the Mishnah and the writings of Philo of Alexandria (1880: 71).[21]

In contrast to Wellhausen, who argued that "the written word took the place of the spoken, and the people of the word became a 'people of the book,'"[22] Maybaum declares that "the spoken word was always in the service of the written word" (1883: 138); therefore,

> It is entirely clear that this [the period of the Law beginning with Ezra, the end of prophecy, and the rise of commentary] does not signify the start of a decline. Of course in Christian theological circles they see the period of the "Law" as a time of disintegration of the religion of Jehovah – but they err! The goal toward which the prophets strove was from first to last the enactment of an authoritative law in order to put an end to the eternal straying of the people; immediately when it was formed, that is, at the final separation of the prophecy from its ancient source, the seed was discovered of the development which was brought to a temporary end by Ezra's consecration of the Torah. Just by virtue of this success, the period of the Law deserves to be considered in every way as progress relative to the prophetic era (1883: 142).

---

21 Maybaum refers to Philo's *De Festo Cophini* and to Mishnah *Bikkurim* 3:3-8, *Sukkah* 5:1.
22 Wellhausen 1878, 425, quoted from Wellhausen 1885, 279.

In contrast to the perception that held Christianity as the continuation of the prophetic spirit and of the absence of Law in ancient Israel, and later Judaism as a deviation thereof, Maybaum depicts Judaism as a synthesis of the priesthood and the prophecy. He strongly emphasizes the antithesis between the prophets and the priests – which Wellhausen considered relatively insignificant – only to conclude the history of their struggle in synthesis. Thus he creates a picture of historical progress from ancient Israel to Judaism.

Criticizing the Criticism

At the end of his second book Maybaum comes out against the Christology implicit in Wellhausen's approach (without mentioning him by name):

> Clearly, one should not adopt the biased perspective that sees the prophetic religion in its entirety as nothing but a preliminary stage of Christianity, while the "Law" is seen as a reaction that "entered midway" and interrupted its natural development (1883: 142).

Paul's verse about the Law which "entered in-between"[23] was, as already seen, the epigraph to the third part of Wellhausen's book. Moreover Wellhausen, again, used the verse in order to testify to the similarity between his approach and Paul's. Maybaum responds in precisely the same vein:

> Paul,[24] incidentally, appreciated the prophets more accurately than some modern theologians, because he saw them clearly as loyal representatives of the "Law," and for that reason his teachings did not latch on to the prophets, but instead to Abraham (1883: 142).

In other words, if Paul had believed, like Wellhausen, that the prophets represented the opposite of the Law, he would have sought the basis for his outlook in them; in Paul's reliance on Abraham, Maybaum actually finds support for his own understanding that the prophets fought on the side of the Law and not against it.

Here Maybaum expands his criticism and applies it to modern theologians in general – to their attitude toward Judaism, toward Christianity, and toward the scientific ethos. He comes out against traditional accusations regarding the alleged particularism of the prophets and the Jewish Law: the best fruit of the prophetic religious worldview,

---

23   Romans 5:20; see p. 106 above.
24   Maybaum gives as a reference: Romans 4:16ff.; Galatians 3:6-9. Both mention Abraham, not the prophets, as the father of the believers.

Maybaum declares, is the "servant of the Jehovah," who suffers for the salvation of mankind. Only one who perceives the "era of the Law" from the start as deterioration and petrifaction which Christianity escaped, could direct such accusations at the prophets (1883: 143).

Maybaum berates, with their own accusation, the theologians who accused Jewish scholars of approaching the Bible with insufficient intellectual independence; they too always regard the Old Testament as a preliminary stage to the New, and cannot even imagine that the New Testament is, at least in some respects, a degeneration, even if an historically unavoidable one.

As for modern theologians' perception of Christianity, Maybaum argues that they ignore the fact that Christianity too (meaning Catholicism) deviates from Paul's antinomian position, because it too developed sacrificial practice, the *opera operata*, and the rituals demanded by the new religion;

> And even Protestantism, which Richard Simon has called the Christian Karaism, is for the most part quite well on its way to the materialization of the concept, that is, to becoming an independent religion, because the people cannot long adhere to a concept of direct communion with God (1883: 144f.).

Here Maybaum uses the concept of the Law to strike at Protestantism itself: the number and quality of the deeds – of the *opera operata* – is unimportant; they are determined by each people and in each period according to its level of development; but even the smallest number of deeds breaks the antinomian principle, and the principle was indeed broken – in Judaism, and Catholicism, and even in Protestantism.

Therefore it is foolish and simultaneously unscholarly to still rely in the modern era on Paul and dub the ceremonial law of the Priestly Code, which seeks to sanctify all of human life, "not only immoral but also truly godless"[25] – just as unscholarly, on the other hand, as to denigrate Christianity for undeniably contaminating the concept of monotheism, instead of explaining the historical process that inevitably led to this contamination (1883: 145).

The role of scholarship, according to Maybaum, is to explain (*erklären*) phenomena in their historical context, not to judge them from a biased confessional perspective. At the end of his second book Maybaum not only calls for impartial scholarship, but concludes on a personal note, expressing a wish:

> That on the Christian side its adulteration of monotheism and all the implications thereof gradually disappear, and that on the Jewish side the ceremonial law will gradually shed its national clothing and assume a pure

---

25   Here Maybaum quotes Duhm.

humanist form, in order to fulfill the prophet's messianic words: "And the Lord will become king over all the earth; on that day the Lord will be one and his name one (Zechariah 14:9)" (1883: 146).

This is a supremely enlightened vision, in which the two religions approach a pure, universalist, monotheistic faith, and simultaneously approach each other.

The Image of Modern Judaism

A distinction must be made between two spheres of struggle over the meaning of Torah / Law in Maybaum's work: the first is historiography, between Maybaum and Christian scholars; the other is history itself, between Jews (or "Israelites") and themselves. In the latter sphere, Maybaum focuses on the conflict between the prophets and the priests during the biblical period, but it turns out that the conflict is not limited to ancient history and still remains undecided:

> The great struggle between prophets and priests, which would be resumed later again and again in different forms and between different parties and continues to this very day, revolved around the content of the "Torah" (1880: 62).

"To this very day": here Maybaum interweaves a link to the struggle over the image of Judaism in his own time, bitterly criticizing Graetz. He ridicules the conservatism of the latter, who was willing to critically examine later Judaism but rejected Pentateuchal criticism:

> The so-called liberal direction wishes to apply the law of historical development in full and in its entirety to the second half of our race's lifetime, yet in contrast to keep well away from that law in the first half. But if one proves with unlimited scientific tools that Judaism from the days of Ezra to our present day is an unbroken chain of religious development, can one still dare to argue that during the period that lasted from Moses to Ezra there was no development at all? That the beginning and end of this long period mark exactly the same point in religious theory? This is entirely unreasonable! (1880: 125).

Graetz's argument[26] that biblical criticism turned the composers of the Pentateuch into a band of forgers (*Bande von Fälschern*) is rejected by Maybaum out of hand: there is no question here of forgery, but of emptying old content into a new vessel; the same processes of copying and redaction which Graetz was willing to apply to the books of Prophets and Writings apply to the Pentateuch as well; "It almost seems as though Graetz would prefer that the Pentateuch remain a holy of holies

---

26   Graetz 1902, 438f.

(*Sanctissimum*) to criticism, while the other books of Scripture are declared free as birds" (1880: 121). And in a crushing attack on Graetz's historical writing he adds:

> And since something that undergoes no development necessarily has no history, perhaps it would be better if the history of the period, which is said to have been subject to no development, had not been written at all (1880: 125).

At the conclusion of his book, after this attack on Graetz, Maybaum lays out in detail his views of Judaism and its development:

> But in truth Judaism, from the first impetus it received in the revelation at Sinai to our present day, turns out to be a continuous line of religious development [...] A central period in this development begins with the prophecy's separation from the priesthood, that is, with the independence of thought from form, of the spiritual from the material – and the struggle that burst out in its wake between these two elements of religious life which were originally united, a struggle that marks the most important turning point in the religious consciousness of our race. Twice, with the destruction of the First and Second Temples, history decided in favor of prophecy, but each time the priesthood rose anew: the first time as a historical reality, the second time as hope on the one hand, and in a symbolic form on the other (1880: 126).

"Hope" apparently hints at the Jewish national Messianic hope; as we have seen, Maybaum wished that the ceremonial law would eventually shed its national character and take on a purely humanist form (needless to say, he objected to Zionism). The "symbolic form" of priesthood evidently refers to the (Orthodox) rabbis.

> This struggle has not since calmed, but remains the essential element of religious development. It rises in a different form but with the same power and decisiveness in the disputes between the Pharisees and the Sadducees, between Rabbinic Jews and Karaites. [...] We encounter it in the struggles of the later Jewish philosophers against the crude, materialist conception of God, as well as in the struggle of modern religious development against the narrow limitations in which codification imprisoned religious life. For the struggle is as eternal as progress! Therefore we can calm those who work for the development of Judaism and are subject to censure from all sides, if they are but aware that they are deeply bound to the past and have not broken the chain of development. Because this natural historical development is the will of God; its latest link is as legitimate as all those before it, its newest form has the same sanctified character as all its forerunners (1880: 126).

Thus Maybaum weaves his biblical criticism into his overarching perception of Judaism, a perception whose core is legitimacy for innovation and for reform that prefers the spirit to the material, the thought to the form. He views the contemporary reformers of Judaism as heirs of the prophets, and considers their work no less legitimate but perhaps even more so than that of the anti-reformist "priests." In his sympathetic review of the book, Steinthal remarked: "With the aid of the priests, everyone should be prophetic. A hint suffices for the wise."[27]

Maybaum's alternative historiography, his revision-to-the-revision of the Graf-Wellhausen narrative, thus consciously and explicitly served contemporary ideological needs – the struggle over the image of Reform Judaism – and simultaneously offered overt criticism of both Orthodox Judaism and the Positive–Historical stream.

---

27   Steinthal 1886, 364.

Conclusion

Scientific thought in Western Judaism
was thus conquered by biblical criticism
which rose up around it. And this spiritual treasure
which was accumulated in German
became the property of the *Wissenschaft des Judentums*
even in other lands and other tongues.

Menachem Soloveitchik and Zalman Rubasheff, 1925[1]

Judaism's engagement with biblical criticism, expressed in the work of the *Wissenschaft des Judentums* in Germany from its beginnings in the 1920s to the end of the century, represents a unique combination of continuity and innovation, of scholarship and politics, of affinity and segregation. It was the work of intellectuals who belonged to a religious and ethnic minority subject to a struggle of a colonialist type at once internal and external: a struggle over the image of modern Judaism from within, as well as over Judaism's place in the modern world. The struggle was in some ways an additional link in the old tradition of Jewish–Christian theological polemic and the Hebraist discourse which framed it; it was also partly an attempt to construct a revised image of the past using modern, scholarly tools against the background of the modern academic Orientalist discourse.

At the start of the nineteenth century there was among Jewish scholars a sense of enthusiasm for all things new — a revolutionism that aimed its arrows inward at the old orthodoxy and was eagerly prepared to adopt the tools and conclusions of modern, scholarly biblical criticism. Jost was delighted by biblical criticism, but even his own work proposes a counter-history of Israel and the Jews to correct the picture of the past constructed by the Christian biblical criticism of Jost's time. The political context is evident: in postulating a schism be-

---

1   Soloveitchik and Rubasheff 1925, 142.

tween Israelites on the one hand and Jews on the other, where the former were a nation and the latter only a religious community, the intent
was to serve the ideology of emancipation, as well as Jews' integration
into modern Central European society and states as one amongst several religious communities. At the same time, Jost's diminution of the
importance of the Law in the history of Israel, which was also politically motivated, continued the Jewish–Christian polemical tradition that
had existed for ages.

During the middle third of the century – a period of reaction and
conservatism – the reactive character of Jewish biblical criticism stood
out: with the decline of Christian engagement in radical critical scholarship, Jewish work in the field came to a near-complete halt. Steinheim,
the highly eccentric Jewish physician and theologian, was a sort of exception that proved the rule; he chose in a comprehensive book specifically to debate a scholar who would eventually become one of the most
important and influential non-Jewish biblical critics, namely Vatke.
Steinheim's work is a sweeping attempt to deal with the negative implications of the Hegelian developmental approach toward Israel and
Scripture and skillfully uncovers its ideological, religious, and political
biases. Steinheim's Archimedean point – Revelation – was perhaps not
in particular traditionally Jewish (on the contrary, it reveals a clear
Christian influence), but it allowed him to expose the prejudices that
lay behind Vatke's developmental framework and to debate them, even
though he could not propose an alternative framework of his own.
Here too the centrality of the Law stands out as a new-old bone of contention in the depiction of Judaism.

During the final third of the century, which saw the rise of the Graf-
Wellhausen school, German Jewry was already divided into clear
camps, and the *Wissenschaft des Judentums* itself was divided into three
streams: Orthodox, Positive–Historical, and Reform. Orthodox Jews
attempted to reformulate the traditional approach using the terminology of "biblical criticism," or pointed to the inconsistencies of radical
criticism in order to strengthen the traditional image through elimination. Positive–Historical Jewish scholars like Graetz refrained from
engaging with the theologically more difficult implications of biblical
criticism and pointed to its anti-Jewish ideological biases. Yet Reform
Jewish scholars, though aware of these biases, took up biblical criticism
wholeheartedly. Particularly interesting is the work of Siegmund Maybaum, who did not flinch from adopting the principles of the Graf-
Wellhausen view of the formation of the Pentateuch, but created an
alternative historical narrative that corrected the hostile aspects of contemporary biblical criticism while at the same time utilizing a signifi-

cant portion of its conclusions in order to rehabilitate the picture of the Jewish past and serve the polemic between Reform and Orthodox Jews about the image of modern Judaism.

Several basic features characterize Jewish engagement with biblical criticism during this period. First, we must bear in mind the discrimination that existed at the institutional and financial foundation of scholarly activity: while non-Jewish biblical scholars operated within the framework of universities' theological faculties and benefited from their services and resources, Jews could at best study at such institutions as students and were excluded from holding academic tenures. Attempts to establish Jewish studies as an independent field within the greater academic framework came to nothing. Thus there remained a significant gap in the financial and intellectual resources available to Jewish and non-Jewish scholars: the former were obliged to conduct their research in their free time and to obtain their livelihoods by other means. Some were employed by the religious establishment of the Jewish community as rabbis and teachers, positions which by their very nature imposed a certain restraint on their scholarly work when sensitive subjects of religion were at stake.

Secondly, it must be emphasized that biblical scholarship, and particularly biblical criticism, were not a central occupation of the *Wissenschaft des Judentums*. Ideologically this was due to the preference, already evident in Zunz's early manifesto, to concentrate on the later, less-studied and more maligned periods of Jewish history; as well as to the tendency to avoid the ancient national period in Jewish history, which was less suited to German Jews' needs regarding their self-image during the era of emancipation. From a practical perspective it was also due to the clear advantage in resources and expertise that Protestant theology had in the field of biblical studies. Nonetheless, already at the birth of the *Wissenschaft des Judentums* efforts were made to deal with biblical criticism, even if in quantity they fell short of the work devoted to later historical periods.

Third, the present study shows that the Jewish reception of biblical criticism was largely reactive in nature. This finding derives partially from the very definition of the research in this study: reception is by its nature reactive. Nevertheless, reception can occur in different ways. In particular, it may initiate autonomous development on the receiver's side. This was not true of Jewish biblical criticism in the nineteenth century: though that work did have an internal Jewish aspect, it was primarily a heteronomous chain of reactions to non-Jewish criticism; only in the Reform camp, toward the end of the century, is it possible to discover inklings of autonomous Jewish biblical criticism creating its own tradition. The question of reciprocity between Jews and non-Jews in the field of biblical criticism – that is, Christian attitudes toward Jewish scholarship – is not examined here; current research has concluded that such reciprocity was minimal.[2]

Fourth, Jews were aware of the change in the basic premises of Christian biblical criticism, primarily the relinquishment of the Christological perspective, and they hoped it would lead to objective, nonconfessional scholarship that would correct the traditional anti-Jewish biases. These hopes were disappointed over the course of the century. As biblical criticism developed, so did the Christian anti-Jewish biases in that discipline stand out. It was clear to Jews that despite all its innovation and promise, modern biblical criticism was yet another chapter in the Christian exegesis of the Old Testament; indeed, more than a few of the verses that modern biblical scholarship relied upon were part of the traditional Christian anti-Jewish arsenal (Jeremiah 7:22, Ezekiel 20:25-27, and more). It appears that at the end of the century all Jewish biblical scholars, whether they rejected or supported biblical criticism, were aware of its Christian biases even if they did not mention them explicitly. At the same time, Jews (except, perhaps, part of the Orthodoxy) did not reject biblical criticism as a whole; they attempted to reconcile it with Judaism and even to make use of its conclusions in shaping that religion.

In conclusion let us briefly note the thematic side of the polemic. Interestingly, a central theme in the struggle prompted by biblical criticism, in both the Jewish–Christian and internal Jewish arenas, was "the Law" – its origin, meaning, and religious and historical significance. The Law was a central theme in the Jewish–Christian polemic from the start, and the continuity of the polemic is evident here. As Kaufmann Kohler wrote, "Like the entire New Testament, all of Christianity's theological studies to this day are tendentious. 'Nomism,' borrowed from Paul, is the slogan."[3] Jost, who operated at a time when the antiquity of the Law was still accepted in non-Jewish research, attempted to prove that the Israelites had never followed the Law, and thereby to minimize the Law's influence on Judaism and emphasize the influence of the Hebrew Bible instead. Steinheim, who addressed Vatke's postdating of the Law, objected to the identification of the Hebrew Bible with the Law and attempted, in contrast with Vatke, to prove the former's antiquity (at the same time refuting the lateness of the Law). Maybaum, who contended with the theory of the lateness of the Law

2   Wiese 1999.
3   Kohler 1909, 345.

and its ascription to the priesthood of the Graf-Wellhausen school, attempted to prove that the Law (the Priestly Codex) was the fruit of an extended process of development that finally became consolidated under prophetic hegemony.

The very same theme, which stood at the heart of the Jewish–Christian polemic, also held a central place in the internal Jewish struggle. Progressive Jewish scholars walked a thin line: on the one hand, a sweeping defense of the Law against Christian attacks was liable to corner them into a conservative Orthodox position in the internal Jewish sphere. On the other hand, a sweeping acceptance of a hostile position toward the Law would undermine a central element of Judaism. Steinheim and Maybaum tried, each in his own way, to find the golden mean – the former by minimizing the Law's status in Judaism and emphasizing the moral elements of the religion; the latter by presenting Judaism (and the Law in particular) as the result of a continual struggle between the priesthood and the prophecy – between a legalistic, formalistic approach and a dynamic, conceptual–moral one – of which the struggle between Orthodoxy and Reform was the most recent incarnation.

An additional central theme was the question of the continuity of the Jewish people, or the relationship between the terms "Israelites" and "Jews". Jost adopted the dichotomy between these two concepts, which originated in the biblical criticism of his time (and had roots in the Christian outlook that strictly distinguished between the Judaism that existed before and after Jesus); he did his best to prove the existence of a break, rather than continuity, between those two historical phenomena, one of which he described as a nation and the other as a religious community. The political motivation with respect to emancipation was clear: to present the Jews as one of many communities within the modern state rather than as a separate nation. During the second half of the century this strict dichotomy receded in Jewish historiography, and Maybaum specifically emphasized the continuous nature of Jewish history – but as the dynamic continuity of an ongoing struggle rather than as a static, a-historical fixture.

Applying the terminology of narrative and counter-narrative, or history and counter-history – terminology characteristic of a colonial context – we can say that non-Jewish biblical criticism (particularly at the end of the century) proposed a counter-history to the traditional picture of the past as expressed in what Judaism and traditional Christianity saw (with a great deal of consensus) as the literal meaning of the Bible: the Pentateuch revealed to Moses at Sinai, the prophets existing in the wake of the Law, Ezra as an updater rather than author. The

Jewish Orthodoxy (as in Christianity) adhered to this traditional narrative. Steinheim, followed by the conservative Graetz, successfully pointed out the Christian and anti-Jewish biases of the new counter-history, but neither presented a corrected counter-history of his own; as a result Graetz was left supporting an inconsistent and intermediate position which applied biblical criticism only to the later parts of the Hebrew Bible but not to the Pentateuch. As for Reform Judaism (Maybaum), it attempted to propose a Jewish counter-history to the non-Jewish one without returning to the traditional narrative – a counter-counter-history that would serve the construction of a new outward and inward Jewish identity.

The present study, which begins with the birth of the *Wissenschaft des Judentums*, concludes toward the end of the nineteenth century with the beginning of the retreat of the Graf-Wellhausen school in the face of other schools of biblical scholarship; with the rise of ancient Near East studies which relied on extra-biblical sources, first among them the discoveries and findings from archaeological digs in the East; and with the expansion and changing character of the struggle between Judaism and academic scholarship, as evident in the Bibel-Babel dispute that began in 1903 and is addressed in other studies.[4] Thus, when in 1909 the conservative scholar Sigmund Jampel published his book *Vom Kriegsschauplatze der israelitischen Religionswissenschaft. Eine gemeinverständliche Schilderung der Kämpfe auf dem Gebiete der modernen Bibelwissenschaft* (On the Battlefield of Israelite Religious Studies: A Generally Comprehensible Description of the Wars in the Field of Modern Biblical Scholarship),[5] he did not restrict himself just to the Wellhausen school but distinguished between the "extreme-radical school" – Wellhausen and his followers, who saw the Jewish religion as a post-Israelite creation – and the "pan-Babylonian" school – namely Assyriology, which considered Judaism a pre-Israelite Babylonian creation.

Not only biblical criticism but also the *Wissenschaft des Judentums* underwent change at the turn of the century. The German Jewish hegemony within that movement was undermined: Jewish studies became more global in nature during the twentieth century, because of the proliferation in centers of scholarship (France, Britain, the United States, Jerusalem) and Jewish scholars' greater mobility between them. The cultural background through which we have attempted to interp-

---

4   On the growth in Jewish interest in archeology, see: Shavit 1987. On the Babel-Bibel polemic, see: Johanning 1988, and recently, in detail: Shavit and Eran 2007.

5   Jampel 1909. The rabbi Sigmund Jampel (1874–1934) dealt frequently in biblical criticism.

ret the German-Jewish engagement with biblical criticism thus evolved during the twentieth century. However, it is clear that Jewish engagement with biblical criticism, and with the Wellhausen school in particular, did not come to an end. It would be continued by Jewish scholars during the twentieth century, and not only in Germany: Benno Jacob (1862–1945), Umberto Cassuto (1883–1951), and Yehezkel Kaufmann (1889–1963) were among the most prominent, publishing professional and comprehensive works in that field.[6] The history of Jewish biblical scholarship in the twentieth century, its professionalization, and the (full?) integration of Jewish scholars into global biblical scholarship remain a subject for further studies.[7]

---

6   On Jacob see the anthology: Jacob and Jürgensen 2002. On Kaufmann see: Krapf 1990. On Cassuto see: Uffenheimer 1976; Gottlieb 1966.

7   On the gap and integration between Jewish and Christian biblical scholarship, primarily in the twentieth century, see Goshen-Gottstein 1983.

Bibliography

Abbreviations

ADB   *Allgemeine deutsche Biographie.* Vol. I-LVI. Leipzig: Duncker & Humblot 1875-1912.

BBK   *Biographisch-Bibliographisches Kirchenlexikon.* Bd. I-XVIII. Herzberg: Traugott Bautz 1990-2001.

EB   *Encyclopaedia Biblica* 1972-1982. Vol. I-VIII. Jerusalem: Bialik Institute [Hebrew].

EH   *Encyclopaedia Hebraica* 1949-1983. Vol. I-XXXII. Jerusalem: Hevrah le-hotsa'at entsiklopedyot [Hebrew].

EJ   *Encyclopaedia Judaica. Das Judentum in Geschichte und Gegenwart.* Vol. I-X. Berlin 1928-1934.

GWP   *Grote Winkler Prins.* Vol. I-XXVI. Amsterdam: Elsevier 1991.

HBOT   *Hebrew Bible / Old Testament. The History of Its Interpretation.* Göttingen: Vandenhoeck & Ruprecht 1996 – .

JL   *Jüdisches Lexikon. Ein enzyklopädisches Handbuch des jüdischen Wissens.* Vol. I-V. Berlin 1927-1930.

TRE   *Theologische Realenzyklopädie.* Vol. I-XXXVI. Berlin, New York: de Gruyter 1977-2006.

Sources

Ben Ze'ev, Yehuda Leb 1810. *Mavo el mikra'e kodesh.* Wien: Anton Schmid [Hebrew].

Bendavid, Lazarus 1823. "Ueber geschriebenes und mündliches Gesetz", *Zeitschrift für die Wissenschaft des Judenthums* 1.3, 472-500.

Bernstein, A[aron] 1871. *Ursprung der Sagen von Abraham, Isaak und Jakob.* Berlin: Duncker.

Bernstein, A[aron] 1893. "Aus dem Nachlasse A. Bernsteins. III, IV", *Allgemeine Zeitung des Judenthums* 57, 69-70, 90-92.

Bohlen, P[eter] von 1835. *Die Genesis historisch-kritisch erläutert.* Königsberg: Bornträger.

Cassel, David 1872. *Geschichte der jüdischen Literatur.* Vol. I-II. Berlin: Gerschel.

Cohen, Hermann 1907. "Religion und Sittlichkeit", in idem, *Jüdische Schriften*. Vol. III. Berlin: Schwetschke, 98-168.

Dozy, R[einhart] 1864a. *De Israëlieten te Mekka, van Davids tijd tot in de vijfde eeuw onzer tijdrekening*. Haarlem: Kruseman.

Dozy, R[einhart] 1864b. *Die Israeliten zu Mekka, von Davids Zeit bis in's fünfte Jahrhundert unserer Zeitrechnung. Ein Beitrag zur alttestamentlichen Kritik und zur Erforschung des Ursprungs des Islams*. Leipzig: Engelmann, Haarlem: Kruseman.

[Dünner, Josef Zebi Hirsch] 1865-1866. "Boekbeschouwing: De Israelieten te Mekka [...]", *Nieuw Israelietisch Weekblad* I:3 (18.VIII.1865), 5 (1.IX.1865), 11 (11.X.1865), 13 (27.X.1865), 17 (24.XI.1865), 22 (29.XII.1865), 29 (16.II.1866).

Dünner, [Josef Zebi Hirsch] 1869. "Drei Verse in Ezechiel Kap. 20", *Monatsschrift für Geschichte und Wissenschaft des Judenthums* 18, 459-465.

[Eichhorn, Johann Gottfried] 1789. "[Review of:] Essai sur la régénération physique, morale et politique des Juifs [...] par M. Grégoire [...] Metz 1789", *Allgemeine Bibliothek der biblischen Litteratur* 2, 293-302.

Eichhorn, J[ohann] G[ottfried] 1790. *Einleitung ins Alte Testament* [2nd ed.]. Reutlingen.

[Eichhorn, Johann Gottfried] 1796. "Nachricht", *Allgemeine Bibliothek der biblischen Litteratur* 4, 393.

[Eichhorn, Johann Gottfried] 1821. "[Review of:] Geschichte der Israeliten [...] von J. M. Jost [Vol. I-II]", *Göttingische gelehrte Anzeigen* I:15 (27.1.1821), 137-139.

[Eichhorn, Johann Gottfried] 1822. "[Review of:] Geschichte der Israeliten [...] von J. M. Jost [Vol. III]", *Göttingische gelehrte Anzeigen* II:126 (10.8.1822), 1249-1255.

Einhorn, David 1854. *Das Princip des Mosaismus und dessen Verhältnis zum Heidenthum und rabbinischen Judenthum*. Leipzig: Fritzsche.

Ewald, Heinrich 1843-1859. *Geschichte des Volkes Israel bis Christus*. Göttingen: Dieterich.

Formstecher, S[alomon] 1863. *Buchenstein und Cohnberg. Ein Familiengemälde aus der Gegenwart*. Frankfurt a.M.: Bechhold.

[Frankel, Zacharias] 1874a. "Mißverstandene Stellen in der Genesis", *Monatsschrift für Geschichte und Wissenschaft des Judenthums* 23, 113-122.

[Frankel, Zacharias] 1874b. "Die Echtheit des Buches des Propheten Ezechiel", *Monatsschrift für Geschichte und Wissenschaft des Judenthums* 23, 433-446.

Friedländer, David 1793. *Akten-Stücke, die Reform der Jüdischen Kolonieen in den preußischen Staaten betreffend*. Berlin: Voss.

Friedländer, David 1823. "Briefe über das Lesen der heiligen Schriften, nebst einer Uebersetzung des sechsten und siebenten Capitels des Micha, als Beilage", *Zeitschrift für die Wissenschaft des Judenthums* 1.1, 68-94.

Fürst, Julius 1867. *Geschichte der biblischen Literatur und des jüdisch-hellenistischen Schriftthums.* Vol. I. Leipzig: Tauchnitz.

Geiger, Abraham 1844. "Das Verhältnis des natürlichen Schriftsinnes zur thalmudischen Schriftdeutung", *Wissenschaftliche Zeitung für jüdische Theologie* 5, 53-81.

G[eiger, Abraham] 1847. "Literarisch-kritische Übersicht: Bibel", *Wissenschaftliche Zeitung für jüdische Theologie* 6, 114-115.

Geiger, Abraham 1928 <1857>. *Urschrift und Übersetzungen der Bibel in ihrer Abhängigkeit von der inneren Entwicklung des Judenthums* [2nd ed.]. Frankfurt a.M.: Madda.

[Geiger, Abraham] 1862a. "[Review of:] Der biblische Bericht über die Stiftshütte [...] von Dr. Julius Popper", *Jüdische Zeitschrift für Wissenschaft und Leben* 1, 122-140.

[Geiger, Abraham] 1862b. "Hupfeld über 'die heutige theosophische oder mythologische Theologie und Schrifterklärung", *Jüdische Zeitschrift für Wissenschaft und Leben* 1, 160-163.

[Geiger, Abraham] 1863. "Christliche Gelehrsamkeit in Beziehung auf Judenthum", *Jüdische Zeitschrift für Wissenschaft und Leben* 2, 292-297.

[Geiger, Abraham] 1864. "Christliche Gelehrsamkeit und Judenthum", *Jüdische Zeitschrift für Wissenschaft und Leben* 3, 299-303.

[Geiger, Abraham] 1867. "Die neuesten Fortschritte in der Erkenntnis der Entwickelungsgeschichte des Judenthums und der Entstehung des Christenthums", *Jüdische Zeitschrift für Wissenschaft und Leben* 5, 252-282.

[Geiger, Abraham] 1869a. "Kritische Behandlung der biblischen Schriften, namentlich ihres historischen Theiles", *Jüdische Zeitschrift für Wissenschaft und Leben* 7, 96-111.

[Geiger, Abraham] 1869b. "Das Ewald'sche Geschichtswerk", *Jüdische Zeitschrift für Wissenschaft und Leben* 7, 195-199.

[Geiger, Abraham] 1869c. "[Review of:] Materialien zur Geschichte und Kritik des Pentateuchs. Herausgegeben von Paul de Lagarde", *Jüdische Zeitschrift für Wissenschaft und Leben* 7, 309-315.

[Geiger, Abraham] 1871. "Ein theologischer Briefwechsel", *Jüdische Zeitschrift für Wissenschaft und Leben* 9, 255-275.

[Geiger, Abraham] 1872. "[Review of:] Der Text der Bücher Samuelis untersucht von Lic. Julius Wellhausen [...]", *Jüdische Zeitschrift für Wissenschaft und Leben* 10, 84-103.

[Geiger, Abraham] 1875. "Kuenen über unsern hebräischen Bibeltext", *Jüdische Zeitschrift für Wissenschaft und Leben* 11, 195-196.

[Geiger, Abraham] 1875. "Zunz' Bibelkritisches", *Jüdische Zeitschrift für Wissenschaft und Leben* 11, 247-250.

Geiger, Abraham 1875-1878. *Nachgelassene Schriften.* Vol. I-V. Berlin: Gerschel.

George, J. F. L[eopold]. 1835. *Die älteren jüdischen Feste mit einer Kritik der Gesetzgebung des Pentateuch.* Berlin: Schröder.

Goeje, M[ichael] J. de 1864. "Een stap vooruit. De Israëlieten te Mekka [...] Door Dr. R. Dozy", *De Gids* 28, 297-312.

Goeje, M[ichael] J. de 1883. *Biographie de Reinhart Dozy.* Translated by Victor Chauvin. Leiden: Brill.

Goethe, Johann Wolfgang von 1914. *The West-Eastern Divan.* Translated by Edward Dowden. Lodon & Toronto: Dent & Sons.

Goethe, Johann Wolfgang von 1962. *The Sorrows of Young Werther, and Selected Writings.* Translated by Catherine Hutter. New York: New American Library.

Goethe, Johann Wolfgang von 1987. *From My Life, Poetry and Truth.* Ed. by Thomas P. Saine and Jeffrey L. Sammons. New York: Suhrkamp.

G[raetz, Heinrich] 1854. "[Review of:] Staats- und Religionsgeschichte der Königreiche Israel und Juda, von Karl Adolf Menzel [...]", *Monatsschrift für Geschichte und Wissenschaft des Judenthums* 3, 68-73.

Graetz, Heinrich 1875. *Geschichte der Juden.* Vol. II:1. Leipzig: Leiner.

Graetz, Heinrich 1886. "Die allerneuste Bibelkritik, Wellhausen-Renan", *Monatsschrift für Geschichte und Wissenschaft des Judenthums* 35, 193-251.

Graetz, Heinrich 1887. "Judaism and Biblical Criticism", *Jewish Chronicle* 5.VIII.1887, 9.

Graetz, Heinrich 1902. *Geschichte der Juden.* Vol. II:1 [2nd ed.]. Leipzig: Leiner.

Graetz, Heinrich 1975. *The Structure of Jewish History and Other Essays.* Translated, edited, and introduced by Ismar Schorsch. New York: Jewish Theological Seminary.

Graf, K[arl] H[einrich] 1865. "[Review of:] Die Israeliten zu Mekka [...] von Dr. R. Dozy", *Zeitschrift der deutschen morgenländischen Gesellschaft* 19, 330-351.

Graf, K[arl] H[einrich] 1866. *Die geschichtlichen Bücher des Alten Testaments. Zwei historisch-kritische Untersuchungen.* Leipzig: Weigel.

Graf, K[arl] H[einrich] 1869. "Die sogenannte Grundschrift des Pentateuchs", *Archiv für wissenschaftliche Erforschung des Alten Testaments* 1, 466-477.

Grimm, Jacob and Wilhelm Grimm 1877. *Deutsches Wörterbuch*. Vol. IV:2. Leipzig.

Gugenheimer, J[osef]. 1867-1869. "Die Hypothesen der Bibelkritik und der Commentar von Herrn Rabbiner S. R. Hirsch", *Jeschurun* 13, 293-312, 397-409; 14, 1-17, 173-190, 312-324; 15, 81-100, 179-192.

Hegel, Georg Wilhelm Friedrich 1907. "Der Geist des Christentums und sein Schicksal", in Herman Nohl (ed.), *Hegels theologische Jugendschriften*. Tübingen: Mohr (Paul Siebeck), 242-342.

Hegel, Georg Wilhelm Friedrich 1961. *Vorlesungen über die Philosophie der Geschichte*. Stuttgart: Reclam.

Heine, Heinrich 1970. *Heinrich Heine Säkularausgabe*. Berlin: Akademie Verlag, Paris: Editions du CNRS.

Herder, J[ohann] G[ottfried] 1833. *The Spirit of Hebrew Poetry*. Translated by James Marsh. Burlington: Edward Smith.

Herzfeld, L[evi] 1863. *Geschichte des Volkes Israel von Vollendung des zweiten Tempels bis zur Einsetzung des Mackabäers Schimon zum hohen Priester und Fürsten*. Leipzig: Wilfferodt.

Hirsch, Samson Raphael 1904. *Gesammelte Schriften*. Vol. II. Frankfurt a.M.: Kauffmann.

Hirsch, Samson Raphael 1912. *Gesammelte Schriften*. Vol. IV. Frankfurt a.M.: Kauffmann.

Hirsch, Samson Raphael 1919. *Neunzehn Briefe über Judentum*. Berlin: Welt-Verlag.

Hoffmann, D[avid] 1876. "Das Alter des Versöhnungsfestes", *Magazin für die Wissenschaft des Judenthums* 3, 1-20, 61-77.

Hoffmann, D[avid] 1877. "Einheit und Integrität der Opfergesetze", *Magazin für die Wissenschaft des Judenthums* 4, 1-16, 62-75, 125-141, 210-218.

Hoffmann, D[avid] 1879-1880. "Die neueste Hypothese über den pentateuchischen Priestercodex", *Magazin für die Wissenschaft des Judenthums* 6, 1-19, 90-114, 209-237; 7, 137-156, 237-254.

Hoffmann, D[avid] 1890. "Priester und Leviten. Eine Beurtheilung der Schrift [...] von Dr. H. Vogelstein", *Magazin für die Wissenschaft des Judenthums* 17, 74-87, 136-151.

Hoffmann, D[avid] 1904. *Die wichtigsten Instanzen gegen die Graf-Wellhausensche Hypothese*. Heft I. Berlin: Itzkowski.

Hoffmann, David 1914-1919. "Probleme der Pentateuch-Exegese", *Jeschurun* 1, 43-50, 114-119, 272-280, 390-396; 2, 18-21, 132-137, 213-223, 308-320, 501-506; 3, 20-35, 159-164; 4, 14-20, 177-185, 310-319, 373-383, 535-545; 5, 289-301, 501-513; 6, 12-21, 133-143.

Hoffmann, D[avid] 1916. *Die wichtigsten Instanzen gegen die Graf-Wellhausensche Hypothese*. Heft II. Berlin: Itzkowski.

Hoffmann, David 1928. *Re'ayot makhri'ot neged Wellhausen.* Translated by Eliezer Barishenski. Jerusalem: Darom.

Hoofiën, Jacob 1875. "Zur Pentateuch-Kritik", *Monatsschrift für Geschichte und Wissenschaft des Judenthums* 24, 301-310.

Horwitz, Avraham Halevy 1965. *Yesh nohalin.* Jerusalem: Agudat TDHTZ [Hebrew].

Ilgen, Karl David 1798. *Die Urkunden des Jerusalemischen Tempelarchivs in ihrer Urgestalt als Beytrag zur Berichtigung der Geschichte der Religion und Politik.* Halle: Hemmerde & Schwetschke.

Jampel, Sigmund 1909. *Vom Kriegsschauplatze der israelitischen Religionswissenschaft. Eine gemeinverständliche Schilderung der Kämpfe auf dem Gebiete der modernen Bibelwissenschaft.* Frankfurt a.M.: Kauffmann.

Jastrow, M[arcus] 1864. "[Review of:] Die Israeliten zu Mekka [...]", *Monatsschrift für Geschichte und Wissenschaft des Judenthums* 13, 313-317.

Joël, M[anuel]. 1857. "[Review of:] Der Lehrbegriff der Synagoge als exacte Wissenschaft von Dr. S. L. Steinheim", *Monatsschrift für Geschichte und Wissenschaft des Judenthums* 6, 37-41, 73-79.

Jost, I[saak] M[arkus] 1820-1828. *Geschichte der Israeliten seit der Zeit der Maccabäer bis auf unsre Tage, nach den Quellen bearbeitet.* Vol. I-IX. Berlin: Schlesinger.

Jost, I[saak] M[arkus] 1832. *Allgemeine Geschichte des Israelitischen Volkes, sowohl seines zweimaligen Staatslebens als auch der zerstreuten Gemeinden und Sekten bis in die neueste Zeit.* Vol. I-II. Berlin: Amelang [2nd ed. 1850, Leipzig: Amelang].

Jost, I[saak] M[arkus] 1854. "Vor einem halben Jahrhundert. Skizzen aus meiner frühesten Jugend", in Wolf Pascheles (ed.), *Sippurim, eine Sammlung jüdischer Volkssagen, Erzählungen, Mythen, Chroniken, Denkwürdigkeiten und Biographien berühmter Juden. 3. Sammlung.* Prag: Wolf Pascheles, 141-166.

Jost, I[saak] M[arkus] 1857. *Geschichte des Judenthums und seiner Secten.* Vol. I-III. Leipzig: Dörffling und Franke.

Kirchheim, Raphael 1864. "[Review of:] Die Israeliten zu Mekka [...]", *Ben Chananja* 7, 974-977, 1000-1001.

Kohler, K[aufmann] 1867. *Der Segen Jacob's mit besonderer Berücksichtigung der alten Versionen und des Midrasch kritisch-historisch untersucht und erklärt.* Berlin: Benzian.

Kohler, Kaufmann 1868. "Die Bibel und die Todesstrafe", in Kohler 1931, 149-173.

Kohler, Kaufmann 1902. "The Attitude of Christian Scholars towards Jewish Literature", in Kohler 1931, 413-425.

Kohler, Kaufmann [1909]. *Grundriss einer systematischen Theologie des Judentums auf geschichtlicher Grundlage*. Frankfurt a.M.: Kauffmann.

Kohler, Kaufmann 1916. *Hebrew Union College and Other Addresses*. Cincinnati: Ark.

Kohler, Kaufmann 1931. *Studies, Addresses, and Personal Papers*. New York: Bloch.

Kuenen, A[braham] 1886. *An Historico-Critical Inquiry into the Origin and Composition of the Hexateuch (Pentateuch and the Book of Joshua)*. Translated by Philip H. Wicksteed. London: Macmillan.

Lazarus, M[oritz] 1894. *Der Prophet Jeremias*. Breslau: Schottlaender.

Lazarus, Moshe [Moritz] 1897. *Yirmiyah ha-navi*. Translated by Reuven Breinin. Warsaw: Achiasaf [Hebrew].

Löwy, Moritz 1903. "Die Paulinische Lehre vom Gesetz", *Monatsschrift für Geschichte und Wissenschaft des Judenthums* 47, 322-339, 417-433, 534-544; 48, 268-276, 321-327, 400-416.

Luther, Martin 1520. "Von der Freiheit eines Christenmenschen", in *Martin Luthers Werke, kritische Gesamtausgabe*. Weimar: Bohlaus 1883-1966 VII, 3-38.

Manasseh ben Israel 1972. *The Conciliator of R. Manasseh ben Israel*. New York: Hermon Press.

Maybaum, S[iegmund] 1880. *Die Entwicklung des altisraelitischen Priesterthums. Ein Beitrag zur Kritik der mittleren Bücher des Pentateuch*. Breslau: Koebner.

Maybaum, S[iegmund] 1883. *Die Entwicklung des israelitischen Prophetenthums*. Berlin: Dümmler.

Maybaum, S[iegmund] 1883b. "Zur Pentateuchkritik", *Zeitschrift für Völkerpsychologie* 14, 191-202.

Maybaum, S[iegmund] 1896. *Methodik des jüdischen Religionsunterrichts*. Berlin: Koebner.

Merx, A[dalbert] 1865. "Aphoristische Bemerkungen über die Pentateuchkritik nebst einer Besprechung von Popper Dr. Jul. Der Biblische Bericht über die Stifthütte [...]", *Protestantische Kirchenzeitung für das evangelische Deutschland* 12, 377-388.

Michaelis, Johann David 1770-75. *Mosaisches Recht*. Vol. I-VI. Frankfurt a.M.: Johann Gottlieb Garbe.

Michaelis, John David 1814. *Commentaries on the Laws of Moses*. Translated by Alexander Smith. London: Rivington.

--r-- [Moser, Moses] 1822. "Recension: Der Bibel'sche Orient. Eine Zeitschrift in zwanglosen Heften", *Zeitschrift für die Wissenschaft des Judenthums* 1, 177-196.

Nöldeke, Theodor 1869. *Untersuchungen zur Kritik des Alten Testaments*. Kiel: Schwers.

Paul, Jean 1959 – . *Werke.* Ed. by Norbert Miller and Gustav Lohmann. München: Hanser.

[Philippson, Ludwig] 1857. "Die Bibel und ihre Auslegung", *Allgemeine Zeitung des Judenthums* 21, 41-43.

Philippson, Ludwig 1858. *Die Israelitische Bibel.* [Vol. I:] *Der Pentateuch, die fünf Bücher Moscheh* [2nd ed.]. Leipzig: Baumgärtner.

[Philippson, Ludwig] 1864a. "Das Judenthum und die Schriftkritik", *Allgemeine Zeitung des Judenthums* 28, 539-540.

[Philippson, Ludwig] 1864b. [Review of: "Die Israeliten zu Mekka" of R. Dozy,] *Allgemeine Zeitung des Judenthums* 28, 589-590.

[Philippson, Ludwig] 1868. "Literarischer Wochenbericht", *Allgemeine Zeitung des Judenthums* 32, 834.

[Philippson, Ludwig] 1871-1872. "Vom Sinai bis Esra", *Allgemeine Zeitung des Judenthums* 35, 977-981, 1020-1022, 1039-1041; 36, 2-3.

[Philippson, Ludwig] 1879. "Die Einheit der Ideen in der heiligen Schrift Israels", *Allgemeine Zeitung des Judenthums* 43, 1-4, 33-35, 49-52, 131-133, 145-147, 243-245, 257-259, 321-325, 370-373, 386-388, 418-421.

[Philippson, Ludwig] 1885a. "Die biblische Wissenschaft", *Allgemeine Zeitung des Judenthums* 49, 681-683.

[Philippson, Ludwig] 1885b. "Die Propheten und das mosaische Gesetz", *Allgemeine Zeitung des Judenthums* 49, 729-731, 747-749, 765-766.

[Philippson, Ludwig] 1889. "Die Bibelkritik in Frankreich", *Allgemeine Zeitung des Judenthums* 53, 559-561.

Philippson, Ludwig 1911. *Gesammelte Abhandlungen.* Vol. I-II. Leipzig: Fock.

Popper, Julius 1854. *Israelitsche Schulbibel und Spruchbuch zum Gebrauch beim israelitischen Religionsunterricht nebst einem kurzen Abriß der Geschichte der Juden bis auf die neueste Zeit.* Dessau: Stange.

Popper, Julius 1862. *Der biblische Bericht über die Stifthütte. Ein Beitrag zur Geschichte der Composition und Diaskeue des Pentateuchs.* Leipzig: Hunger.

Popper, Julius 1879. *Der Ursprung des Monotheismus, eine historische Kritik des hebräischen Altertums, ins besondere der Offenbarungsgeschichte. Kritik der Patriarchengeschichte.* Berlin: Heymann.

Rabbinische Gutachten über die Verträglichkeit der freien Forschung mit dem Rabbineramte. [1. Sammlung:] 1842; [2. Sammlung:] 1843. Breslau: Freund.

Schechter, S[olomon] 1903. "Higher Criticism – Higher Anti-Semitism", in idem, *Seminary Addresses and Other Papers.* Cincinnati: Ark, 35-39.

Spinoza, Benedict de 2007. *Theological-Political Treatise*. Edited by Jonathan Israel, translated by Michael Silverthorne and Jonathan Israel. Cambridge: University Press.

Steinheim, Salomon Ludwig 1835. *Die Offenbarung nach dem Lehrbegriffe der Synagoge*. Vol. I. Frankfurt a.M.: Schmerber.

Steinheim, S[alomon] L[udwig] 1840. *Die Offenbarung vom Standpuncte der höheren Kritik. Eine Prüfung der Darstellung des Herrn Professors W. Vatke in dessen Schrift: "Die Religion des Alten Testaments nach den kanonischen Büchern entwickelt. Berlin, 1835"*, Kiel: Universitäts-Buchhandlung.

Steinheim, Salomon Ludwig 1856. *Die Offenbarung nach dem Lehrbegriffe der Synagoge*. [Vol. II:] *Die Glaubenslehre als exacte Wissenschaft*. Frankfurt a.M.: Schmerber.

Steinheim, Salomon Ludwig 1863. *Die Offenbarung nach dem Lehrbegriffe der Synagoge*. [Vol. III:] *Die Glaubenslehre als exacte Wissenschaft*. Frankfurt a.M.: Schmerber.

Steinheim, Salomon Ludwig 1865. *Die Offenbarung nach dem Lehrbegriffe der Synagoge*. [Vol. IV:] *Die Glaubenslehre als exacte Wissenschaft*. Frankfurt a.M.: Schmerber.

[Steinschneider, Moritz] 1864. "[Review of:] Dozy, R. Die Israeliten zu Mekka [...]", *Ha-maskir* VII.41, 103-106.

Steinthal, [Heymann] 1886. "[Review of:] Maybaum, Dr., Die Entwicklung des altisraelitischen Priesterthums [...] Desselben, Die Entwicklung des altisraelitischen Prophetenthums [...]", *Zeitschrift für Völkerpsychologie* 16, 361-367.

Strauss, David Friedrich 1835. *Das Leben Jesu, kritisch bearbeitet*. Tübingen: Osiander.

Vatke, W[ilhelm] 1835. *Die biblische Theologie wissenschaftlich dargestellt. 1, Die Religion des Alten Testaments nach den kanonischen Büchern entwickelt*. Berlin: Bethge.

Vogelstein, [Heinemann] 1881. "Recension. Die Entwickelung des altisraelitischen Priesterthums [...] von Dr. S. Maybaum", *Monatsschrift für Geschichte und Wissenschaft des Judenthums* 30, 179-192.

Vogelstein, H[einemann] 1889. *Der Kampf zwischen Priestern und Leviten seit den Tagen Ezechiels*. Stettin: Nagel.

Vogelstein, H[einemann] 1890. "Erwiderung", *Magazin für die Wissenschaft des Judenthums* 17, 236-249.

Wechsler, B. 1863. "Zur Geschichte der Versöhnungsfeier", *Jüdische Zeitschrift für Wissenschaft und Leben* 2, 113-125.

Weisel, Naftali Herz 1889. *Sefer divre shalom ve-emet*. Warsaw: Sablinski [Hebrew].

Wellhausen, J[ulius] 1878. *Geschichte Israels*. Vol. I. Berlin: Greimer.

Wellhausen, Julius 1885. *Prolegomena to the History of Israel.* Translated by J. Sutherland Black and Allan Menzies. Edinburgh: Black.

Wette, W[ilhelm] M[artin] L[eberecht] de 1806-1807. *Beiträge zur Einleitung in das Alte Testament.* Vol. I-II. Halle: Schlimmelpfennig.

Zunz, Leopold 1818. "Etwas über die rabbinische Literatur", in Zunz 1875, 1-31.

Zunz, Leopold 1873. "Bibelkritisches", *Zeitschrift der deutschen morgenländischen Gesellschaft* 27, 669-689.

Zunz, L[eopold] 1875. *Gesammelte Schriften.* Vol. I. Berlin: Gerschel.

Zunz, L[eopold] 1892. *Die gottesdienstlichen Vorträge der Juden, historisch entwickelt* [2nd ed.]. Frankfurt a.m.: Kauffmann [orig. Berlin 1832].

Zunz, L[eopold] 1931. *Das Buch Zunz, künftigen ehrlichen Leuten gewidmet.* Ed. by Fritz Bamberger. [Berlin:] Soncino Gesellschaft.

Studies

Altmann, Alexander 1956. "Theology in Twentieth Century German Jewry", *Leo Baeck Institute Year Book* 1, 193-216.

Anderson, Benedict R. 1991. *Imagined Communities* [Revised ed.]. London: Verso.

Baron, Salo W. 1964. "I. M. Jost the Historian", in idem, *History and Jewish Historians.* Philadelphia: Jewish Publication Society of America, 240-262.

Barr, James 1993. "Modern Biblical Criticism", in Bruce M. Metzger and Michael D. Coogan (eds.), *The Oxford Companion to the Bible.* Oxford: University Press, 318-324.

Barth, Karl 1961. *Evangelium und Gesetz.* München: Kaiser.

Bechtoldt, Hans-Joachim 1995. *Die jüdische Bibelkritik im 19. Jahrhundert.* Stuttgart: Kohlhammer.

Beinert, Wolfgang (ed.) 1991. *Lexikon der katholischen Dogmatik.* Freiburg, Basel, Wien: Herder.

Benecke, Heinrich 1883. *Wilhelm Vatke in seinem Leben und seinen Schriften.* Bonn: Strauß.

Blau, Yehoshua 1958. "Jacob Barth", in Federbush 1958, 47-52 [Hebrew].

Breuer, Mordechai 1992. *Modernity Within Tradition: the Social History of Orthodox Jewry in Imperial Germany.* Translated by Elizabeth Petuchowski. New York: Columbia University Press.

Breuer, Mordechai (ed.) 1987. *Torah im Derekh Eretz Movement.* Ramat-Gan: Bar-Ilan University Press [Hebrew].

Breuer, Edward 1996. *The Limits of Enlightenment. Jews, Germans, and Eighteenth-Century Study of Scripture.* Cambridge, Mass. and London: Harvard University Press.

Brömse, M[ichael] 1973. *Studien zur 'Biblischen Theologie' Wilhelm Vatkes.* Ph.D. dissertation, Kiel University.

Cazelles, Henri 1980. "Torah et Loi: préalables à l'étude historique d'une notion juive", in Gérard Nahon and Charles Touati (eds.), *Hommage à Georges Vajda. Études d'histoire et de pensée juives.* Louvain: Peeters, 1-12.

Cohen, Jeremy (ed.) 1991. *Essential Papers on Judaism and Christianity in Conflict. From Late Antiquity to the Reformation.* New York and London: New York University Press.

Cohen, Jeremy 1999. *Living Letters of the Law: Ideas of the Jew in Medieval Christianity.* Berkeley: University of California Press.

Cohen, Jonathan N. 1982. "De historicus I. M. Jost (1793-1860) in de Duitse geschiedtraditie", in Lea Dasberg and Jonathan N. Cohen (eds.), *Neveh Ya'akov, Jubilee Volume Presented to Dr. Jaap Meijer on the Occasion of his Seventieth Birthday.* Assen: Van Gorcum, 133-145.

Dahrendorf, Ralf 1961. "Demokratie und Sozialstruktur in Deutschland", in idem, *Gesellschaft und Freiheit. Zur soziologischen Analyse der Gegenwart.* München: Piper 1961, 260-299.

Denzler, Geoerg and Carl Andresen 1997. *Wörterbuch Kirchengeschichte* [5th ed.]. München: dtv.

Das deutsche Judentum und der Liberalismus 1986. *Dokumentation eines internationalen Seminars der Friedrich-Naumann-Stiftung in Zusammenarbeit mit dem Leo Baeck Institute, London.* Sankt Augustin: COMDOK.

Dinur, B[en] Z[ion] 1978. *Dorot u-reshumot.* Jerusalem: Bialik Institute [Hebrew].

Dunn, James D. G. (ed.) 1996. *Paul and the Mosaic Law.* Tübingen: Mohr.

Elbogen, Ismar 1922. "Ein hundertjähriger Gedenktag unserer Wissenschaft", *Monatsschrift für Geschichte und Wissenschaft des Judenthums* 66, 89-97.

Eliav, Mordechai 1992. "Das orthodoxe Rabbinerseminar in Berlin", in Julius Carlebach (ed.), *Wissenschaft des Judentums. Anfänge der Judaistik in Europa.* Darmstadt: Wissenschaftliche Buchgesellschaft, 59-73.

Ellenson, David and Richard Jacobs 1988. "Scholarship and Faith: David Hoffman[n] and his Relationship to *Wissenschaft des Judentums*", *Modern Judaism* 8:1, 27-40.

Ellenson, David 1992. "German Jewish Orthodoxy: Tradition in the Context of Culture", in Jack Wertheimer (ed.), *The Uses of Tradition:*

Jewish Continuity in the Modern Era. New York: Jewish Theological Seminary of America, 5-22.

Ettinger, Shmuel 1969. "Yahadut ve-toldot ha-yehudim bi-tefisato shel Graetz", in Heinrich Graetz, *Essays, Memoirs, Letters*. Translated by Yerucham Tolkes. Jerusalem: Bialik Institute [Hebrew], 7-36.

Federbush, Simon (ed.) 1958. *Hokhmat Yisra'el be-ma'arav Eropah*. Tel-Aviv: Ogen [Hebrew].

Fishman, Isidore 1944. *The History of Jewish Education in Central Europe. From the End of the Sixteenth to the End of the Eighteenth Century*. London: Edward Goldston.

Foucault, Michel 1970. *The Order of Things, an Archaeology of the Human Sciences*. Translated by Alan Sheridan. London: Tavistock.

Frei, Hans W. 1974. *The Eclipse of Biblical Narrative*. New Haven and London: Yale University Press.

Funkenstein, Amos 1990. *Signonot be-farshanut ha-mikra bi-yeme ha-benayim*. Tel Aviv: Universita meshuderet [Hebrew].

Funkenstein, Amos 1991. "Historiah, historiah she-ke-neged ve-siper", *Alpayim* 4, 206-223 [Hebrew].

Geiger, Ludwig (ed.) 1878. *Abraham Geiger's Leben in Briefen*. Berlin: Gerschel.

Geiger, Ludwig 1896a. "Abraham Geigers Briefe an J. Dérenbourg (1837-1842)", *Allgemeine Zeitung des Judenthums* 60 (1896), 187-190.

Geiger, Ludwig 1896b. "Zunz im Verkehr mit Behörden und Hochge-stellten", *Allgemeine Zeitung des Judenthums* 60, 245-262, 321-347.

[Geiger, Ludwig] 1910. "S. Maybaum", *Allgemeine Zeitung des Judenthums* 74, 19-20.

Geiger, Ludwig et al. 1910. *Abraham Geiger, Leben und Lebenswerk*. Berlin: Reimer.

Glatzer, Nahum N. (ed.) 1958. *Leopold and Adelheid Zunz: an Account in Letters, 1815-1885*. London: East and West Library.

Glatzer, Nahum N. 1964. *Leopold Zunz. Jude – Deutscher – Europäer*. Tübingen: Mohr.

Goshen-Gottstein, Moshe 1983. "Modern Jewish Bible Research", *World Congress of Jewish Studies* 9:5, 1-18.

Gottlieb, Isaac Boaz 1966. "The Documentary Hypothesis by U. Cassuto", *Gesher* 3:1, 100-111.

Graupe, Heinz Mosche 1966. "Die philosophischen Motive der Theologie S. L. Steinheims", in Schoeps 1966, 40-76.

Greenberg, Moshe 1982. "Tanakh, parshanut", EB VIII, 641-649 [Hebrew].

Grossman, Avraham 1986. "Ha-pulmus ha-yehudi–notzri veha-parshanut ha-yehudit la-mikra ba-me'ah ha-12", *Zion* 51, 29-60 [Hebrew].

Haberman, Jacob 1998. "Kaufmann Kohler and his Teacher Samson Raphael Hirsch", *Leo Baeck Institute Year Book* 43, 73-102.

Haberman, Joshua O. 1990. *Philosopher of Revelation. The Life and Thought of S. L. Steinheim.* Philadelphia – New York, Jewish Publication Society.

Halbertal, Moshe 1997. *People of the Book. Canon, Meaning and Authority.* Cambridge, Mass.: Harvard University Press.

Harris, Jay Michael 1992. "Modern Students of *Midrash Halakhah*: Between Tradition And *Wissenschaft*", in Jack Wertheimer (ed.), *The Uses of Tradition: Jewish Continuity in the Modern Era.* New York: Jewish Theological Seminary of America, 261-277.

Harris, Jay Michael 1995. *How do we know it? Midrash and the fragmentation of modern Judaism.* Albany: State University of New York Press.

Hechter, Michael 1975. *Internal Colonialism: the Celtic Fringe in British National Development, 1536-1966.* Berkeley: University of California Press.

Heschel, Susannah 1998. *Abraham Geiger and the Jewish Jesus.* Chicago: University of Chicago Press.

Heschel, Susannah 1999. "Revolt of the Colonized: Abraham Geiger's *Wissenschaft des Judentums* as a Challenge to Christian Hegemony in the Academy", *New German Critique* 77, 61-85.

Hess, Jonathan M. 1998. "Sugar Island Jews? Jewish Colonialism and the Rhetoric of 'Civic Improvement' in Eighteenth-Century Germany", *Eighteenth-Century Studies* 32.1, 92-100.

Hess, Jonathan M. 2000. "Johann David Michaelis and the Colonial Imaginary: Orientalism and the Emergence of Racial Antisemitism in Eighteenth-Century Germany", *Jewish Social Studies* 6.2, 56-101.

Heuer, Renate (ed.) 1982-1988. *Bibliographia Judaica. Verzeichnis jüdischer Autoren in deutscher Sprache.* Frankfurt a.M.: Campus.

Hirshman, Marc 1996. *A Rivalry of Genius: Jewish and Christian Biblical Interpretation in Late Antiquity.* Translated by Batya Stein. Albany: State University of New York Press.

Hoffmann, Christhard 1988. *Juden und Judentum im Werk deutscher Althistoriker des 19. und 20. Jahrhunderts.* Leiden, New York, København, Köln: Brill.

Hoheisel, Karl 1978. *Das antike Judentum in christlicher Sicht: ein Beitrag zur neueren Forschungsgeschichte.* Wiesbaden: Harrassowitz.

Horwitz, Rivka 1984. *Zacharias Frankel and the Beginnings of Positive-Historical Judaism.* Jerusalem: Zalman Shazar [Hebrew].

Horwitz, Rivka 1996. "Al historiografiah, mitos ve-dialog notzri-yehudi be-Germaniah be-reshit ha-me'ah ha-19", *Eshel Be'er-Sheva* 4, 317-341 [Hebrew].

Houtman, Cees 1994. *Der Pentateuch. Die Geschichte seiner Erforschung neben einer Auswertung.* Kampen: Pharos.

Jacob, Walter and Almuth Jürgensen (eds.) 2002. *Die Exegese hat das erste Wort: Beiträge zu Leben und Werk Benno Jacobs.* Stuttgart: Calwer

Johanning, Klaus 1988. *Der Bibel-Babel-Streit. Eine forschungsgeschichtliche Studie.* Frankfurt a.M.: Peter Lang.

Kalmar, Ivan Davidson and Derek J. Penslar (eds.) 2005. *Orientalism and the Jews.* Waltham, Mass.: Brandeis University Press.

Kamin, Sarah 1991. *Jews and Christians Interpret the Bible.* Jerusalem: Magnes Press.

Katz, Jacob 1973. *Out of the Ghetto: the Social Background of Jewish Emancipation, 1880-1870.* Cambridge, Mass.: Harvard University Press.

Katz, Jacob 1987. "Rabbi Samson Raphael Hirsch, ha-memin vehamasmil", in Breuer 1987, 13-31 [Hebrew].

Katz, Jacob 1988. *From Prejudice to Destruction.* Cambridge, Mass.: Harvard University Press.

Klugman, Eliyahu Meir 1996. *Rabbi Samson Raphael Hirsch, Architect of Torah Judaism for the Modern World.* New York: Mesorah Publications.

Kochan, Lionel 1993. "Steinheim und der Bilderdienst im Judentum", in Schoeps et al. 1993, 135-141.

Kohler, Max J. 1913. "Biographical Sketch of Dr. K. Kohler", in David Philipson, David Neumark and Julian Morgenstern (eds.), *Studies in Jewish Literature issued in Honor of Professor Kaufmann Kohler.* Berlin: Reimer, 1-10.

Kraeling, Emil G. 1969. *The Old Testament Since The Reformation.* New York: Schocken.

Krapf, Thomas 1990. *Yehezkel Kaufmann. Ein Lebens- und Erkenntnisweg zur Theologie der Hebräischen Bibel.* Berlin: Institut Kirche und Judentum.

Kraus, Georg 1991. "Gesetz und Evangelium", in Wolfgang Beinert (ed.), *Lexikon der katholischen Dogmatik.* Freiburg, Basel, Wien: Herder, 186-191.

Kraus, Hans-Joachim 1982. *Geschichte der historisch-kritischen Erforschung des Alten Testaments* [3rd ed.]. Neukirchen-Vluyn: Neukirchener.

Krauss, Samuel 1995. *The Jewish-Christian Controversy from the Earliest Times to 1789.* [Vol. I:] *History.* Edited and revised by William Horbury. Tübingen: Mohr (Paul Siebeck).

Krey, Henning 1991. *Gott und Krieg, Nation und Geschichte. Zeitgeschicht- liche Einflüsse auf die Rekonstruktion der Geschichte Israels in der deut- schen alttestamentlichen Forschungsgeschichte von 1870-1971.* M.A. the- sis, Heidelberg University.

Kugel, James 1987. "Torah", in Arthur A. Cohen and Paul Mendes- Flohr (eds.), *Contemporary Jewish Religious Thought.* New York: Free Press, London: Collier Macmillan, 995-1005.

Kuhn, Thomas S. 1970. *The Structure of Scientific Revolutions* [2nd ed.]. Chicago: University of Chicago Press.

Kusche, Ulrich 1991. *Die unterlegene Religion. Das Judentum im Urteil deutscher Alttestamentler.* Berlin: Institut Kirche und Judentum.

Lease, Gary 1984. "Salomon Ludwig Steinheim's Influence: Hans- Joachim Schoeps, A Case Study", *Leo Baeck Institute Year Book* 29, 383-402.

Lease, Gary 1993. "Die Steinheim-Rezeption in der Gegenwart", in Schoeps et al. 1993, 275-292.

Levy, Ze'ev 1994a. *Judaism in the Worldview of J. G. Hamman, J. G. Herder and W. v. Goethe.* Jerusalem: Mosad Bialik and Leo Baeck Institute [Hebrew].

Levy, Ze'ev 1994b. "Ben tevunah le-hitgalut, al filosofiat ha-dat shel Steinheim", in Shear-Yashuv 1994, 114-126 [Hebrew].

Liberles, Robert 1985. *Religious Conflict in Social Context: the Resurgence of Orthodox Judaism in Frankfurt am Main, 1838-1877.* Westport, Conn.: Greenwood Press.

Liebeschütz, Hans 1967. *Das Judentum im deutschen Geschichtsbild von Hegel bis Max Weber.* Tübingen: Mohr (Siebeck).

Liebeschütz, Hans 1978. "Past, Present and Future of German-Jewish Historiography", *Leo Baeck Institute Year Book* 23, 3-21.

Livnè-Freudenthal, Rachel 1991. "Der 'Verein für Cultur und Wissen- schaft der Juden' (1819-1824). Zwischen Staatskonformismus und Staatskritik", *Tel-Aviver Jahrbuch für deutsche Geschichte* 20, 103-125.

Livnè-Freudenthal, Rachel 1996. *'Ha-igud le-tarbut u-mada shel ha- yehudim' (1819-1824) be-hipus ahar musag hadash shel yahadut.* Ph.D. dissertation, Tel Aviv University [Hebrew].

Löwenbrück, Anna-Ruth 1994. "Johann David Michaelis und Moses Mendelssohn, Judenfeindschaft im Zeitalter der Aufklärung", in Michael Albrecht, Eva J. Engel and Norbert Hinske (eds.), *Moses Mendelssohn und die Kreise seiner Wirksamkeit.* Tübingen: Max Nie- meyer, 315-332.

Löwenbrück, Anna-Ruth 1995. *Judenfeindschaft im Zeitalter der Aufklä- rung. Eine Studie zur Vorgeschichte des modernen Antisemitismus am*

Beispiel des Göttinger Theologen und Orientalisten Johann David Michaelis. Frankfurt a.M.: Peter Lang.

Maier, Johann 1977. "Jude und Judentum – Bezeichnungen und Selbstbezeichnungen im Wandel der Zeiten", *Lebendiges Zeugnis* 32.1/2, 52-63.

Manuel, Frank E. 1992. *The Broken Staff: Judaism Through Christian Eyes.* Cambridge, Mass.: Harvard University Press.

Maybaum, S[iegmund] 1894. *Aus dem Leben von Leopold Zunz.* Berlin: Rosenthal (Bericht über die Lehranstalt für die Wissenschaft des Judenthums in Berlin 12).

Mendes-Flohr, Paul R. 1979. *Modern Jewish Studies, Historical and Philosophical Perspectives.* Jerusalem: Zalman Shazar (Issues in Jewish History 9) [Hebrew].

Mendes-Flohr, Paul R. 1991a. "Fin de Siècle Orientalism, the *Ostjude,* and the Aesthetics of Jewish Self-Affirmation", in idem, *Divided Passions, Jewish Intellectuals and the Experience of Modernity.* Detroit: Wayne State University Press, 77-132.

Mendes-Flohr, Paul R. 1991b. "Law and Sacrament: Ritual Observance in Twentieth-Century Jewish Thought", in idem, *Divided Passions, Jewish Intellectuals and the Experience of Modernity.* Detroit: Wayne State University Press, 341-369.

Meyer, Michael A. 1971. "Jewish Religious Reform and Wissenschaft des Judentums. The Positions of Zunz, Geiger and Frankel", *Leo Baeck Institute Year Book* 16, 19-41.

Meyer, Michael A. 1974. *Ideas of Jewish History.* New York: Behrman House.

Meyer, Michael A. 1975. "Abraham Geiger's Historical Judaism", in Jakob Josef Petuchowski (ed.), *New Perspectives on Abraham Geiger: An HUC-JIR Symposium.* Cincinnati: Hebrew Union College-Jewish Institute of Religion, 3-16.

Meyer, Michael A. 1988. *Response to Modernity: a History of the Reform Movement in Judaism.* New York: Oxford University Press.

Meyer, Michael A. 1992. "Jewish Scholarship and Jewish Identity: Their Historical Relationship in Modern Germany", in Peter Y. Medding (ed.), *A New Jewry? America Since the Second World War.* New York, Oxford: Oxford University Press (Studies in Contemporary Jewry VIII), 181-193.

Meyer, Michael A. 1993. "Salomon Ludwig Steinheim and the Reform Movement", in Schoeps et al. 1993, 143-158.

Meyer, Michael A. 1997. *German-Jewish History in Modern Times.* [Vol. II:] *Emancipation/Acculturation 1780-1871.* New York: Columbia University Press.

Michael, Reuven 1983. *I. M. Jost, Founder of the Modern Jewish Historiography*. Jerusalem: Magnes [Hebrew].

Michael, Reuven 1993. *Jewish Historiography from the Renaissance to the Modern Time*. Jerusalem: Mosad Bialik [Hebrew].

Miles, Jack 1995. *God, a Biography*. New York: Knopf.

Morgan, Robert with John Barton 1988. *Biblical Interpretation*. Oxford: University Press.

Morgenstern, Matthias 2000. "Jüdisch-orthodoxe Wege zur Bibelkritik", *Judaica* 56, 178-192, 234-249.

Muller, Richard A. 1985. *Dictionary of Latin and Greek Theological Terms*. Michigan: Baker Books.

Nipperdey, Thomas 1983. *Deutsche Geschichte 1800-1866. Bürgerwelt und starker Staat*. München: Beck.

Nipperdey, Thomas 1992. *Deutsche Geschichte 1866-1918. Machtstaat vor der Demokratie*. Vol. I-II. München: Beck.

Olender, Maurice 1992. *The Languages of Paradise: Race, Religion and Philology in the Nineteenth Century*. Translated by Arthur Goldhammer. Cambridge, Mass.: Harvard University Press.

Parush, Iris 2004. "Another Look at "the Life of 'Dead' Hebrew": Intentional Ignorance of Hebrew in Nineteenth-Century Eastern European Jewish Society", *Book History* 7, 171-214.

Perles, Felix 1910. "Bibel", in Ludwig Geiger et al. 1910. *Abraham Geiger, Leben und Lebenswerk*. Berlin: Reimer, 317-327.

Perlitt, Lothar 1965. *Vatke und Wellhausen. Geschichtsphilosophische Voraussetzungen und historiographische Motive für die Darstellung der Religion und Geschichte Israels*. Berlin: Töpelmann.

Philipson, David 1967. *The Reform Movement in Judaism*. New York: Ktav.

Porges, N[athan] 1917. "Graetz als Exeget", in Brann, M[arkus] (ed.), *Heinrich Graetz, Abhandlungen zu seinem 100. Geburtstag*. Wien, Berlin: Löwit, 47-64.

Raz-Krakotzkin, Amnon 1999. "Orientalism, mada'ey ha-yahadut vehahevrah ha-yisra'elit: mispar he'arot", *Jama'a* 3, 34-61 [Hebrew].

Rendtorff, Rolf 1980. "Die jüdische Bibel und ihre antijüdische Auslegung", in Rolf Rendtorff and E. Stegemann (eds.), *Auschwitz – Krise der christlichen Theologie*. München: Kaiser, 99-116.

Richarz, Monika 1974. *Der Eintritt der Juden in die akademischen Berufe. Jüdische Studenten und Akademiker in Deutschland 1678-1848*. Tübingen: Mohr (Paul Siebeck).

Rogerson, John 1984. *Old Testament Criticism in the Nineteenth Century England and Germany*. London: SPCK.

Rogerson, John 1988. "The Old Testament", in Paul Avis (ed.), *The History of Christian Theology*. [Vol. II:] *The Study and Use of the Bible*. Basingstoke: Marshall Pickering, Grand Rapids: Eerdmans, 3-150.

Rogerson, John 1992. *W. M. L. de Wette, Founder of Modern Biblical Criticism. An Intellectual Biography*. Sheffield: JSOT (Journal for the Study of the Old Testament, Supplement Series 126).

Rohls, Jan 1997. *Protestantische Theologie der Neuzeit I. Die Voraussetzungen und das 19. Jahrhundert*. Tübingen: Mohr (Paul Siebeck).

Rosenberg, Shalom 1993. "Hitgalut", in Arthur A. Cohen and Paul Mendes-Flohr (eds.), *Contemporary Jewish Religious Thought*. Tel-Aviv: Am Oved, 166-176 [Hebrew].

Rotenstreich, Nathan 1987. *Ha-mahshavah ha-yehudit ba-et ha-hadashah* [3rd ed.]. Tel-Aviv: Am Oved [Hebrew].

Ruether, Rosemary Radford 1974. *Faith and Fratricide. The Theological Roots of Anti-Semitism*. New York: Seabury.

Said, Edward W. 1978. *Orientalism*. London: Penguin.

Salomonski, M[artin] 1919. "Siegmund Maybaum", *Allgemeine Zeitung des Judenthums* 83, 354-355.

Sandler, Perez 1968. *Mendelssohn's Edition of the Pentateuch*. Jerusalem: Rubin Mass [Hebrew].

Sarna, Nahum M. 1975. "Abraham Geiger and Biblical Scholarship", in Jakob Josef Petuchowski (ed.), *New Perspectives on Abraham Geiger: An HUC-JIR Symposium*. Cincinnati: Hebrew Union College-Jewish Institute of Religion, 17-30.

Schmidt, Johann Michael 1969. *Die jüdische Apokalyptik. Die Geschichte ihrer Erforschung von den Anfängen bis zu den Textfunden von Qumran*. Neukirchen: Verlag des Erziehungsvereins.

Schoeps, Julius H. (ed.) 1966. *Salomon Ludwig Steinheim zum Gedenken. Ein Sammelband*. Leiden: Brill.

Schoeps, Julius H. 1992. *Bürgerliche Aufklärung und liberales Freiheitsdenken. A. Bernstein in seiner Zeit*. Stuttgart, Bonn: Burg.

Schoeps, Julius H., Anja Bagel-Bohlan, Margret Heitmann and Dieter Lohmeier (eds.) 1993, *"Philo des 19. Jahrhunderts", Studien zu Salomon Ludwig Steinheim*. Hildesheim, Zürich, New York: Georg Olms.

Schorsch, Ismar 1994. *From Text to Context. The Turn to History in Modern Judaism*. Hanover, NH: Brandeis University Press.

Schulin, Ernst 1997. "Nationalismus und jüdische Geschichtsschreibung in Deutschland", in Wolfgang Küttler, Jörn Rüsen and Ernst Schulin, *Geschichtsdiskurs*. Frankfurt a.M.: Fischer III, 198-217.

Schwartz, E[duard]. 1938. "Julius Wellhausen", in idem, *Vergangene Gegenwärtigkeiten*. Berlin: Berlin: de Gruyter I, 326-361.

Schwartz, Moshe 1967. "Shene perakim al Steinheim", in Shear-Yashuv 1994, 67-77 [Hebrew].

Schweid, Eliezer 1994. "Ha-dat ha-yehudit ben ratsionalism le-mistikah", in Shear-Yashuv 1994, 100-113 [Hebrew].

Seidel, Bodo 1993. *Karl David Ilgen und die Pentateuchforschung im Umkreis der sogenannten Älteren Urkundenhypothese.* Berlin, New York: De Gruyter.

Shavit, Yaacov 1987. "'Emet me-eretz titsmah': kavim le-hitpathut ha-inyan ha-tsiburi ha-yehudi be-arkheologiah", *Katedra* 44, 27-54 [Hebrew].

Shavit, Yaacov and Mordechai Eran 2007. *The Hebrew Bible Reborn: From Holy Scripture to the Book of Books.* Translated by Chaya Naor. Berlin, New York: Walter de Gruyter (Studia Judaica 38).

Shavit, Zohar and Hans-Heino Ewers, in co-operation with Annegret Völpel and Ran HaCohen 1996. *Deutsch-jüdische Kinder- und Jugendliteratur von der Haskala bis 1945. Die deutsch- und hebräischsprachigen Schriften des deutschsprachigen Raums. Ein bibliographisches Handbuch.* Stuttgart, Weimar: Metzler.

Shear-Yashuv, Aharon 1986. *The Theology of Salomon Ludwig Steinheim.* Leiden: Brill.

Shear-Yashuv, Aharon 1993. "Die Theologie des Salomon Ludwig Steinheim in ihrer Beziehung zur europäischen Philosophie", in Schoeps et al. 1993, 77-96.

Shear-Yashuv, Aharon (ed.) 1994. *Salomon Ludwig Steinheim, Studies in His Thought.* Jerusalem: Magnes Press [Hebrew].

Shear-Yashuv, Aharon 1994a. "Ha-filosofiah be-mivhan ha-hitgalut – lefi Steinheim", in Shear-Yashuv 1994, 48-66 [Hebrew].

Sheehan, James J. 1989. *German History 1770-1866.* Oxford: Clarendon Press.

Sheehan, Jonathan 2005. *The Enlightenment Bible: Translation, Scholarship, Culture.* Princeton: University Press.

Shohat, Ella 1992. "Notes on the Post-Colonial", *Social Text* 31/32, 99-113.

Shohat, Ella and Robert Stam 1994. *Unthinking Eurocentrism: Multiculturalism and the Media.* London: Routledge.

Shohet, Azriel 1960. *Beginnings of the Haskalah Among German Jewry.* Jerusalem: Mosad Bialik [Hebrew].

Smend, Rudolf 1958. *Wilhelm Martin Leberecht de Wettes Arbeit am Alten und am Neuen Testament.* Basel: Helbing & Lichtenhahn.

Smend, Rudolf 1959. *Das Mosebild von Heinrich Ewald bis Martin Noth.* Tübingen: Mohr (Paul Siebeck).

Smend, Rudolf 1982. "Wellhausen und das Judentum", *Zeitschrift für Theologie und Kirche* 79, 249-282.

Smend, Rudolf 1989. Deutsche *Alttestamentler in drei Jahrhunderten.* Göttingen: Vandenhoeck & Ruprecht.

Soloveitchik, Menahem and Salman Rubasheff 1925. *The History of the Bible Criticism.* Berlin: Dwir-Mikra [Hebrew].

Sperling, S[halom] D[avid] 1980. "Judaism and Modern Biblical Research", in L[awrence] Boadt (ed.), *Biblical Studies: Meeting Ground of Jews and Christians.* New York: Ramsey, 19-44.

Stemberger, Günther 2000. "Elements of Biblical Interpretation in Medieval Jewish-Christian Disputation", in HBOT I/2, 578-590.

Stern, Alfred 1885. *Abhandlungen und Aktenstücke zur Geschichte der preußischen Reformzeit 1807-1811.* Leipzig: Duncker & Humblot.

Tal, Uriel 1963. *Antisemitism in the Second Reich, 1870/1-1914.* Ph.D. dissertation, Tel Aviv University [Hebrew].

Tal, Uriel 1975. *Christians and Jews in Germany: Religion, Politics, and Ideology in the Second Reich, 1870-1914.* Translated by Noah Jonathan Jacobs. Ithaca: Cornell University Press.

Talmage, Ephraim F. 1982. "Ha-parshanut ha-notzrit bi-yeme ha-benayim ve-zikat ha-gomlin benah le-ven ha-parshanut ha-yehudit", EB VIII, 714-722 [Hebrew].

Thompson, R. J. 1970. *Moses and the Law in a Century of Criticism since Graf.* Leiden: Brill.

Toury, Jacob 1960. *Jewish Political Orientations in XIXth Century Germany.* Ph.D. dissertation, Tel Aviv University [Hebrew].

Toury, Jacob 1966. *Die politischen Orientierungen der Juden in Deutschland. Von Jena bis Weimar.* Tübingen: Mohr (Paul Siebeck).

Ucko, Sinai (Siegfried) 1934. "Geistesgeschichtliche Grundlagen der Wissenschaft des Judentums (Motive des Kulturvereins vom Jahre 1819)", in Wilhelm 1967 I, 315-352.

Uffenheimer, Binyamin 1976: "Cassuto as a Biblical Commentator", *Immanuel* 6, 20-29.

Urbach, Ephraim E. 1975. *The Sages, Their Concepts and Beliefs.* Translated by Israel Abrahams. Jerusalem: Magnes Press.

Volkov, Shulamit 1997. *Ihud ve-herut be-Germaniah mi-Napoleon ad Bismarck.* Tel Aviv: Universita meshuderet [Hebrew].

Volkov, Shulamit 2006. *Germans, Jews, and Antisemites.* Cambridge: University Press.

Wachsman, Meir 1958. "Prof. David Hoffmann", in Federbush 1958, 199-209 [Hebrew].

Wallach, Luitpold 1959. *Liberty and Letters. The Thoughts of Leopold Zunz.* London: East and West Library.

Wasserstein, David J. 1999. "Evariste Lévi Provençal and the Historio-graphy of Iberian Islam", in Kramer 1999, 273-289.

Werblowsky, R[aphael] J[ehuda] Zwi 1960. "Mada ha-mikra ki-be'ayah datit", *Molad* 18, 162-168 [Hebrew].

Werblowsky, R[aphael] J[ehuda] Zwi 1990. "Hitgalut be-idan ha-positivism", in Shear-Yashuv 1994, 41-47 [Hebrew].

Whitelam, Keith W. 1996. *The Invention of Ancient Israel, the Silencing of Palestinian History*. London and New York: Routledge.

Wiederbach, Hartwig and Annette Winkelmann (eds.) 2002. *Chajim H. Steinthal, Sprachwissenschaftler und Philosoph im 19. Jahrhundert / Linguist and Philosopher in the 19th Century*. Leiden, Boston, Köln: Brill.

Wiener, Max 1933. *Jüdische Religion im Zeitalter der Emanzipation*. Berlin: Philo.

Wiener, Max 1962. *Abraham Geiger and Liberal Judaism. The Challenge of the Nineteenth Century*. Philadelphia: Jewish Publication Society.

Wiese, Christian 1999. *Wissenschaft des Judentums und protestantische Theologie im wilhelminischen Deutschland. Ein Schrei ins Leere?* New York: Leo Baeck Institut, Tübingen: Mohr Siebeck.

Wiese, Christian 2002. "Struggling for Normality: The Apologetics of *Wissenschaft des Judentums* in Wilhelmine Germany as an Anti-colonial Intellectual Revolt against the Protestant Construction of Judaism", in Rainer Liedtke and David Rechter (eds.), *Towards Normality? Acculturation and Modern German Jewry*, Tübingen: Mohr Siebeck, 77-101.

Wilhelm, Kurt (ed.) 1967. *Wissenschaft des Judentums im deutschen Sprachbereich*. Tübingen: Mohr (Paul Siebeck).

Yerushalmi, Yosef Hayim 1982. *Zakhor, Jewish History and Jewisg Memory*. Seattle: University of Washington Press.

Young, Robert J. C. 2001. *Postcolonialism: an Historical Introduction*. Malden: Blackwell.

Yuval, Israel Jacob 2006. *Two Nations in Your Womb: Perceptions of Jews and Christians in the Middle Ages*. Translated by Barbara Harshav and Jonathan Chipman. Berkeley: University of California Press.

Zantop, Susanne 1997. *Colonial Fantasies: Conquest, Family and Nation in Precolonial Germany, 1770-1870*. Durham: Duke University Press.

Zureik, Elia 1979. *The Palestinians in Israel: a Study in Internal Colonialism*. London: Routledge & Kegan Paul.

Index of Names